T0331178

Artificial Intelligence for Blockchain and Cybersecurity Powered IoT Applications

The objective of this book is to showcase recent solutions and discuss the opportunities that AI, blockchain, and even their combinations can present to solve the issue of Internet of Things (IoT) security. It delves into cutting-edge technologies and methodologies, illustrating how these innovations can fortify IoT ecosystems against security threats. The discussion includes a comprehensive analysis of AI techniques such as machine learning and deep learning, which can detect and respond to security breaches in real time. The role of blockchain in ensuring data integrity, transparency, and tamper-proof transactions is also thoroughly examined. Furthermore, this book will present solutions that will help analyze complex patterns in user data and ultimately improve productivity.

Artificial Intelligence for Blockchain and Cybersecurity Powered IoT Applications

Edited by
Mariya Ouaissa, Mariyam Ouaissa,
Zakaria Boulouard, Abhishek Kumar,
Vandana Sharma, and Keshav Kaushik

CRC Press
Taylor & Francis Group
Boca Raton London New York

CRC Press is an imprint of the
Taylor & Francis Group, an **informa** business

Cover: Shutterstock

First edition published 2025
by CRC Press
2385 Executive Center Drive, Suite 320, Boca Raton, FL 33431

and by CRC Press
4 Park Square, Milton Park, Abingdon, Oxon, OX14 4RN

CRC Press is an imprint of Taylor & Francis Group, LLC

© 2025 selection and editorial matter, Mariya Ouaissa, Mariyam Ouaissa, Zakaria Boulouard, Abhishek Kumar, Vandana Sharma and Keshav Kaushik; individual chapters, the contributors

Reasonable efforts have been made to publish reliable data and information, but the author and publisher cannot assume responsibility for the validity of all materials or the consequences of their use. The authors and publishers have attempted to trace the copyright holders of all material reproduced in this publication and apologize to copyright holders if permission to publish in this form has not been obtained. If any copyright material has not been acknowledged please write and let us know so we may rectify in any future reprint.

Except as permitted under U.S. Copyright Law, no part of this book may be reprinted, reproduced, transmitted, or utilized in any form by any electronic, mechanical, or other means, now known or hereafter invented, including photocopying, microfilming, and recording, or in any information storage or retrieval system, without written permission from the publishers.

For permission to photocopy or use material electronically from this work, access www.copyright.com or contact the Copyright Clearance Center, Inc. (CCC), 222 Rosewood Drive, Danvers, MA 01923, 978-750-8400. For works that are not available on CCC please contact mpkbookspermissions@tandf.co.uk

Trademark notice: Product or corporate names may be trademarks or registered trademarks and are used only for identification and explanation without intent to infringe.

ISBN: 9781032802381 (hbk)
ISBN: 9781032805924 (pbk)
ISBN: 9781003497585 (ebk)

DOI: 10.1201/9781003497585

Typeset in Sabon
by Newgen Publishing UK

Contents

Preface

The Internet of Things (IoT) is now a major part of our daily lives. Billions of intelligent and autonomous objects around the world are connected and communicate with each other. The great power of the IoT lies in the fact that its objects communicate, analyze, process, and manage data autonomously and without any human intervention. However, security concerns are a major obstacle to the development and rapid deployment of this technology. Information theft, intrusion, misfunction in the authentication mechanisms, and other flaws can make IoT devices vulnerable to cyberattacks.

IoT security has become a major concern of the scientific community, and several solutions are being presented in the literature. Among these solutions, Blockchain technology presents itself as a rising star as it has the potential to secure the IoT environment through cryptography. Blockchain builds on the idea of peer-to-peer (P2P) networks and provides a universal data set that every actor can trust, even though they might not know or trust each other. It provides a shared and trusted ledger of transactions, where immutable and encrypted copies of information are stored on every node in the network.

Another rising star in the solutions provided to secure IoT systems is artificial intelligence (AI). AI approaches have emerged as powerful tools that can provide intelligent communication designs and enhance the level of security aspects against cyberattacks and malfunctions to improve the overall network efficiency. The objective of this book is to exhibit recent solutions and to discuss the opportunities that AI, Blockchain, and even their combinations can present to solve the issue of IoT security.

The book aims to propose the recent solutions and to discuss the opportunities that AI, Blockchain, and even their combinations can present to solve the issue of IoT security. Furthermore, this book will display solutions that will help analyze complex patterns in user data and ultimately improve productivity.

Let's take a closer look at the specific themes and contributions of each chapter:

- The first and foundational chapter provides a comprehensive review of the existing foundational models, ranging from rule-based systems to advanced machine learning algorithms.
- Chapter 2 explores critical aspects of protecting IoT networks against the emerging threats by examining security vulnerabilities unique to IoT devices and networks, including issues related to data breaches, unauthorized access, and cyberattacks.
- Chapter 3 investigates the primary obstacles and proposes effective countermeasures in the convergence of these cutting-edge domains. Key challenges include scalability issues, data privacy concerns, computational resource constraints, and the complexities of ensuring interoperability among diverse systems.
- Chapter 4 comprehensively surveys the existing literature on the applications of blockchain to enhance cybersecurity.
- Chapter 5 delves into an outline of blockchain technology, detailing its historical development, key concepts, and current applications.
- Chapter 6 reviews the advancements in machine learning and deep learning techniques for detecting distributed denial of service (DDoS) attacks in IoT; researchers interested in IoT security will also benefit from this chapter's addition to their expertise.
- Chapter 7 conducts an in-depth study, focusing on the current state of cybersecurity in IoV, synthesizing findings from a comprehensive analysis of recent literature.
- Focusing on cloud storage, Chapter 8 introduces 'Cloud Sync,' a web-based cloud storage platform that grants access in both online and offline modes.
- Chapter 9 looks ahead to the benefits and opportunities offered by the use of Blockchain in the field of biometric identification.
- Chapter 10 conducts a thorough review of current methodologies, highlights the synergies between AI and Blockchain, and proposes a novel integrated architecture that addresses data privacy, system scalability, and interoperability challenges of face detection and human tracking systems in IoT applications.
- Chapter 11 presents the confluence of IoT, augmented reality (AR), and virtual reality (VR) technologies is bringing about a revolutionary transformation in training and education, providing possibilities for organizations, educators, and learners to adopt new paradigms.
- Chapter 12 provides a specific use case of the feasibility of a non-invasive remote neurostimulation system using IoMT-based transcranial direct current stimulation by developed a hardware

prototype of a device that can be controlled via an Android application over the internet.

- In the context of healthcare, Chapter 13 showcases the revolutionary potential of generative AI frameworks and their use in healthcare contexts. However, Chapter 14 demonstrates how intelligent systems can to track and analyze various health parameters in real time.

About the Editors

Mariya Ouaissa is currently a professor in cybersecurity and networks at the Faculty of Sciences Semlalia, Cadi Ayyad University, Marrakech, Morocco. She holds a Ph.D. obtained in 2019 in computer science and networks from the Laboratory of Modelisation of Mathematics and Computer Science at ENSAM-Moulay Ismail University, Meknes, Morocco. She is a networks and telecom engineer, graduating in 2013 from National School of Applied Sciences, Khouribga, Morocco. She is a co-founder and IT consultant at IT Support and Consulting Center. She was working for the School of Technology of Meknes, Morocco, as a visiting professor from 2013 to 2021. She is a member of the International Association of Engineers and International Association of Online Engineering, and since 2021, she is an ACM Professional Member. She is and expert reviewer with Academic Exchange Information Centre (AEIC) and brand ambassador with Bentham Science. She has served and continues to serve on technical program and organizer committees of several conferences and events and has organized many symposiums, workshops, and conferences as a general chair also as a reviewer of numerous international journals. Ouaissa has made contributions in the fields of information security and privacy, Internet of Things security, and wireless and constrained networks security. Her main research topics are IoT, machine-to-machine (M2M), device-to-device (D2D), wireless sensor network (WSN), cellular networks, and vehicular networks. She has published over 40 papers (book chapters, international journals, and conferences/workshops), 15 edited books, and 10 special issues as a guest editor.

Mariyam Ouaissa is currently an assistant professor in networks and systems at ENSA, Chouaib Doukkali University, El Jadida, Morocco. She received her Ph.D. in 2019 from National Graduate School of Arts and Crafts, Meknes, Morocco, and her engineering degree in 2013 from the National School of Applied Sciences, Khouribga, Morocco. She is a communication and networking researcher and practitioner with industry and academic experience. Ouaissa's research is multidisciplinary focusing on

Internet of Things, machine to machine (M2M), wireless sensor network (WSN), vehicular communications and cellular networks, security networks, congestion overload problem, and the resource allocation management and access control. She is serving as a reviewer for international journals and conferences including *IEEE Access*, *Wireless Communications*, and *Mobile Computing*. Since 2020, she is a member of International Association of Engineers (IAENG) and International Association of Online Engineering, and since 2021, she is an ACM Professional Member. She has published more than 30 research papers (this includes book chapters, peer-reviewed journal articles, and peer-reviewed conference manuscripts), 12 edited books, and six special issues as a guest editor. She has served on program committees and organizing committees of several conferences and events and has organized many symposiums, workshops, and conferences as a general chair.

Zakaria Boulouard is currently a professor at the Department of Computer Sciences in the Faculty of Sciences and Techniques Mohammedia, Hassan II University, Casablanca, Morocco. In 2018, he joined the Advanced Smart Systems Research Team at the Computer Sciences Laboratory of Mohammedia. He received his PhD in 2018 from Ibn Zohr University, Morocco and his engineering degree in 2013 from the National School of Applied Sciences, Khouribga, Morocco. His research interests include artificial intelligence, big data visualization and analytics, optimization, and competitive intelligence. Since 2017, he is a member of Draa-Tafilalet Foundation of Experts and Researchers, and since 2020, he is an ACM Professional Member. He has served on program committees and organizing committees of several conferences and events and has organized many symposiums, workshops, and conferences as a general chair. He has served and continues to serve as a reviewer of numerous international conferences and journals. He has published several research papers. This includes book chapters, peer-reviewed journal articles, peer-reviewed conference manuscripts, edited books, and special issue journals.

Abhishek Kumar is currently working as an assistant director/associate professor in the computer science and engineering department in Chandigarh University, Punjab, India. He holds a doctorate in computer science from University of Madras and is a post-doctoral fellow in Ingenium Research Group Lab, Universidad De Castilla-La Mancha, Ciudad Real, Spain. He has done M.Tech in Computer Science & Engineering and B.Tech in I.T. from Rajasthan Technical University, Kota, India. He has total academic teaching experience of more than 13 years along with 2 years of teaching assistantship. He has more than 170 publications in reputed, peer-reviewed national and international journals, books, and conferences He has guided more than 30 M.Tech projects at national and international levels and 4

Ph.D. scholars who completed their degree under his guidance. His research area includes artificial intelligence, renewable energy image processing, computer vision, data mining, and machine learning. He has been session chair and keynote speaker of many international conferences and webinars in India and abroad. He has been the reviewer for *IEEE* and *Inderscience Journal*. He has authored/co-authored 7 books published internationally and edited 45 books (published and ongoing) with IET, Elsevier, Wiley, IGI GLOBAL Springer, Apple Academic Press, Degruyter, and CRC Press. He has been a member of various national and international professional societies in the field of engineering and research like senior member of IEEE, IAENG (International Association of Engineers), associate member of IRED (Institute of Research Engineers and Doctors). He is a patent holder and got Sir CV Raman National Award for 2018 in young researcher and faculty category from IJRP Group. He is serving as series editor for four books series, Quantum Computing with Degruyter Germany, Intelligent Energy System with Elsevier, and Mathematical Methods in the Digital Age with Degruyter Germany, AI for environment Sustainability with Degruyter Germany.

Vandana Sharma is an associate professor at CHRIST (Deemed to be University), Delhi National Capital Region, India. Sharma has served NAAC-accredited A++ institutions like Guru Gobind Singh Indraprastha University, Delhi and Galgotias University, Greater Noida Campus, and Amity Institute of Information Technology, Amity University, Noida Campus, India. Sharma has 15 + years of teaching experience at the postgraduate level and has guided 100+ student dissertations. Sharma obtained her doctoral degree from Amity University, Masters of Technology and Bachelor of Electronic Commerce degrees from Guru Gobind Singh Indraprastha University, a Delhi state university in India. She is a Senior Member of IEEE, member of Women in Engineering Society, and member of IEEE Consumer Technology Society, popularly known as CTSoc. As a keen researcher, she has published 50+ research papers in SCI- and Scopus-indexed international journals and conferences. Sharma has contributed voluntarily as a keynote speaker, session chair, reviewer and technical program committee (TPC) member for reputed international journals and IEEE conferences and has presented her work across India and abroad. Currently, she is a post-doctoral fellow at Lincoln University College, Malaysia. Also, she is an honorary adjunct professor and senior fellow of Scientific Innovation Research Group (SIRG) at Beni Suef University, Egypt, and adjunct professor at Perdana University, Malaysia. Her primary areas of interest include artificial intelligence, blockchain technology, and the Internet of Things (IoT).

Keshav Kaushik is an accomplished academician, cybersecurity, and digital forensics expert currently serving as an assistant professor at the Amity

School of Engineering and Technology, Amity University Punjab, India. As a key member of the Cybersecurity Centre of Excellence, he has been instrumental in advancing the field of cybersecurity through his dedicated teaching and innovative research. In addition to his academic role, he holds the prestigious position of vice-chairperson for the Meerut ACM Professional Chapter, highlighting his leadership and commitment to the professional community. His academic journey includes a notable stint as a faculty intern during the Summer Faculty Research Fellow Programme 2016 at the Indian Institute of Technology (IIT) Ropar, reflecting his continuous pursuit of knowledge and professional development. His scholarly contributions are extensive and impactful, with over 135 publications to his credit. This includes 25 peer-reviewed articles in SCI/SCIE/Scopus-indexed journals and 50+ publications in Scopus-indexed conferences. He is also an inventor, holding one granted patent and six published patents, alongside five granted copyrights. His editorial expertise is showcased by publishing 30 books and 25 book chapters, further cementing his reputation as a thought leader in the field. His professional certifications are a testament to his expertise and commitment to excellence. He is a certified ethical hacker (CEH v11) by EC-Council, a CQI and IRCA Certified ISO/IEC 27001:2013 Lead Auditor, a Quick Heal Academy Certified Cyber Security Professional (QCSP), and an IBM cybersecurity analyst. His recognition as a Bentham Ambassador by Bentham Science Publishers and his role as a guest editor for the *IEEE Journal of Biomedical and Health Informatics* underscore his influence and authority in cybersecurity. He is a dynamic speaker, having delivered over 50 national and international talks on cybersecurity and digital forensics topics. His mentorship was acknowledged during the Smart India Hackathon 2017, under the aegis of the Indian Space Research Organization (ISRO), with a certificate of appreciation from AICTE, MHRD, and i4c. A two-time GATE qualifier with an impressive 96.07 percentile (2012 and 2016), he has also received accolades from the Uttarakhand Police for his significant contributions to cybercrime investigation training. With a career marked by significant achievements and a profound impact on cybersecurity and digital forensics, he continues to inspire and lead in both academic and professional circles.

Contributors

Thota Akshitha
Stanley College of Engineering and Technology for Women
Hyderabad, India

Mohamed Alhyan
Chouaib Doukkali University
El Jadida, Morocco

Veeramalla Anitha
Stanley College of Engineering and Technology for Women
Hyderabad, India

Taran Singh Bharati
Jamia Millia Islamia
New Delhi, India

Rejwan Bin Sulaiman
Northumbria University
Newcastle upon Tyne, United Kingdom

Srinath Doss
Faculty of Engineering and Technology Botho University
Gaborone, Botswana

Mohamed El Ghazouani
Chouaib Doukkali University
El Jadida, Morocco

Zakaria Abou El Houda
INRS, University of Québec
Québec City, Québec, Canada

My Ahmed El Kiram
Cadi Ayyad University
Marrakech, Morocco

Latifa Er-rajy
Cadi Ayyad University
Marrakech, Morocco

Amine Idelhaj
ENSICAEN, Normandy University
Caen, France

Ali Kartit
Chouaib Doukkali University
El Jadida, Morocco

Yasir Khan
Department of Science and Technology & Information Technology (ST&IT)
Peshawar, Pakistan

Lyes Khoukhi
ENSICAEN, Normandy University
Caen, France

Oussama Lachihab
Cadi Ayyad University
Marrakech, Morocco

Kari Lippert
University of South Alabama
Mobile, Alabama, USA

Priyanka Maan
SRM University, Sonepat
Haryana, India

Mohammad Sultan Mahmud
Shenzhen University
Shenzhen, China

T. Monika Singh
Stanley College of Engineering and Technology for Women
Hyderabad, India

Sahiti Mummadi
Stanley College of Engineering and Technology for Women
Hyderabad, India

Zineb Nadifi
Chouaib Doukkali University
El Jadida, Morocco

Mariya Ouaissa
Cadi Ayyad University
Marrakech, Morocco

Mariyam Ouaissa
Chouaib Doukkali University
El Jadida, Morocco

A. Prasanth
Vel Tech Rangarajan Dr. Sagunthala R&D Institute of Science and
   Technology
Chennai, Tamil Nadu, India

C. Kishor Kumar Reddy
Stanley College of Engineering and Technology for Women
Hyderabad, India

D. Manoj Kumar Reddy
Vardhaman College of Engineering
Hyderabad, India

Garima Sharma
The NorthCap University
Gurugram, India

Jaspreet Singh
Drexel University College of Computing & Informatics
Philadelphia, Pennsylvania, USA

Md Sakib Ullah Sourav
Shandong University of Finance and Economics
Shandong, China

Ch. Sumalakshmi
Koneru Lakshmaiah Education Foundation (Deemed to be university)
Andhra Pradesh, India

Md Simul Hasan Talukder
Bangladesh Atomic Energy Regulatory Authority
Bangladesh

Mohammad Zahid
Jamia Millia Islamia
New Delhi, India

Chapter 1

Foundations models in cybersecurity

A comprehensive review and future direction

Amine Idelhaj, Zakaria Abou El Houda, and Lyes Khoukhi

1.1 INTRODUCTION

In an increasingly interconnected world, where digital technologies permeate every aspect of our lives, cybersecurity has emerged as a critical concern. With the proliferation of cyber threats ranging from data breaches and ransomware attacks to sophisticated state-sponsored espionage, safeguarding sensitive information and ensuring the integrity of digital systems have become paramount. Traditional approaches to cybersecurity, such as firewalls and antivirus software, are no longer sufficient to combat the evolving tactics of cybercriminals and malicious actors.

In this context, the role of foundational models in cybersecurity has garnered significant attention. These models provide the theoretical underpinnings and methodological frameworks necessary for understanding, analyzing, and mitigating cyber threats. From rule-based systems that enforce predefined security policies to advanced machine learning algorithms capable of detecting anomalous behavior, foundational models form the backbone of modern cybersecurity defenses.

However, as the cyber threat landscape continues to evolve with the emergence of new attack vectors and sophisticated adversaries, there is a pressing need to reassess and enhance existing foundational models. Moreover, the advent of artificial intelligence and natural language processing has opened up new possibilities for bolstering cybersecurity capabilities through the integration of language models and advanced analytics techniques.

Against this backdrop, this chapter seeks to delve into the current landscape of foundational models in cybersecurity, examining their efficacy, limitations, and potential for future advancements. By providing a comprehensive review of the existing models and proposing future directions for research and development, this study aims to contribute to the ongoing discourse on strengthening cybersecurity resilience in an ever-changing digital landscape.

DOI: 10.1201/9781003497585-1

1.2 FOUNDATION MODELS

1.2.1 Definition

Foundation models have primarily been developed in the field of natural language processing (NLP), which is where our focus lies for now. However, similar to how deep learning first gained traction in computer vision but later expanded beyond it, we view foundation models as a broader AI paradigm, not confined exclusively to NLP [1].

Foundation models are a class of machine learning models characterized by their extensive training on broad datasets, often using self-supervised learning techniques. These models are designed to be adaptable to a wide range of downstream tasks. Examples include Bidirectional Encoder Representations from Transformers (BERT), Generative Pre-Trained Transformer 3 (GPT-3), and Contrastive Language-Image Pre-Training (CLIP). The term "foundation models" underscores their central yet incomplete nature, indicating that while they provide a robust starting point, they require further fine-tuning or adaptation to specific applications. The models are built using standard deep learning and transfer learning approaches but at a scale that brings forth new emergent capabilities. These capabilities and the model's adaptability make them particularly powerful and versatile, though they also come with risks such as the potential to perpetuate or accentuate biases and other harms[2].

1.2.2 What is hallucination in foundation model?

In the context of foundation models, hallucination refers to a situation where the model generates content that deviates from factual or accurate information. This phenomenon occurs when the model produces text containing details, facts, or claims that are fictional, misleading, or entirely fabricated, rather than providing reliable and truthful information.

The issue arises because the model can generate plausible-sounding text based on patterns learned from its training data, even if the content does not align with reality. Hallucination may be unintentional and can result from factors such as biases in the training data, lack of access to real-time or up-to-date information, or inherent limitations in the model's ability to comprehend and generate contextually accurate responses [3].

1.2.3 The lifecycle of the foundation model system

The lifecycle of foundation model systems, as detailed in Figure 1.1, comprises four primary stages, designated as 1, 2, 3, and 4, that encapsulate the comprehensive development and operational phases of these systems [4].

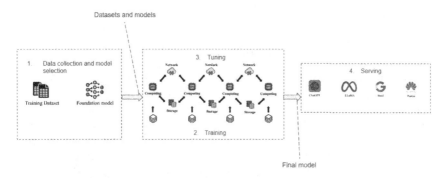

Figure 1.1 Lifecycle of the foundation model system.

1. *Data collection and preprocessing*: This stage involves the acquisition and preparation of data that are essential for training the foundation models. High-quality, diverse datasets are gathered and preprocessed to ensure they are in the appropriate format and structure for model training. This step is foundational, as the quality and variety of the data can significantly influence the performance and capabilities of the resulting model.

2. *Model training*: In this phase, the selected models are trained using the prepared datasets. The training process involves adjusting the model's parameters through algorithms like backpropagation, and it requires substantial computational resources to optimize the model's fit to the data. This phase is both resource-intensive and critical, as it determines the model's ability to perform its intended tasks effectively.

3. *Model evaluation and fine-tuning*: Once a model has been trained, it must be evaluated to assess its performance. This involves using test data to measure how well the model generalizes to new, unseen examples. Fine-tuning adjustments are made based on the evaluation results to enhance the model's performance further and ensure it meets the desired criteria for its applications.

4. *Model serving*: The final stage is the deployment of the model into a serving system where it can process real-world tasks. Model serving focuses on performance optimization, which includes strategies such as model quantization and hardware acceleration, to ensure the model can operate with high efficiency, low latency, and in harmony with the existing systems.

This lifecycle reflects the complexity and the iterative nature of developing foundation model systems, highlighting the need for both methodical progression through each stage and ongoing refinements to maintain and improve the model's performance in practical applications [5].

1.2.4 Transformers for foundation models

Transformers have cemented their role as the core architecture within foundation models, significantly impacting the field of cybersecurity [55]. The crux of the transformer architecture lies in its self-attention mechanism, which grants the model the capability to weigh the significance of different parts of the input data (Figure 1.2). In the context of cybersecurity, this means the ability to discern intricate patterns and relationships in textual data, which could indicate malicious activity or inform about the security landscape [6].

Foundation models like GPT and BERT, built upon transformer architectures, excel in processing large and diverse datasets, capturing the subtleties and complexities of language that are integral to cyber communications. Unlike their predecessors, these models eschew sequential data processing for parallel computation, enabling them to rapidly

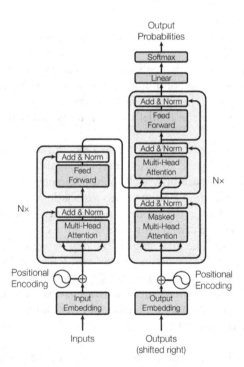

Figure 1.2 The transformer architecture.

assimilate and analyze information, a critical feature in the fast-paced domain of cybersecurity.

The strength of transformer-based foundation models in cybersecurity stems from their sophisticated understanding of context and their ability to handle the nuances of technical language. These models learn to parse through security reports, logs, and threat descriptions, extracting relevant features that contribute to a robust representation of cybersecurity knowledge.

However, such powerful models come with inherent challenges when deployed in the cybersecurity domain. Their performance is heavily dependent on the quality and scope of the training data. Given the dynamic nature of cyber threats, the models must be continuously updated with the latest data to maintain their effectiveness. Additionally, the self-attention mechanism, while powerful, does not inherently distinguish between benign and malicious patterns, necessitating careful tuning and oversight to ensure that the models' outputs are reliable and not swayed by adversarial inputs [7].

In summary, transformer-based foundation models stand as critical technological advancements in cybersecurity. Their unique architecture equips them with the potential to elevate the efficiency and accuracy of cybersecurity threat detection and analysis.

1.3 LARGE LANGUAGE MODELS (LLMS)

Large language models (LLMs), typified by groundbreaking models such as GPT-3, have become a focal point in the realm of artificial intelligence, showcasing remarkable performance in a spectrum of natural language processing tasks without the need for task-specific training. These models are distinguished by their vast scale, both in terms of the sheer number of parameters and the breadth of the pretraining corpus, which endow them with capabilities that push the boundaries of machine understanding and generation of human language [8].

The evolution of LLMs began with OpenAI's introduction of GPT-3, which set in motion an era where the size of a model and the corpus on which it was trained were scaled up significantly. Subsequent models, including ChatGPT and GPT-4, have continued this trend, contributing to a rapidly growing body of research that taps into their expanded capabilities. The proliferation of LLMs, particularly within the research community, has underscored the necessity for comprehensive reviews that consolidate the multifaceted progress and provide insightful directives for future exploration.

These models, being foundational, serve as the architecture upon which the fabric of current AI capabilities is woven. They are pre-trained on a wide-ranging array of text data, facilitating a broader grasp of language nuances

Table 1.1 Data preparation process for training a large language model

Raw Corpus	Quality filtering	Deduplication	Privacy reduction	Tokenization	Output
Dataset	Language filtering, Metric filtering, Statistic filtering, Keyword filtering	Sentence-level, Document-level, Set-level	Detect Personally Identifiable Information (PII), Remove PII	Reuse Existing Tokenizer, Sentence Piece, Byte-level BPE	Ready to pre-train

and applications across various domains. Such comprehensive training empowers them to generate responses and analyses that reflect a deep contextual understanding, a prerequisite for tackling complex problems within the AI sphere.

One of the transformative characteristics of LLMs is their inherent ability to approach any natural language processing task as a problem of conditional text generation. By being conditioned on a given input prompt, which may comprise task descriptions and examples, LLMs generate text outputs that align with the specified conditions. This mechanism, rooted in the models' design, enables them to operate effectively even with limited task-specific data.

In the context of cyberthreats and security, the ability of LLMs to parse, understand, and generate text can be invaluable. Their robust feature extraction capabilities mean they can analyze security protocols, threat intelligence reports, and incident logs with a high degree of accuracy (Table 1.1). Their predictive nature can anticipate potential security breaches, and their generative abilities could be utilized to simulate and prepare for a range of cyberattack scenarios [9].

1.3.1 GPT

The generative pre-trained transformer (GPT) series, developed by OpenAI, has significantly advanced the field of artificial intelligence, particularly in natural language processing. From GPT-1 to the latest iteration, GPT-4 (Table 1.2), these models have demonstrated remarkable abilities in understanding and generating human-like text, propelling the boundaries of machine learning [10].

GPT-4, the successor to GPT-3.5, marks a significant progress in generative AI. It showcases an increased model size and a new rule-based reward model approach during training. These innovations have led to notable

Table 1.2 Different versions and evolution of OpenAI's GPT

Model	Details
GPT-1	Trained with Books Corpus
GPT-2	Trained with Books WebText (Reddit Articles)
GPT-3	32 TPU, trained for 1 week, cost $43k
GPT-4	Trained with Books WebText, Wikipedia
	2019.4 MuseNet, MIDI Generation
	2020.4 Jukebox
	2020.9 Reinforcement Learning trained with Reddit TLDR dataset
	Trained with a large corpus of texts, Increased word limit (25,000) and performance,
	Multimodal: can also take images as input
	2021.9 Information Cutoff
	2023.3 ChatGPT Plus (Paid subscription)
	GPT-4 Passes the Bar Exam (75%-90th percentile)
	2023.5 Bing AI

improvements in model performance and safety, such as a marked reduction in hallucination incidents. With a remarkable 170 trillion parameters, GPT-4 boasts enhanced capabilities for complex language processing tasks, achieving higher accuracy than its predecessors.

Yet, despite these enhancements, GPT-4 shares certain limitations with earlier models, such as generating harmful content and potential for disinformation abuse. OpenAI's publication of the GPT-4 system card represents a step toward mitigating these risks, enhancing transparency around the model's capabilities and the measures taken to ensure safety.

A standout feature of GPT-4 is its ability to process multimodal inputs, broadening its applicability beyond text to include images. This feature signifies a substantial leap in the field of AI, given that previous models like GPT-3 were restricted to text-only inputs.

Moreover, GPT-4's proficiency in benchmark exams suggests human-competitive performance, further demonstrated by its top percentile scores across various academic disciplines. It also exhibits vast improvements in understanding and generating multiple languages.

The potential of GPT-4 and other LLMs to revolutionize diverse industries cannot be understated. However, there's an imperative need to focus on enhancing non-functional aspects, like safety and reliability, to preclude malicious use [11].

The evolution from GPT-3.5 to GPT-4 exemplifies major progress in language model development. This iteration brings forward greater sophistication in processing abilities due to advancements in scale, modality, context window length, and rule-based training. Nonetheless, to fully harness GPT models' potential, ongoing efforts must address persistent challenges. It is essential to continually refine these models, focusing not only on functional performance but also on ethical AI deployment to ensure beneficial use while minimizing the possibility of misuse [12].

1.3.1.1 Impact of ChatGPT on cybersecurity

Generative AI significantly impacts cybersecurity by enhancing threat detection and automating responses, yet it also introduces new challenges through its potential for misuse in cyber-attacks. The advanced language capabilities of models like GPT-3 and GPT-4 can aid in defense but also be exploited for malicious purposes (Figure 1.3). This dual-use nature necessitates a balanced approach, focusing on ethical usage, robust security measures, and oversight to ensure the benefits of AI are realized while minimizing risks [13].

1.3.2 BERT

The Bidirectional Encoder Representations from Transformers (BERT) model represents a significant advancement in the application of NLP to cybersecurity. As a powerful language understanding model, BERT can be fine-tuned to enhance various cybersecurity tasks such as threat detection, phishing recognition, and security-related text classification [14].

BERT's deep learning architecture, pre-trained on a vast corpus of text, is adept at capturing the subtle nuances of language, making it particularly effective for analyzing the linguistic patterns found in cyber threat intelligence reports, malicious emails, and other security-related documents. By learning contextual relationships between words, BERT provides a nuanced

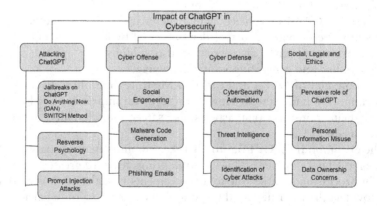

Figure 1.3 Impact of ChatGPT in cybersecurity.

understanding that goes beyond the capabilities of traditional, rule-based cybersecurity systems.

In the context of cybersecurity, BERT can be leveraged to automate the extraction of indicators of compromise (IoCs) from unstructured data, identify phishing attempts by analyzing the language used in emails, and classify security incidents based on the textual descriptions. This automation contributes to a more efficient and timely response to security incidents, thereby enhancing the overall threat intelligence process.

However, the deployment of BERT in cybersecurity is not without its challenges. The model requires substantial amounts of labeled data for fine-tuning, which can be difficult to obtain in the cybersecurity domain due to the sensitive nature of the data. Moreover, the adaptability of BERT to ever-evolving cyber threats depends on continuous retraining, which necessitates access to up-to-date and representative datasets.

Despite these challenges, BERT's potential for transforming cybersecurity practices is evident. Its ability to learn from context and improve over time promises a new level of intelligence in cyber defenses. As the field continues to evolve, the integration of BERT and similar models into cybersecurity tools will likely become a standard, driving forward the next generation of cyber defense technologies [15].

1.3.3 Encoder–decoder and attention mechanisms

Encoders and decoders in transformer models employ the notion of 'attention,' which involves emphasizing relevant information while disregarding the irrelevant. This can be likened to the practice of speed reading—instead of poring over entire articles or books, one might skim chapter titles, opening sentences, and search for key terms to locate the desired information.

Within transformer models, 'queries,' 'keys,' and 'values' are instrumental in pinpointing this attention, all represented by vectors. When a query vector aligns closely with a key, it indicates a match. Keys are sophisticated encodings of values, which, in straightforward scenarios, may be identical (Figure 1.4).

Attention mechanisms can be realized through various algorithms. A simple approach to understanding this is to consider words that frequently appear in tandem within sentences to have a stronger connection [16].

1.3.4 Positional encoding

Figure 1.5 illustrates the initial components of a transformer model's encoder, focusing on the integration of word embeddings and positional encodings.

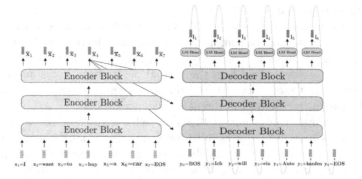

Figure 1.4 Encoder–decoder architecture.

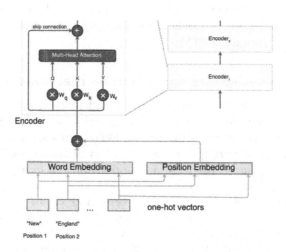

Figure 1.5 Positional encoding and word embedding.

The lower part of the diagram shows "Word Embedding" and "Position Embedding." Word embeddings are vector representations of words that capture their meaning and context within the text. For example, the word "New" at position 1 and "England" at position 2 are converted into numerical vectors that encapsulate semantic information about the words.

Positional embeddings, also shown, add information about the position of each word within the sequence. This is important because, unlike models such as Recurrent Neural Networks (RNNs) or Long Short-Term

Table 1.3 Example of positional encoding

Sequence	Index of token	Pk0	Pk1	Pk2	Pk3
I	0	sin(0)=0	cos(0)=1	sin(0)=0	cos(0)=1
am	1	sin(1) = 0.84	cos(1) = 0.54	sin(1/10) = 0.10	cos(1/10) = 1.00
a	2	sin(2) = 0.91	cos(2) =-0.42	sin(2/10) = 0.20	cos(2/10) = 0.98
Robot	3	sin(3) =0.14	cos(3) =-0.99	sin(3/10) = 0.30	cos(3/10) = 0.96

Memories (LSTMs), the transformer does not process words sequentially. It processes all words at once and hence needs a way to take into account the order of words. The positional encodings ensure that the sequence's order is preserved and that the model can recognize patterns based on the position of words in a sentence. These one-hot vectors represent a unique position in the sequence, providing the model with the ability to understand the sequence order.

These two types of embeddings are then combined, typically by element-wise addition, to give a comprehensive representation that carries both semantic and positional information for each word. This combined representation is then fed into the multi-head attention mechanism, which allows the model to focus on different parts of the sentence for a given task.

The "Multi-Head Attention" module takes queries (Q), keys (K), and values (V) as inputs, all derived from the same word representations, and applies the attention mechanism multiple times in parallel (hence "multi-head"). This process enables the model to capture various aspects of the sentence, like context and relationships between words, which is crucial for understanding the sentence as a whole.

The outputs from the multi-head attention mechanism are then typically passed through a feedforward neural network, and each sub-layer in the encoder, including the multi-head attention and feedforward network, has a skip connection around it followed by layer normalization (not shown in this image).

This process is repeated in each encoder block (Encoder1, Encoder2, etc., shown on the right side), with the output of one block serving as the input to the next, building deeper levels of understanding at each step (Table 1.3) [17].

1.4 RELATED WORK

The emergence of CySecBERT signifies a notable development in domain-specific language models, expanding upon CyBERT's approach by integrating comprehensive pre-training alongside targeted fine-tuning on cybersecurity corpora. This advancement yields a model that exhibits a profound understanding of cybersecurity vernacular, demonstrated by its exemplary performance across a range of NLP tasks within this domain. Empirical results, particularly the Silhouette Score, attest to CySecBERT's effectiveness in creating more cohesive and distinct data clusters compared to its predecessors.

In addition, CySecBERT has shown remarkable results in word similarity tasks, significantly outstripping the performance of baseline models like BERT. This is indicative of its nuanced semantic understanding, which is also evident in Named Entity Recognition (NER) tasks where CySecBERT excels in identifying specific cybersecurity-related entities such as software versions and names.

Classification tasks also benefit from the sophistication of CySecBERT. It adeptly handles complex datasets and outperforms BERT in generating precise F1 scores, suggesting its potential as a benchmark for specialized language model development in cybersecurity.

The role of generative AI, with models such as GPT-3 and GPT-4, cannot be understated in the cybersecurity domain. These models contribute significantly to the advancement of threat detection capabilities while also presenting potential risks due to their capacity for misuse. ChatGPT, in particular, has demonstrated its dual utility in both enhancing defense strategies and its possible exploitation for cyber-attacks. Such developments underscore the necessity for an equitable approach to leverage AI's strengths while mitigating associated risks and upholding ethical standards.

CySecBERT's performance across various NLP tasks positions it as a leading model for cybersecurity applications, marking a crucial point in the evolution of language models. Its development underscores the need for models that can navigate the technicalities of sector-specific lexicons. The rise of CySecBERT catalyzes discussions about the continuous innovation required in NLP to develop practical, ethical, and effective AI tools for cybersecurity [18].

1.4.1 SecurityBERT

The integration of large language models (LLMs) like BERT into cybersecurity realms has catalyzed significant advancements in cyber threat detection. SecurityBERT, a novel adaptation of BERT, has been specifically architected for IoT networks, exhibiting a lightweight and privacy-preserving structure that makes it ideally suited for embedded devices within such environments. In the work by Ferrag et al., SecurityBERT is fine-tuned and pre-trained with a focus on cybersecurity-related datasets, enabling it to outperform traditional machine learning (ML) and deep learning (DL) models in cyber threat detection tasks.

One of the pivotal innovations in SecurityBERT is the incorporation of a novel encoding technique, Privacy-Preserving Fixed-Length Encoding

(PPFLE), which allows for the structured representation of network traffic data, significantly enhancing the model's performance metrics. Tested against the Edge-IIoTset cybersecurity dataset, SecurityBERT achieved an impressive accuracy rate, exceeding the efficiency of preceding hybrid models and setting a new benchmark for real-time traffic analysis on IoT devices. The compact model size, coupled with its rapid inference capability, underscores its potential to operate within resource-constrained environments while maintaining data confidentiality during classification tasks on untrusted servers.

Furthermore, the empirical evaluation demonstrates that SecurityBERT's sophisticated architecture, with a strategic number of encoder layers and a carefully calibrated parameter configuration, ensures not only high accuracy but also addresses challenges of model complexity, paving the way for its seamless integration into real-world scenarios.

1.5 CONCLUSION AND FUTURE WORKS

This review has extensively covered the foundational models in cybersecurity, evaluating their strengths and shortcomings across various scenarios involving cyber threats and attacks. The discussion highlighted the essential role of rule-based systems, machine learning algorithms, and the integration of advanced technologies like AI and natural language processing in enhancing cybersecurity measures.

As we look toward the future, several areas stand out for further research and development:

- *Enhanced model adaptability*: Continuous refinement of foundational models is necessary to keep pace with the rapidly evolving cyber threat landscape. This includes integrating real-time data feeds into model training to ensure responsiveness to new threats.
- *Ethical AI use*: There is a critical need to address the ethical considerations surrounding AI in cybersecurity. Developing guidelines and frameworks for responsible AI usage will help mitigate risks associated with machine learning models in security applications.
- *Advanced threat detection systems*: Future research should focus on creating more sophisticated systems capable of detecting subtle, nuanced threats, which often bypass conventional security measures. Employing deep learning and complex pattern recognition technologies could be pivotal.
- *Cross-domain applications*: Exploring the application of cybersecurity foundational models in other domains, such as IoT security and mobile network defense, could provide comprehensive protection strategies across all digital platforms.

- *Collaborative frameworks*: Encouraging collaboration between academia, industry, and government bodies to share knowledge, tools, and best practices can accelerate the advancement of cybersecurity solutions and their deployment.

In conclusion, while the current foundational models offer robust frameworks for managing cyber risks, the dynamic nature of cyber threats necessitates ongoing innovations and adaptations. The future of cybersecurity lies in the ability to anticipate changes, adapt methodologies swiftly, and implement solutions that are not only reactive but also proactive in securing digital assets [20–55].

REFERENCES

[1] B. Kereopa-Yorke (2023). Building Resilient SMEs: Harnessing Large Language Models for Cyber Security in Australia. Proceedings of the Artificial Intelligence for Cyber Security (AICS) Workshop 2020.

[2] R. Bommasani, D. A. Hudson, E. Adeli, R. Altman, S. Arora, S. von Arx, ... D. Zhou (2021). On the opportunities and risks of foundation models. arXiv preprint arXiv:2108.07258. https://doi.org/10.48550/arXiv.2108.07258.

[3] V. Rawte, A. Sheth, A. Das (2023). A survey of hallucination in large foundation models. arXiv preprint arXiv:2309.05922. https://doi.org/10.48550/arXiv.2309.05922.

[4] Y. Xu, M. Zhao, J. Liu, X. Zhang (2024). Training and serving system of foundation models: A comprehensive survey. *IEEE Open Journal of the Computer Society*. https://doi.org/10.1109/OJCS.2024.338082

[5] Y. Chang et al., A survey on evaluation of large language models. *ACM Trans. Intell. Syst. Technol.*, pp. 1–45, 2023.

[6] Z. Wu, H. Zhang, P. Wang, Z. Sun (2022). RTIDS: A robust transformer-based approach for intrusion detection. *IEEE Access*. https://doi.org/10.1109/ACCESS.2022.3182333

[7] S. Karita, N. E. Y. Soplin, S. Watanabe, M. Delcroix, A. Ogawa, and T. Nakatani (2019). Improving transformer-based end-to-end speech recognition with connectionist temporal classification and language model integration, in Proc. Interspeech, Sep., pp. 1–

[8] J. Radford, R. Wu, D. Child, D. Luan, Amodei, I. Sutskever (2018). Language models are unsupervised multitask learners, *OpenAI Blog*, 1(8), 9.

[9] G. de J.C. da Silva, C. B. Westphall (2023). A survey of large language models in cybersecurity. arXiv. https://doi.org/10.48550/arXiv.2402.16968

[10] M. Al-Hawawreh, A. Aljuhani, Y. Jararweh (2023). ChatGPT for cybersecurity: practical applications, challenges, and future directions, *Cluster Computing*. https://doi.org/10.1007/s10586-023-04124-5

[11] A. Kolides, A. Nawaz, A. Rathor, D. Beeman, M. Hashmi, S. Fatima, D. Berdik, M. Al-Ayyoub, Y. Jararweh (2023). Artificial intelligence

foundation and pre-trained models: fundamentals, applications, opportunities, and social impacts. *Simul. Modell. Pract. Theory* 126, 102754

[12]   OpenAI. GPT-4 technical report. March 2023.

[13]   M. Gupta, C.K. Akiri, K. Aryal, E. Parker, L. Praharaj (2023). From ChatGPT to ThreatGPT: impact of generative AI in cyber-security and privacy. *IEEE Access*, 11, 1–1, doi: 10.1109/AC- CESS.2023.3300381

[14]   W. Zhu, X. Qiu, Y. Ni, G. Xie (2020). AutoRC: Improving BERT based relation classification models via architecture search. arXiv preprint arXiv:2009.10680.

[15]   J. Devlin, M.-W. Chang, K. Lee, K. Toutanova (2018). BERT: Pre-training of deep bidirectional transformers for language understanding. arXiv preprint arXiv:1810.04805.

[16]   Neural Machine Translation by Jointly Learning to Align and Translate Dzmitry Bahdanau, Kyunghyun Cho, Yoshua Bengio (Submitted on 1 Sep 2014 (v1), last revised 19 May 2016 (this version, v7)).

[17]   X. Chu, Z. Tian, B. Zhang, X. Wang, C. Shen (2021). Conditional positional encodings for vision transformers. arXiv preprint arXiv:2102.10882. https://doi.org/10.48550/arXiv.2102.10

[18]   M. Bayer, P. Kuehn, R. Shanehsaz, C. Reuter (2024). CySecBERT: A domain-adapted language model for the cybersecurity domain. *ACM Transactions on Privacy and Security*, 27(2), Article 18, 1–20. https://doi.org/10.1145/3652594

[19]   M. A. Ferrag, M. Ndhlovu, N. Tihanyi, L. C. Cordeiro , M. Debba, T. Lestable, N. S. Thandi (2024). Revolutionizing cyber threat detection with large language models: A privacy-preserving BERT-based lightweight model for IoT/IIoT devices. *IEEE Access.* https://doi.org/10.1109/ACC ESS.2024.3363469

[20]   Z. A. E. Houda, H. Moudoud, B. Brik, L. Khoukhi. (2024). Blockchain-enabled federated learning for enhanced collaborative intrusion detection in vehicular edge computing. *IEEE Transactions on Intelligent Transportation Systems*, doi: 10.1109/TITS.2024.3351699.

[21]   Z. A. E. Houda, H. Moudoud, B. Brik (2024). Federated deep reinforcement learning for efficient jamming attack mitigation in O-RAN. *IEEE Transactions on Vehicular Technology*, doi: 10.1109/TVT.2024.3359998.

[22]   Z. A. El Houda, L. Khoukhi, A. Hafid (2018). ChainSecure – A scalable and proactive solution for protecting blockchain applications using SDN. 2018 IEEE Global Communications Conference (GLOBECOM), Abu Dhabi, United Arab Emirates, pp. 1–6, doi: 10.1109/GLOCOM.2018.8647279.

[23]   Z. A. El Houda, A. Hafid, L. Khoukhi (2019). Co-IoT: A collaborative DDoS mitigation scheme in IoT environment based on blockchain using SDN. 2019 IEEE Global Communications Conference (GLOBECOM), Waikoloa, HI, USA, pp. 1–6, doi: 10.1109/GLOBECOM38437.2019.9013542.

[24]   Z. Abou El Houda, A. S. Hafid, L. Khoukhi (2019). Cochain-SC: an intra- and inter-domain ddos mitigation scheme based on blockchain using SDN and smart contract," *IEEE Access*, 7, 98893–98907, doi: 10.1109/ACCESS.2019.2930715.

[25]   Z. A. E. Houda, A. Hafid, L. Khoukhi (2020). Blockchain meets AMI: towards secure advanced metering infrastructures. ICC 2020 – 2020 IEEE

International Conference on Communications (ICC), Dublin, Ireland, pp. 1–6, doi: 10.1109/ICC40277.2020.9148963.

[26] Z. A. E. Houda, A. Hafid, L. Khoukhi (2020). BrainChain – A machine learning approach for protecting blockchain applications using SDN. ICC 2020 – 2020 IEEE International Conference on Communications (ICC), Dublin, Ireland, pp. 1–6, doi: 10.1109/ICC40277.2020.9148808.

[27] Z. Abou El Houda, L. Khoukhi, A. Senhaji Hafid (2020). Bringing intelligence to software defined networks: mitigating DDoS attacks. *IEEE Transactions on Network and Service Management*, 17(4), 2523–2535, doi: 10.1109/TNSM.2020.3014870.

[28] H. Moudoud, W. Hamhoum, S. Cherkaoui (2023). Strengthening open radio access networks: advancing safeguards through ZTA and deep learning. GLOBECOM 2023 – 2023 IEEE Global Communications Conference, Kuala Lumpur, Malaysia, pp. 80–85, doi: 10.1109/GLOBECOM54140.2023.10437829.

[29] Z. A. El Houda, A. S. Hafid, L. Khoukhi (2021). Blockchain-based Reverse Auction for V2V charging in smart grid environment. ICC 2021 – IEEE International Conference on Communications, Montreal, QC, Canada, pp. 1–6, doi: 10.1109/ICC42927.2021.9500366.

[30] Z. A. El Houda, A. S. Hafid, L. Khoukhi (2021). A novel machine learning framework for advanced attack detection using SDN. 2021 IEEE Global Communications Conference (GLOBECOM), Madrid, Spain, pp. 1–6, doi: 10.1109/GLOBECOM46510.2021.9685643.

[31] Z. A. El Houda, L. Khoukhi, B. Brik (2022). A low-latency fog-based framework to secure IoT applications using collaborative federated learning. 2022 IEEE 47th Conference on Local Computer Networks (LCN), Edmonton, AB, Canada, pp. 343–346, doi: 10.1109/LCN53696.2022.9843315.

[32] Z. Abou El Houda, L. Khoukhi (2022). A hierarchical fog computing framework for network attack detection in SDN. ICC 2022 – IEEE International Conference on Communications, Seoul, Republic of Korea, pp. 4366–4371, doi: 10.1109/ICC45855.2022.9838560.

[33] Z. A. El Houda, D. Naboulsi, G. Kaddoum (2022). Cost-efficient federated reinforcement learning- based network routing for wireless networks. 2022 IEEE Future Networks World Forum (FNWF), Montreal, QC, Canada, pp. 243–248, doi: 10.1109/FNWF55208.2022.00050.

[34] Z. A. E. Houda, B. Brik, A. Ksentini, L. Khoukhi, M. Guizani (2022). When federated learning meets game theory: A cooperative framework to secure IIoT applications on edge computing. *IEEE Transactions on Industrial Informatics*, 18(11), 7988–7997, doi: 10.1109/TII.2022.3170347.

[35] Z. A. E. Houda, B. Brik, L. Khoukhi (2022) "Why should I trust your IDS?": an explainable deep learning framework for intrusion detection systems in internet of things networks. *IEEE Open Journal of the Communications Society*, 3, 1164–1176, , doi: 10.1109/OJCOMS.2022.3188750.

[36] Z. A. El Houda, B. Brik, S. -M. Senouci (2022). A novel IoT-based explainable deep learning framework for intrusion detection systems. *IEEE Internet of Things Magazine*, 5(2), 20–23, doi: 10.1109/IOTM.005.2200028.

[37]   Z. A. El Houda, D. Nabousli, G. Kaddoum (2023). Advancing security and efficiency in federated learning service aggregation for wireless networks. 2023 IEEE 34th Annual International Symposium on Personal, Indoor and Mobile Radio Communications (PIMRC), Toronto, ON, Canada, pp. 1–6, doi: 10.1109/PIMRC56721.2023.10293790.

[38]   Z. A. El Houda, H. Moudoud, B. Brik, L. Khoukhi (2023). Securing federated learning through blockchain and explainable AI for robust intrusion detection in IoT networks. IEEE INFOCOM 2023 – IEEE Conference on Computer Communications Workshops (INFOCOM WKSHPS), Hoboken, NJ, USA, pp. 1–6, doi: 10.1109/INFOCOMWKS HPS57453.2023.10225769.

[39]   Z. A. E. Houda, J. Beaugeard, Q. Sauvêtre, L. Khoukhi (2023). Towards a secure and scalable access control system using blockchain. 2023 IEEE International Conference on Blockchain and Cryptocurrency (ICBC), Dubai, United Arab Emirates, pp. 1–8, doi: 10.1109/ICBC56567.2023.10174880.

[40]   Z. A. El Houda, H. Moudoud, L. Khoukhi (2023). Secure and efficient federated learning for robust intrusion detection in IoT networks. GLOBECOM 2023 – 2023 IEEE Global Communications Conference, Kuala Lumpur, Malaysia, pp. 2668–2673, doi: 10.1109/ GLOBECOM54140.2023.10436768.

[41]   Z. A. E. Houda, A. S. Hafid, L. Khoukhi, B. Brik (2023). When collaborative federated learning meets blockchain to preserve privacy in healthcare. *IEEE Transactions on Network Science and Engineering*, 10(5), 2455–2465, doi: 10.1109/TNSE.2022.3211192.

[42]   Z. A. E. Houda, A. S. Hafid, L. Khoukhi (2023). MiTFed: A privacy preserving collaborative network attack mitigation framework based on federated learning using SDN and blockchain. *IEEE Transactions on Network Science and Engineering*, 10(4), 1985–2001, doi: 10.1109/ TNSE.2023.3237367.

[43]   Z. A. El Houda, B. Brik, A. Ksentini, L. Khoukhi (2023). A MEC-based architecture to secure IoT applications using federated deep learning. *IEEE Internet of Things Magazine*, 6(1), 60–63, doi: 10.1109/ IOTM.001.2100238.

[44]   A. Taïk, H. Moudoud, S. Cherkaoui (2021). Data-quality based scheduling for federated edge learning. 2021 IEEE 46th Conference on Local Computer Networks (LCN), Edmonton, AB, Canada, pp. 17–23, doi: 10.1109/ LCN52139.2021.9524974.

[45]   Z. A. E. Houda, D. Naboulsi, G. Kaddoum (2024). A privacy-preserving collaborative jamming attacks detection framework using federated learning. *IEEE Internet of Things Journal*, 11(7), 12153–12164, doi: 10.1109/ JIOT.2023.3333870.

[46]   H. Moudoud, S. Cherkaoui and L. Khoukhi (2021). Towards a scalable and trustworthy blockchain: IoT use case. ICC 2021 – IEEE International Conference on Communications, Montreal, QC, Canada, pp. 1–6, doi: 10.1109/ICC42927.2021.9500535.

[47]   H. Moudoud, S. Cherkaoui, L. Khoukhi (2019). An IoT blockchain architecture using oracles and smart contracts: the use-case of a food supply chain. 2019 IEEE 30th Annual International Symposium on Personal,

Indoor and Mobile Radio Communications (PIMRC), Istanbul, Turkey, pp. 1–6, doi: 10.1109/PIMRC.2019.8904404.

[48] H. Moudoud, S. Cherkaoui (2023). Empowering security and trust in 5G and beyond: A deep reinforcement learning approach. *IEEE Open Journal of the Communications Society*, 4, 2410–2420, doi: 10.1109/ OJCOMS.2023.3313352.

[49] Z. A. El Houda, H. Moudoud, L. Khoukhi (2023). Secure and efficient federated learning for robust intrusion detection in IoT networks, GLOBECOM 2023 – 2023 IEEE Global Communications Conference, Kuala Lumpur, Malaysia, pp. 2668–2673, doi: 10.1109/ GLOBECOM54140.2023.10436768.

[50] H. Moudoud, S. Cherkaoui (2023). Enhancing open RAN security with zero trust and machine learning. GLOBECOM 2023 – 2023 IEEE Global Communications Conference, Kuala Lumpur, Malaysia, pp. 2772–2777, doi: 10.1109/GLOBECOM54140.2023.10437043.

[51] H. Moudoud, S. Cherkaoui (2023). Federated learning meets blockchain to secure the metaverse. 2023 International Wireless Communications and Mobile Computing (IWCMC), Marrakesh, Morocco, pp. 339–344, doi: 10.1109/IWCMC58020.2023.10182956.

[52] H. Moudoud, L. Khoukhi, S. Cherkaoui (2021). Prediction and detection of FDIA and DDoS attacks in 5G enabled IoT. *IEEE Network*, 35(2), 194–201, doi: 10.1109/MNET.011.2000449.

[53] H. Moudoud, S. Cherkaoui (2022). Toward secure and private federated learning for IoT using blockchain. GLOBECOM 2022 – 2022 IEEE Global Communications Conference, Rio de Janeiro, Brazil, pp. 4316–4321, doi: 10.1109/GLOBECOM48099.2022.10000623.

[54] H. Moudoud, Z. Mlika, L. Khoukhi, S. Cherkaoui (2022). Detection and prediction of FDI attacks in IoT systems via hidden Markov model. *IEEE Transactions on Network Science and Engineering*, 9(5), 2978–2990, 1 Sept.-Oct., doi: 10.1109/TNSE.2022.3161479.

[55] A. Vaswani, N. Shazeer, N. Parmar, J. Uszkoreit, L. Jones, A.N. Gomez, L. Kaiser, I. Polosukhin (2017). Attention is all you need. ArXiv. /abs/ 1706.03762.

Chapter 2

Security, privacy, and trust in IoT networks

Zineb Nadifi, Mariyam Ouaissa, Mariya Ouaissa,
Mohamed Alhyan, and Ali Kartit

2.1 INTRODUCTION

The Internet of Things (IoT) is a new architecture dedicated to facilitating users' lives in several domains: medicine and healthcare, smart buildings, wearables, transportation, and logistics [1]. To achieve this, many pieces of information should be exchanged, treated, and carried out with multiple devices, which should be connected over the internet. This generates new challenges and risks such as privacy and confidentiality [2].

While gradually using and initializing IoT services, many vulnerabilities show up more and more, as does the hackers' interest in their exploitation [3]. Since IoT has reported a huge change in the world on different levels, like the treatment of data, controlling devices, and sensitive sensation thresholds remotely, securing this architecture becomes a big challenge to the security expert vis-à-vis hacker attacks [4].

In this chapter, we will discuss the challenges that IoT has to face, as well as the famous attacks launched by attackers, the prerequisites, and the security measures that must be implemented and put in place to keep our architecture secure and minimize risks and violations.

2.2 BACKGROUND TO IOT

2.2.1 IoT concept

Two terms are included in the phrase "Internet of Things": The Internet is defined as a global network that interconnects a billion pieces of equipment around the world, to facilitate communication between them, and Things that may be anything from these pieces of equipment, such as cameras, cars, insulin pumps, pacemakers, and vehicles.

Therefore, IoT is a world of interconnected things and an ecosystem that connects and relates a number of devices, such as vehicles, medical staff,

DOI: 10.1201/9781003497585-2

cameras, and smartphones in order to collect and exchange data among themselves, and other ones in the cloud over the internet [5].

The IoT spans a wide range of categories and industries, including smart home devices, wearable devices, industrial sensors and equipment, connected cars and vehicles, environmental sensors, and smart cities. And, of course, other sectors.

2.2.2 IoT architecture

The architecture of the IoT generally depends on the environment where it is planned to be implemented in as well as its needs and functionality; however, it can be represented by four common stages: the sensing layer, network layer, data processing layer, and application layer [6] (Figure 1).

2.2.2.1 Sensing/ perception layer

To make the IoT system work, an interaction between the reel and digital world should be assured by a designated device; the sensing layer, is the responsible for this interaction.

Basically, a lot of information that brings meaning and requires actions surrounds the environment, where there is a need for some sensitive devices, which are able to feel and capture these signs and moves, to forward them to the appropriate equipment in order to establish and complete the IoT circle

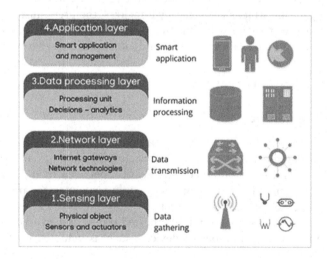

Figure 2.1 IoT architecture.

and let the user be informed regarding the actual situation of the ecosystem. For that, the following devices are used:

- Capture: The device (like a gauge or a probe) that is dedicated to understanding and acquiring the signs of the environment, such as temperature, humidity, light, sound, presence, and pressure, and other physical parameters, in order to provide an input to the higher levels within the architecture; consequently, it is the first level that gets in contact with the real-world indicators.
- Actuators are devices that take charge of converting the analog and digital signs into physical actions in an automatic way, and without human intervention; these signs are received from another tier, such as the capture and control software, and require a specific action to be taken, like cutting off the water at a valve in the event of a disaster, switching on a light, or stopping an assembly line if an imminent failure is detected.

2.2.2.2 Network layer

This is the layer that receives the data sent by the detection devices in the level below and is responsible for its transmission between the applications, devices, severs, and all IoT elements, via different protocols, and technologies [7].

This transmission needs the following components to be achieved:

- Gateway assures the bridge between the internal network and the external system; it's the device that contacts the captures while collecting data, in order to transmit it to the cloud or the user in question.
- Data storage system (DAS) provides data aggregation and conversion functions and efficient data management, enabling the storage, processing, and securing of data collected by connected devices.

2.2.2.3 Data processing layer

In this level, the data collected from the previous stage will be stocked, accumulated, and analyzed via IoT platforms and application programming interfaces (APIs), in order to decide whether these data are efficient for the initial need or not. The main goal is to stock and get as much as possible of the relevant data collected from IoT and non-IoT resources in order to be treated and sent to the application for use and for making decisions.

This stage is considered important since a good treatment and successful implementation of raw data result in beneficial decisions and provide efficient actions that match the expected results and needs.

2.2.2.4 Application layer

The application layer is the one that offers the user a platform so he can interact with the IoT environment and get into specific services. This may be done through the user's mobile or computer using some applications that are dedicated to showing dashboards, statistics, and easy buttons. By clicking on them, the user can enable or disable the IoT equipment, for example, and based on the dashboard results, the user can ask to activate the air conditioner with a simple click.

The goal is for the user to gain a flexible and soft platform that allows him to interact with the devices, so he can meet his needs.

2.3 IOT RISKS AND CHALLENGES

With IoT, everything becomes a computer and a system, making the job that is basically attended to be done from a non-IoT equipment. For example, a light bulb may be considered a computer to light up the home; a car is also a system that drives you places. So based on this statement, and according to some basic knowledge of IT, we can affirm that every computer and system can be hacked; therefore, everything related to the hacked system can also be hacked [8].

On the other hand, the IoT is running within a code that contains over 100 million lines; more the line numbers increase, more it's complicated, and so do the number of bugs. All of that ends up having much more vulnerabilities.

So, what is required to minimize the attack surface?

Before listing what solutions can be used, let's check what risks we will be facing in the event of a hack:

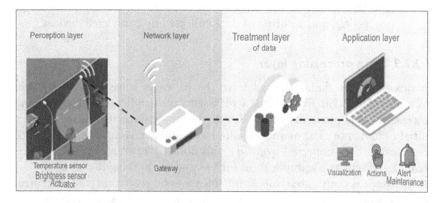

Figure 2.2 IoT components.

- *Privacy*: If one of the security devices is broken, that may lead to checking its data, and maybe it will start recording, seeing, and tracking the user's activities, which impact and damage the user privacy.
- *Safety*: Several IoT devices control physical, and medical systems, such as industrial machinery, defibrillators, or an implantable insulin pump. Compromising the security of these devices could result in havoc, or serious accidents, or vehicle theft, or even much worse!
- *Denial of Service (DoS) attack*: The IoT devices may be hijacked and explored to create and send a huge flood of traffic to a target in order to impact its availability and cause a malfunction of a target service. At the end, the IoT devices are involved and a part of the DoS attack.
- *Data Protection*: To make an IoT ecosystem works in an organized way, a huge amount of data should be transmitting among several equipment and applications, locally, and over the internet. This means that the probability of sniffing these data increases. Also, this fact presents a huge challenge regarding keeping the data safe and secure.
- *Weak authentication*: the IoT devices are known by their weak passwords, as well as the default ones, which cause a major vulnerability and good target for the hackers. For example, The Mirai botnet that scans the internet for insecure smart devices and logs in using default and hardcoded passwords. He then takes control of it to create a network of bots capable of launching devastating cyberattacks.

2.4 PRIVACY AND TRUST IN IOT

In the previous lines, a list of challenges and risks referring to IoT architecture has been mentioned; however, privacy takes the lead of them, since the IoT devices are supposed to collect, treat, and exchange important data over a public network (internet) [9].

With the increase in the rate of use of IoT, and the diversity of fields that it is now present in, such as medicine, agronomy, industry, and banks, the user data exchange becomes increasingly critical and their disclosure can cause major damage for the user, as well as for the architects of the IoT, which involves the risk of impacting the privacy of consumers of this new architecture.

No one can imagine the impact of a leak of medical analysis results, bank statements, or confidential exchanges on a violation of people's privacy. Therefore, the use of an IoT architecture must be imperative and always be respectful of a set of security measures to benefit from the facilities and advantages that it offers, while at the same time not being a victim of vulnerabilities, and a lack of security [10].

Many attacks could cause this kind of violation; some of them have more occurrences than others; next are the common ones.

2.5 IOT CYBERATTACKS

As IoT devices continue to grow in an exponential way, so do cyberattacks, which can take different levels and stages according to the target of the attack, such as the following [11]:

- Device attacks: browser-based, SMS, application attacks, rooted/jailbroken devices.
- Network attacks: DNS cache poisoning, rogue Aps, packet sniffing.
- Data center (Cloud) attacks: databases, photos, etc.

Following are some common and famous IoT attacks:

- *Distributed Denial of Service (DDoS)*: The number of IoT devices grows more and more by the year, and many of them suffer from security issues such as infrequent updates, default credentials, or mis-configuration, making them an easy target for attackers to exploit them as botnets and launch DDoS attacks.

  The cybercriminal uses his machine as a Command and Control (C&C) server that will control, guide, and orchestrate the infected devices called botnets, so they can send a huge amount of data and requests to the victim device.

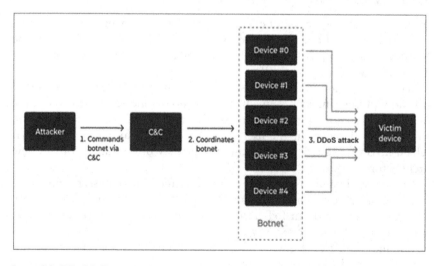

Figure 2.3 DDoS IoT attack.

- *Firmware attacks*: Cybercriminals exploit the vulnerabilities in the firmware and software used by IoT devices to function in order to gain control over the device, compromising their functionality and potentially spreading to other devices on the network.
- *Man in the Middle (MiTM)*: In this attack, the attacker tries to interrupt the original traffic between the source and destination, and gets in the middle, to both intercept the data flow and alter and modify the data flowing. This can lead to data manipulation, unauthorized access, or eavesdropping on communications. Weak encryption, poor authentication, and insecure network connections are prime targets for this type of attack.
- *Physical attacks*: Physical attacks such as theft and tampering are rarely discussed but highly impact in the event of an occurrence. The physical security should assume huge importance as much as the network one does since it's the first line of contact with IoT devices. Therefore a list of measures is required, such as locks, access controls, and tamper-evident packaging, to prevent unauthorized physical access to IoT devices.
- *Radiofrequency jamming*: The cyberattackers use malicious nodes to create and forward radio signals in order to interfere, disrupt, and block authorized and legitimate wireless communication. Jamming can be used to disrupt the communications between the sensors and their control devices or the gateway. An IoT device may not even work if and attacker interferes with the way that it communicates.

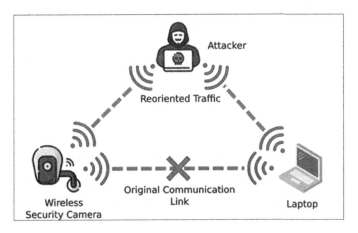

Figure 2.4 MiTM attack.

2.6 IOT SECURITY AND BEST PRACTICES

To improve the device's security, and since there is no way we can avoid all security risks, different kinds of practices are required, either in the office or at home, trying to minimize as much as possible the mentioned risks and obviously others [12]:

2.6.1 Secure the credentials

Each device has its own credentials, such as a user ID and password. The first thing a user can do is change this information for all of his network environment, the router, the Wi-Fi, and the device itself and make use of choosing a strong and long password for each one of them; a password vault can be used to store them all, and then the user may lock and unlock the vault with one password that he has to remember. Adding a multifactor authentication (MFA) would basically improve credential security through biometrics, fingerprints, or iris scanning.

2.6.2 Secure the network

We can secure the IoT network by creating a single network segment or demilitarized zone (DMZ) area dedicated to the IoT architecture. So we can guarantee that if a vulnerability is explored by a threat, it's going to be separated in the IoT segment and won't impact and affect the users' area. Especially if the users have implemented a strong architecture at home, the attack traffic will also be stopped by the firewall configured and the other security policies that have been configured to flow filtering [13].

2.6.3 Chasing for regular patching/updates

One of the most common practices that can make a big difference in terms of security is keeping the software updated.

Launching a patch for each device may take time and effort from the user; worse, it can be forgotten; however, an update can be automatically programmed to take place in different timeslots that have already been scheduled by the user; this can be operated and implemented on all of the network IoT devices without the need for manual intervention.

The patch or update is very important because once the software comes out for use, the hackers always pursue and try hard to discover the software edition vulnerabilities so they can exploit them as an entry point for hijacking. The updates launched by the software editions should be used to mitigate and correct these vulnerabilities and keep the devices safe as long as they can.

2.6.4 Least privilege

The principle of least privilege is to keep only the needed services and devices enabled and to disable the rest. If a user doesn't need access to an IoT camera, the more secure it is to disable this access in order to avoid the privacy risk. Also, if the camera doesn't need to connect to the cloud, this should also be disabled. The main point is that the more services and privileges are enabled, the more the risk of privacy and surface attacks is increasing and occurring [14].

2.6.5 Turning the devices off

If a device is not needed anymore, then it should be turned off. For example, if a user needs a camera at home when he is out for safety reasons, he can turn it off once he is at home because there is no longer a need for this device to be enabled. The rule is that the devices are on since there is a need for the services they provide; when this service is no longer needed, the device could be turned off to reduce the entry points for a malicious intervention.

2.6.6 Policy

The policy is a line of instructions that describe what is allowed to be done and what is not, so that the users can refer to it as a guide and rules to redirect and light them up when they are confused regarding some behavior decisions. This policy should be written with a lot of care and consideration of the office needs and requirements, so the collaborators can benefit from the IoT device services without causing any impact on security; hence, it should be respected and followed by all the office users to keep things organized and in order and to avoid as much risks as possible.

2.6.7 Users' sensibilization

The security administrators should keep the users informed regarding their behavior consequences by scheduling training and awareness campaigns to clarify that even a small activation or irresponsible act on the network may lead to very dangerous consequences and may put the whole network under sniffing and spying by malicious resources. On the other hand, following the policy instructions agreed upon by the office can offer a good level of security and keep the network safe and away from risks.

2.6.8 Keep security in mind

Users should always keep security reflection attitudes whenever they are using IoT services. Never diminish the effect and impact of a simple action on network security; sometimes, a simple click or a little bit of negligence results in big attacks and damages network security and produces a large offense.

2.6.9 Zero-trust network access (ZTNA)

ZTNA is a group of policies, functionalities, and technologies that aim to maintain a secure and strong network, based on "never trust, always verify", by offering least privilege, always authentication, rule access to an application, rule access to a specific service in an application. This will help to limit illegal access and reduce unauthorized entities' ability to gain access to sensitive data and systems.

2.7 CONCLUSION

Privacy concerns are equally crucial, given the potential for misuse of sensitive data. It is imperative to implement robust privacy protection mechanisms to prevent the exploitation of this information. Managing trust in IoT environments is also a key element in ensuring reliable communications and data integrity. Trust mechanisms must be continually developed and improved to meet growing demands and emerging threats. This chapter provided an overview of current security protocols, privacy-preserving techniques, and trust management frameworks needed to protect IoT networks. Additionally, practical case studies and directions for future research highlight the evolving nature of IoT security and the importance of continued efforts to mitigate risks.

REFERENCES

[1]   K. O. M. Salih, T. A. Rashid, D. Radovanovic, and N. Bacanin, "A comprehensive survey on the Internet of Things with the industrial marketplace," *Sensors*, vol. 22, no. 3, 2022, p. 730.

[2]   M. Kavre, A. Gadekar, and Y. Gadhade, "Internet of Things (IoT): a survey," In 2019 IEEE Pune section international conference (PuneCon), p. 1–6, IEEE, 2019.

[3]   M. Ouaissa, A. Rhattoy, and I. Chana, "New security level of authentication and key agreement protocol for the IoT on LTE mobile networks," In 2018 6th International Conference on Wireless Networks and Mobile Communications (WINCOM), p. 1–6, IEEE, 2018.

[4]   M. Ouaissa, and M. Ouaissa, "Cyber security issues for iot based smart grid infrastructure," In IOP Conference Series: Materials Science and Engineering, IOP Publishing. vol. 937, no. 1, p. 012001. 2020.

[5]   K. Ragothaman, Y. Wang, B. Rimal, and M. Lawrence, M. (2023). "Access control for IoT: A survey of existing research, dynamic policies and future directions," *Sensors*, vol. 23, no. 4, 2023, p. 1805.

[6]   M. Ouaissa, M. Ouaissa, and A. Rhattoy, "An efficient and secure authentication and key agreement protocol of LTE mobile network for an IoT system," *International Journal of Intelligent Engineering and Systems*, vol. 12, no.4, p. 212–222, 2019.

[7]   M. Ouaissa, M. Benmoussa, A. Rhattoy, M. Lahmer, and I. Chana, "Performance analysis of random access mechanisms for machine type communications in LTE networks," In 2016 International Conference on Advanced Communication Systems and Information Security (ACOSIS), p. 1–6. IEEE, 2016.

[8]   B. K. Mohanta, D. Jena, U. Satapathy, and S. Patnaik, "Survey on IoT security: Challenges and solution using machine learning, artificial intelligence and blockchain technology," *Internet of Things*, vol. 11, 2020, p. 100227.

[9]   L. Babun, K. Denney, Z. B. Celik, P. McDaniel, and A. S. Uluagac, "A survey on IoT platforms: Communication, security, and privacy perspectives," *Computer Networks*, vol. 192, 2021, p. 108040.

[10] H. Mrabet, S. Belguith, A. Alhomoud, and A. Jemai, "A survey of IoT security based on a layered architecture of sensing and data analysis," *Sensors*, vol. 20, no. 13, 2020, p. 3625.

[11] P. Williams, I. K. Dutta, H. Daoud, and M. Bayoumi, "A survey on security in internet of things with a focus on the impact of emerging technologies," *Internet of Things*, vol. 19, 2022, p. 100564.

[12] A. Kamble, and S. Bhutad, S. (2018, January). "Survey on Internet of Things (IoT) security issues & solutions," In 2018 2nd International Conference on Inventive Systems and Control (ICISC), p. 307–312, IEEE, 2018.

[13] V. Hassija, V. Chamola, V. Saxena, D. Jain, P. Goyal, and B. Sikdar, "A survey on IoT security: application areas, security threats, and solution architectures," *IEEE Access*, vol. 7, 2019, p. 82721–82743.

[14] S. Rachit, Bhatt, and P. R. Ragiri, "Security trends in Internet of Things: A survey," *SN Applied Sciences*, vol. 3, 2021, p. 1–14.

Chapter 3

Challenges and countermeasures for using machine learning and artificial intelligence in blockchain and IoT applications

Latifa Er-rajy, My Ahmed El Kiram, Oussama Lachihab, and Mohamed El Ghazouani

3.1 INTRODUCTION

The convergence of machine learning (ML), artificial intelligence (AI), blockchain, and the Internet of Things (IoT) has ushered in a new era of innovation, promising transformative solutions across a myriad of industries. This chapter explores the synergies and complexities inherent in integrating ML and AI technologies within the context of blockchain and IoT applications. While the integration of these cutting-edge technologies holds immense potential for revolutionizing various domains, it also presents unique challenges and vulnerabilities that must be addressed to realize their full benefits.

The intersection of the four technologies presents unprecedented opportunities for enhancing data-driven decision-making, optimizing processes, and enabling autonomous systems. These algorithms can leverage the vast amounts of data generated by IoT devices to extract valuable insights, predict future trends, and facilitate adaptive behaviors. Meanwhile, blockchain technology offers a decentralized and tamper-resistant platform for securely storing and sharing IoT data, ensuring data integrity, transparency, and auditability [1].

However, this integration also introduces a host of technical, ethical, and security challenges that must be carefully navigated. These challenges include ensuring the privacy and security of IoT data, addressing scalability issues in blockchain networks, mitigating biases in AI algorithms, and reconciling the trade-offs between decentralization and efficiency [2]. Moreover, the interoperability between disparate systems and the need for standardization further complicate the integration process.

In this chapter, we examine the key challenges and vulnerabilities inherent in leveraging ML and AI technologies within blockchain and IoT applications. We also propose a set of countermeasures and best practices to address these challenges, including novel approaches to data privacy, security, and governance. By elucidating the complexities and offering practical solutions, this chapter aims to provide valuable insights for researchers, practitioners,

DOI: 10.1201/9781003497585-3

and policymakers seeking to harness the transformative potential of these technologies in a secure and sustainable manner.

3.2 MACHINE LEARNING: OVERVIEW

Machine learning, in essence, is a multidisciplinary field encompassing various research domains that fortify its breadth, as depicted in Figure 3.1. Machine learning models are intertwined with computational statistics and mathematical optimization, amalgamating models with applications and frameworks within the statistical realm. Their primary objective is to facilitate computer-generated predictions. Additionally, machine learning is intertwined with mathematical optimization, bridging models, applications, and frameworks to the domain of statistics.

Real-world problems often exhibit significant complexity, rendering them prime candidates for the application of machine learning across various computing domains, enabling the development of robust and efficient algorithms. For instance, spam filtering, as previously discussed, fraud detection within social networks, face and shape recognition for authentication purposes, online trading actions analysis, character recognition, product recommendations in electronic stores, medical diagnostics, traffic forecasting, personalized movie and show recommendations such as those provided by Netflix, and friend suggestions on platforms like Facebook [3].

ML has demonstrated its efficacy in tackling highly complex problems, particularly those within the realm of data science. To achieve this, it categorizes problems into distinct groups, allowing for the application of

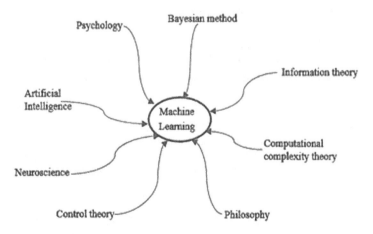

Figure 3.1 Machine learning multi-domains.

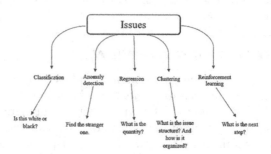

Figure 3.2 Example of the issue categorization.

the most suitable algorithms [4]. Figure 3.2 provides an illustration of how issues are categorized for machine learning applications.

Therefore, depending on the nature of the issue or problem at hand, an appropriate machine learning approach can be selected. The various categories are elucidated below:

Classification: This category pertains to problems where the output can only belong to one of a fixed number of predetermined classes, such as Yes/No or True/False. Depending on the number of output classes, the problem can be classified as either binary or multi-class classification [5].

Anomaly Detection: Problems falling under this category involve analyzing a particular model to identify deviations or anomalies [6]. For instance, banks employ anomaly detection algorithms to detect unusual transaction patterns among their customers and issue alerts accordingly. These problems are primarily concerned with identifying outliers.

Regression: Regression algorithms are utilized to address problems with continuous or digital output. These algorithms are commonly applied to problems that involve answering questions like "how much" or predicting numerical values [7].

Clustering: Clustering is a subset of unsupervised learning algorithms where the objective is to identify structures within the data and group similar data points into clusters [8]. These clusters are then labeled, allowing the algorithm to assign new, unseen data points to appropriate clusters based on their similarity.

Reinforcement Learning: Reinforcement learning algorithms are employed when decisions need to be made based on past learning experiences. In this paradigm, the machine agent learns behavior through trial-and-error interactions with a dynamic environment [9]. Reinforcement learning allows for programming agents using the concept of rewards and penalties without explicitly specifying how tasks should be accomplished. Examples include gaming programs and temperature control systems.

Classification involves leveraging machine learning algorithms to assign a class label to instances within a given domain. To elucidate this concept further, let's consider the scenario of email filtering, where emails are categorized as either "spam" or "not spam." Table 3.1 illustrates the four main types of machine learning classifications.

Table 3.1 Machine learning classification types

Classification type	Meaning	Examples	Algorithm used by
Binary [10]	This type of classification is based on one of two classes to produce the prediction. Usually, binary classification tasks involve one class that is in normal state and another class that is in abnormal state.	Detection of spam by email (spam or not) Churn prediction (churn or not) Conversion prediction (buy or not)	Logistic regression k-Nearest neighbors Decision trees Support vector machine Naive bayes
Multi-labels [11]	Multi-labels classification involves prediction based on one or more classes for each example. This classification refers to classification tasks where the distribution of examples among classes that are not equal.	As an example of this type is the classification of a given photo, which can have multiple objects in the scene and a model can predict the presence of multiple known objects in the photo.	Multi-tagged decision trees Multi-label random forests Multi-label gradient increase
Multi-class [12]	This classification refers to the classification tasks with more than two class labels. Multi-class classification is completely different from binary classification, it is true that we will concede normal and abnormal results; however, the data is classified as belonging to one of a range of known classes.	Classification of the face Classification of plant species Optical character recognition	k-Nearest neighbors Decision trees Naive Bayes Gradient boosting Random forest

(continued)

Table 3.1 (Cont.)

Classification type	Meaning	Examples	Algorithm used by
Imbalance [13]	The imbalanced classification is based on classification tasks which have the number of examples in each class is unevenly distributed. In general, imbalanced classification tasks are binary classification tasks where the majority of the examples in the training data set belong to the normal class on one side; on the one hand, the minorities of the examples belong to the class abnormal.	Detection of outliers Fraud detection Medical diagnostic tests	Logistic regression sensitive to cost Cost-sensitive decision trees Cost-sensitive support vector machines

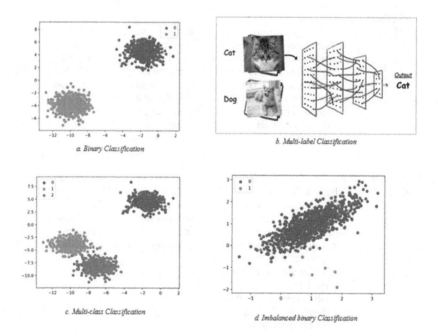

Figure 3.3 Scatter plot dataset of machine learning classification types.

Each classification type generates data uniquely. Figure 3.3 depicts a dataset for each classification type, comprising 1,000 examples, each belonging to one of two classes, with two input features per example.

For binary and unbalanced classifications, the 1,000 samples are divided into input elements (X) and output elements (y). Subsequently, the distribution of class labels is summarized, with instances categorized into class 0 or class 1, leaving 500 examples in each class.

In the case of multi-class classification, where there are three classes and each dataset belongs to one of them, we observe two input features for each class. The distribution of class labels reveals instances belonging to class 0, class 1, or class 2, with approximately 333 samples in each class. Following this, we summarize the first 10 examples, demonstrating that the input values are numeric, and the target values are integers representing class membership.

Finally, a point cloud is generated for the input variables in the dataset, with points colored according to their class value.

Machine learning algorithms can be categorized based on the learning mode they employ:

Supervised Learning: In this mode, classes are predetermined, and examples are known. The system learns to classify using a classification or discriminant analysis model. This process occurs in two phases: learning and testing. An expert labels examples during the learning phase, and the model predicts the label of new data during the testing phase. Examples include linear discriminant analysis or support vector machines [14]. For instance, a system can categorize new patients based on their medical analyses and common symptoms detected in other known patients, estimating their risk of developing a particular disease.

Unsupervised Learning: Here, the system or operator only has examples, but no labels, and the number and nature of classes have not been predetermined. Unsupervised learning or clustering is employed, where the algorithm discovers the hidden structure of the data without expert guidance. The system targets data based on available attributes, grouping them into homogeneous clusters [15]. Similarity is typically calculated based on distance between examples. Examples include data clustering and regression analysis.

Semi-supervised Learning: This type aims to reveal the underlying distribution of examples in their description space using both labeled and unlabeled examples. The model uses unlabeled examples, which can still provide information [16]. For instance, in medicine, it can assist in diagnosis or choosing diagnostic tests.

Partially Supervised Learning: In this type, data labeling is partial, where the model may declare that a data point does not belong to one class but may belong to another [17]. This is common in differential diagnosis scenarios.

Reinforcement Learning: Here, the observation guides the behavior of the algorithm, producing a return value that guides learning. Q-learning is a classic example of this type.

Transfer Learning: This involves applying skills and knowledge gained in previous tasks to new tasks or areas with similar characteristics [33].

3.3 CHALLENGES OF MACHINE LEARNING

Dataset: Over the recent years, there has been a growing demand for utilizing data in various fields. Del Giorgio Solfa and Simonato [18] demonstrated in their paper that employing large datasets leads to improved algorithmic performance. Conversely, Carlini et al. [19] and Ashutosh et al. [20] proposed the notion of "less is more" for tasks like object detection, such as facial action recognition. Additionally, studies like that by Qureshi et al. [21] suggest the merging of existing datasets to address the challenge of data scarcity.

To address the data scarcity issue, researchers such as Morshed et al. [22], Cascella et al. [23], and Alazeb et al. [24] have developed numerous datasets for action recognition tasks. These datasets aim to aid researchers and developers in creating and evaluating their algorithms. Typically, these datasets are curated to present actions in a manner that ensures cleaner data compared to real-world scenarios. Prior to algorithm manipulation, the data is annotated and recorded.

However, machine learning algorithms often require a substantial amount of data for effective training. Unfortunately, limitations in data recording, particularly for events with inherent risks, such as falls or assaults, pose challenges [25]. These events occur infrequently and unpredictably, making data collection difficult. Even if these actions are broken down into steps to mitigate the risk of injury, capturing realistic data remains challenging.

The quality and quantity of data play a crucial role in the performance of machine learning algorithms, classifiers, and functionalities. Barrera-Llanga et al. [26] emphasized that deep learning training necessitates extensive datasets. However, current visual data, especially for tasks like action recognition, are often unrepresentative. Generally, a learning approach is considered robust when compared to the quality and quantity of its data, particularly in the context of deep learning [27]. Algorithms trained on limited or unrepresentative datasets may exhibit questionable performance when applied to real-world scenarios. Additionally, the manual task of adapting and cleaning data to a specific format is time-consuming and labor-intensive, potentially impacting algorithm performance negatively. Inappropriate use of limited or unrepresentative data can significantly affect performance, as highlighted in Table 3.2.

Table 3.2 Difference between machine learning and artificial intelligence

Artificial intelligence (AI)	Machine learning (ML)
The goal of AI is to make a smart computer system like humans to solve complex problems.	The aim of ML is permitting to machines learning from data, accordingly that they are able to provide accurate output.
In AI, we create intelligent systems capable to execute any task as a human being.	In ML, we teach machines with data to perform a particular task and give an accurate result.
AI is a technology which enables a machine to simulate human behavior.	ML is a subset of AI which allows a machine to automatically learn from past data without programming explicitly.
Machine learning and deep learning are the two main subsets of AI.	Deep learning is a main subset of machine learning.
AI is working to create an intelligent system which can perform various complex tasks.	ML is working to create machines that can perform only those specific tasks for which they are trained.
AI has a very wide range of scope. It includes learning, reasoning, and self-correction.	ML has a limited scope. It includes learning and self-correction when introduced with new data.
Among the applications of AI, we find the intelligent humanoid robot operated, for example, by online games, customer support using catboats, the expert system, etc.	For the application of machine learning, we have for example the online recommendation system like the one used by YouTube, the automatic tagging suggestions of Facebook friends, the search algorithms used by Google, etc.
AI completely deals with structured, semi-structured, and unstructured data.	ML deals with structured and semi-structured data.

Functionality: Selecting the appropriate functionalities is crucial for machine learning algorithms to perform specific tasks effectively. Various selection algorithms have been developed to ensure optimal characteristics. However, in supervised learning, researchers often manually generate these features without certainty about their adequacy for the specific classification task. This process relies on human understanding of actions or events and researcher perspectives. While feature selection algorithms aim to ensure the best fit based on provided data, they are limited by the initial feature set. This limitation is challenging to overcome, as demonstrated by studies on automatic feature generation by Kumar et al. [28], which aimed to develop new features for supervised learning based on existing human-made functionalities. On the other hand, Bengio et al. [29] discussed representation algorithms in unsupervised learning and automatic feature extraction using deep learning. Automatic extraction approaches enable unsupervised algorithms to create their own representations for objects or events, moving closer to self-learning algorithms.

Classifier—Universal Approach: Another challenge with data-driven algorithms is the lack of customization, often employing a "one-fits-all" approach. Due to variations in physical characteristics and modes of action among participants, a classifier may only analyze actions within its trained scope. A trainable algorithm requires a sufficiently large dataset to capture natural variations in individual characteristics such as fitness, posture, weight, and height. It is also essential to collect a diverse range of behavioral types, such as gait and physical characteristics. Mastorakis [30] provided an example of this challenge in his paper. Similarly, a random search [31] failed to converge when combining datasets with different modes of action and human physical characteristics variability. Two assessment protocols allow the use of data from different datasets: (a) training on one dataset and testing on another and (b) random selection of samples from combined datasets for training and testing. However, convergence difficulties arise when subjects exhibit different movement behavior patterns and physical characteristics across datasets. Operating on a combined set may hinder convergence because algorithms are based on a single set of parameters for all data, making it challenging to accommodate variability and customization in detection algorithms.

3.3.1 Countermeasures

The increasing demand for diverse data poses a significant challenge in the realm of machine learning, as obtaining and classifying such varied data can be costly and complex. Researchers often face difficulties in acquiring real event data pertaining to specific groups, such as disabled individuals, elderly people, or minors, either due to privacy concerns or limited availability. To address this challenge, approaches have been proposed to generate data through a combination of synthetic data generation or simulation techniques with real observations.

Some researchers have explored the utilization of physics-based modeling, commonly found in literature and computer vision, to tackle this issue. Ezati et al. [32] discussed utilizing physical simulation in bipedal models for gait tracking, while Brubaker [33] explored predicting walking behavior using a simple model, incorporating factors like visual occlusion and varying walking speeds. Other studies have focused on tracking articulated objects based on physics-based frameworks, such as the work by Onofrey et al. [34], who proposed Lagrange equations of motion for synthesizing physically accurate behaviors. Building upon this, Sarafianos et al. [35] implemented a system based on mathematical formulations for precise modeling of general human movement.

In a different approach, Vondrak et al. [36] proposed a method relying on monocular video to estimate human movement, reconstructing three-dimensional models from video for simulating observed human behavior under physical disturbances. Mastorakis et al. [37] suggested monitoring activity using synthetic human data, creating datasets incorporating rigid poses for behavior recognition and scene understanding. Ma et al. [38] proposed action recognition using synthetic data, generating 6 million image frames based on segmentation masks, depth maps, and ground truth, incorporating various backgrounds and foreground people of different sizes.

Li et al. [39] offered a solution in the realm of computer vision, focusing on detecting the stability and likelihood of a rigid object falling using a simulation engine grounded in physics principles. Similarly, Tyc et al. [40] proposed an approach to accurately predict the outcome of collapses by leveraging the behavior of simulated wooden blocks. They created large convolutional network models based on an intuitive physics engine, as advocated by Arulkumaran et al. [41]. Additionally, Von Rueden et al. [42] utilized intuitive physics to develop a human learning model that evolves with age.

3.4 ARTIFICIAL INTELLIGENCE: OVERVIEW

Artificial intelligence refers to the development of computer systems capable of performing tasks that typically require human intelligence. These tasks include learning, reasoning, problem-solving, perception, and language understanding. AI technologies encompass a wide range of approaches, including machine learning, natural language processing, computer vision, robotics, and more.

3.4.1 Issues and solutions

Ethical Concerns: Surrounding the advancement of AI are deeply intertwined with its burgeoning capabilities and pervasive integration into various aspects of modern life. As AI technologies evolve, ethical consider-ations become increasingly complex and pressing. One significant concern is the presence of bias in algorithms, which can inadvertently perpetuate or even exacerbate existing social inequalities. These biases may stem from the data used to train AI systems, reflecting historical prejudices and systemic injustices [43]. Consequently, AI-driven decisions in areas such as hiring, lending, and criminal justice may unwittingly discriminate against certain groups, undermining principles of fairness and equity.

Moreover, the proliferation of AI raises profound privacy concerns as these systems amass vast amounts of personal data for analysis and decision-making. The collection and utilization of such data raise questions about consent, transparency, and individual autonomy. Unauthorized access to sensitive information by malicious actors or misuse of data by corporations and governments further compounds these ethical dilemmas, posing threats to individuals' privacy rights and personal freedoms.

Job Displacement: The potential for job displacement due to automation driven by AI technologies looms large over various industries, stirring profound concerns about the future of work and socioeconomic stability. As AI systems become increasingly adept at performing tasks traditionally carried out by humans, the nature of employment is undergoing a seismic shift, with certain roles and industries particularly vulnerable to disruption. This phenomenon extends beyond routine manual labor to encompass a broad spectrum of professions, including those reliant on repetitive cognitive tasks, data processing, and customer service.

The ramifications of widespread job displacement are far-reaching, with fears of mass unemployment and economic upheaval looming large [44]. Displaced workers may face significant challenges in finding new employment opportunities, particularly if their skills are rendered obsolete by technological advancements. Moreover, the unequal distribution of job losses across different sectors and demographics could exacerbate existing inequalities, widening the gap between the technologically adept and the digitally disenfranchised.

In response to these challenges, there is a growing recognition of the urgent need for retraining and reskilling initiatives to equip workers with the skills necessary to thrive in an increasingly automated economy. Governments, educational institutions, and businesses are called upon to collaborate in designing comprehensive training programs that anticipate emerging skill demands and provide accessible pathways for workers to transition into new roles.

Furthermore, efforts to address the potential negative impacts of automation on employment must be accompanied by broader socioeconomic policies aimed at fostering inclusive growth and mitigating inequality. This may include measures such as universal basic income, job guarantees, and support for lifelong learning to ensure that all individuals have the opportunity to participate meaningfully in the digital economy.

While automation driven by AI technologies holds the promise of increased productivity and innovation, its disruptive effects on the labor market underscore the importance of proactive measures to safeguard workers' livelihoods and promote equitable access to economic opportunities in the digital age. By embracing a holistic approach that prioritizes human-centric solutions and inclusive economic development, societies can navigate the challenges posed by automation while harnessing the transformative potential of AI for the collective benefit of all.

Bias and Fairness: The inadvertent perpetuation or exacerbation of biases within AI systems represents a significant ethical challenge with far-reaching implications for fairness and justice. AI algorithms rely heavily on data to learn patterns and make decisions, but when this data contains inherent biases, the resulting outcomes can be deeply discriminatory. In the context of hiring practices, for example, if historical data used to train AI recruitment tools reflects biases against certain demographic groups, such as gender or race, the algorithms may inadvertently perpetuate these biases by favoring candidates from privileged backgrounds while overlooking qualified candidates from underrepresented groups.

Similarly, in the realm of lending, AI-driven credit scoring models may inadvertently perpetuate systemic biases, resulting in differential treatment of individuals based on factors such as race or socioeconomic status. This can further entrench existing disparities in access to financial opportunities, exacerbating socioeconomic inequalities and hindering economic mobility for marginalized communities [45].

In the criminal justice system, where AI tools are increasingly used for risk assessment and predictive policing, the reliance on biased data can lead to discriminatory outcomes, disproportionately targeting minority groups and perpetuating cycles of injustice. Biased algorithms may erroneously label individuals as high-risk based on factors unrelated to actual criminal behavior, perpetuating systemic discrimination and contributing to wrongful convictions and incarceration rates among marginalized populations.

Addressing these biases within AI systems requires a multifaceted approach that encompasses both technical solutions and broader societal interventions. From a technical standpoint, efforts to mitigate bias must focus on improving the diversity and representativeness of training data, implementing fairness-aware algorithms, and conducting rigorous testing and validation to identify and rectify biased outcomes. Additionally, fostering diversity and inclusion within AI development teams can help mitigate unconscious biases in algorithmic design and decision-making processes.

Beyond technical solutions, addressing biases in AI requires broader societal efforts to challenge and dismantle systemic inequalities that underlie biased data sources. This includes promoting transparency and accountability in algorithmic decision-making, advocating for regulatory oversight and ethical guidelines to govern the use of AI in sensitive domains, and fostering a culture of diversity and equity across all sectors of society.

Ultimately, by acknowledging and actively addressing the biases inherent in AI systems, we can strive toward the development and deployment of more equitable and just technologies that uphold the principles of fairness, dignity, and respect for all individuals.

Security Risks: The vulnerability of AI systems to various forms of attacks poses a significant challenge in ensuring the security and integrity of these increasingly pervasive technologies. Adversarial attacks, in particular, exploit vulnerabilities in AI algorithms by subtly manipulating input data to deceive the system into producing erroneous outputs. These attacks can range from imperceptible modifications to images or text, causing misclassification by image recognition systems or natural language processing algorithms, to more sophisticated techniques that leverage knowledge of the system's inner workings to bypass security measures or compromise sensitive information [46].

Moreover, the emergence of AI-enabled cyber-attacks represents a new frontier in cybersecurity, with malicious actors leveraging AI technologies to automate and enhance the sophistication of their offensive capabilities. AI-powered malware, for instance, can adapt and evolve in real time to evade detection by traditional cybersecurity defenses, posing unprecedented challenges for threat detection and response. Furthermore, the use of AI in orchestrating targeted phishing attacks, social engineering campaigns, and automated botnet operations further amplifies the scale and complexity of cyber threats facing organizations and individuals alike.

These evolving security challenges underscore the critical importance of developing robust defenses and countermeasures to safeguard AI systems against malicious exploitation. This includes integrating security considerations into the design and implementation of AI algorithms, adopting rigorous testing and validation protocols to identify and mitigate vulnerabilities, and deploying advanced intrusion detection and response mechanisms to detect and thwart adversarial attacks in real time.

Collaboration between stakeholders across academia, industry, and government is essential to address the multifaceted nature of AI-related security threats effectively. This includes sharing threat intelligence, best practices, and lessons learned to bolster collective resilience against emerging cyber threats. Additionally, regulatory frameworks and standards for securing AI systems can help incentivize responsible development practices and ensure compliance with security requirements across diverse applications and industries.

The ongoing arms race between defenders and attackers in the realm of AI security underscores the need for continuous innovation and vigilance in safeguarding the integrity, confidentiality, and availability of AI-driven technologies. By embracing a proactive and collaborative approach to cybersecurity, we can mitigate the risks posed by adversarial attacks and ensure the trustworthy and resilient deployment of AI systems in an increasingly interconnected and digitized world.

Lack of Transparency: The opacity of deep learning algorithms poses significant challenges in critical domains such as healthcare and finance, where transparency and interpretability are paramount for informed decision-making and accountability. In healthcare, for example, the deployment of AI systems for diagnostic purposes relies on the ability to understand and trust the rationale behind the algorithm's recommendations. However, the inherent complexity of deep learning models, characterized by millions of interconnected parameters, renders their decision-making processes inscrutable to human experts, raising concerns about reliability and safety [47].

In the context of medical diagnosis, the lack of transparency in deep learning algorithms can lead to diagnostic errors or misinterpretations of patient data, potentially compromising patient outcomes and eroding trust in AI-driven healthcare solutions. Moreover, the inability to explain the underlying reasoning behind algorithmic decisions poses ethical dilemmas regarding patient autonomy and informed consent, particularly when AI systems are used to inform treatment options or clinical interventions.

Similarly, in the financial sector, where AI algorithms are increasingly deployed for tasks such as risk assessment, fraud detection, and algorithmic trading, the lack of transparency in decision-making processes raises concerns about market integrity and systemic stability. The opacity of deep learning models can obscure the factors driving investment decisions or risk predictions, making it difficult for regulators, investors, and stakeholders to assess the fairness, reliability, and potential biases inherent in AI-driven financial services.

Addressing the transparency challenges associated with deep learning algorithms requires a concerted effort to develop interpretable and explainable AI (XAI) techniques that enhance the understandability and trustworthiness of algorithmic outputs. This includes the development of model-agnostic interpretability methods, such as feature attribution techniques and surrogate models, that provide insights into the factors driving algorithmic decisions without compromising model performance or scalability.

Furthermore, promoting transparency and accountability in AI applications requires regulatory oversight and industry standards that mandate disclosure of algorithmic decision-making processes, data usage, and performance metrics. Additionally, fostering collaboration between domain experts, data scientists, and ethicists can help bridge the gap between technical innovation and societal values, ensuring that AI technologies are developed and deployed responsibly in critical applications where human lives and livelihoods are at stake.

By addressing the transparency challenges inherent in deep learning algorithms, we can unlock the full potential of AI to revolutionize healthcare, finance, and other critical domains while upholding principles of fairness, accountability, and human-centric design.

3.5 MACHINE LEARNING VIS-À-VIS ARTIFICIAL INTELLIGENCE

Artificial intelligence and machine learning are integral components of computing that are often intertwined. While these technologies are widely used to develop intelligent systems, they represent distinct concepts.

An AI system incorporates machine learning algorithms alongside its own intelligence. AI is not merely preprogrammed; it involves learning algorithms such as reinforcement learning and deep learning neural networks. Table 3.2 illustrates the differences between machine learning and artificial intelligence.

Despite the significant achievements of AI, it faces three key limitations. Firstly, many current AI algorithms have limited capacity, often struggling when faced with new tasks. Transfer learning can mitigate this to some extent, but AI still lacks the general intelligence of humans. Secondly, training AI algorithms typically requires large datasets, unlike humans who can learn from a small amount of data. For instance, toddlers can differentiate between objects like apples and bananas with minimal exposure. Lastly, AI computations are inefficient compared to the energy efficiency of the human brain, despite the brain's complexity [48]. This inefficiency has environmental implications, with large AI models producing substantial carbon emissions.

Efforts to address these limitations include neuromorphic computing, aiming to mimic the brain's physical substrate. This approach involves creating artificial neurons using phase change materials, which can switch between conductive and non-conductive states. Artificial synapses are also developed, offering more energy-efficient alternatives to conventional neural networks. Quantum computing presents another avenue, potentially revolutionizing AI with its speed and ability to tackle currently unsolvable problems. While current quantum computers have limited qubits, future developments may approach the complexity of the human brain.

Despite these challenges, AI has made significant contributions across various fields, including medicine. Its potential and applications underscore its crucial role in advancing pathology and medicine, as well as numerous other disciplines.

3.6 APPLICATIONS OF AI AND ML

AI and ML technologies are becoming ubiquitous in the realms of blockchain and the Internet of Things (IoT), reshaping the landscape of data management, analysis, and utilization. In the blockchain domain, these technologies are employed across various functions such as fraud detection, anomaly detection, and smart contract analysis. By meticulously analyzing transaction data stored within the blockchain, AI algorithms adeptly uncover patterns indicative of fraudulent activities, significantly bolstering the overall security and integrity of the network [49]. Complementing this, ML models diligently scan network behaviors, swiftly identifying potential security breaches or irregularities that may jeopardize the blockchain's integrity. Furthermore, the implementation of AI-powered smart contract analysis equips organizations with the means to pinpoint vulnerabilities, ensuring the robustness of their smart contracts and effectively mitigating risks associated with code exploits and security breaches.

The integration of AI and ML into blockchain applications not only enhances transaction reliability but also augments transparency and security, thereby instilling a heightened level of trust among network participants. By leveraging these technologies, organizations can navigate the evolving complexities of blockchain ecosystems with greater confidence, positioning themselves for sustained success in an increasingly digitized world [50].

Meanwhile, in the IoT domain, AI and ML play an equally pivotal role in enabling intelligent decision-making and predictive analytics. With the proliferation of connected devices and sensors, vast troves of data are generated, offering invaluable insights across various operational domains, including supply chain management, asset tracking, and predictive maintenance. AI algorithms, operating in real time, meticulously analyze this deluge of data, extracting actionable insights and empowering organizations to make informed decisions promptly [51]. For instance, AI-driven predictive maintenance systems leverage sensor data from IoT devices to anticipate equipment failures, facilitating proactive maintenance scheduling and minimizing downtime, thereby optimizing operational efficiency.

ML algorithms empower IoT devices to adapt and evolve in dynamic environments, continuously enhancing their functionality and performance over time. Through the seamless integration of AI and ML capabilities into IoT solutions, organizations can unlock unprecedented opportunities for automation, optimization, and innovation across diverse industry verticals, ranging from manufacturing and healthcare to transportation and agriculture [52].

As the convergence of AI, ML, blockchain, and IoT technologies continues to evolve, it presents a compelling trajectory for driving innovation and transformative change across various industries. By harnessing the collective power of these technologies, organizations can unlock new frontiers of efficiency, security, and automation, laying the foundation for a more interconnected, intelligent future.

3.6.1 CHALLENGES AND COUNTERMEASURES

One major challenge is the issue of data privacy and security. In both blockchain and IoT environments, vast amounts of data are collected and processed, raising concerns about the protection of sensitive information. AI and ML algorithms require access to large datasets for training, which may include personal or proprietary data. Ensuring the privacy and security of this data, especially in decentralized blockchain networks and IoT ecosystems with numerous interconnected devices, presents a complex challenge [53].

Another challenge is the interoperability of AI and ML systems with blockchain and IoT platforms [54]. Integrating algorithms into existing infrastructure requires compatibility and seamless communication between different technologies and protocols. Achieving interoperability can be challenging due to differences in data formats, communication protocols, and computing architectures across platforms.

Furthermore, scalability poses a significant challenge for AI and ML applications in blockchain and IoT environments. Algorithms often require substantial computational resources and processing power, which may be limited in decentralized networks with constrained IoT devices. Scaling AI and ML systems to handle the growing volume of data generated by blockchain and IoT networks while maintaining performance and efficiency remains a critical challenge.

The complexity of algorithms introduces challenges related to transparency, interpretability, and accountability. In blockchain networks where transactions are immutable and transparent, understanding the decision-making process of models becomes crucial for ensuring trust and accountability. However, complex algorithms, such as deep learning neural networks, are often considered "black boxes," making it difficult to interpret their decisions and ensure transparency in blockchain and IoT applications [55].

Addressing these challenges requires interdisciplinary collaboration and innovative solutions. Researchers and practitioners need to develop privacy-preserving techniques for AI and ML algorithms, design interoperable protocols for seamless integration with blockchain and IoT platforms, and optimize algorithms for scalability and efficiency in decentralized environments. Additionally, efforts to enhance the transparency, interpretability, and accountability of models can foster trust and confidence in their application within blockchain and IoT ecosystems.

Overall, overcoming these challenges will be essential for realizing the full potential of AI and ML in revolutionizing data management, analysis, and utilization in blockchain and IoT applications. By addressing privacy, interoperability, scalability, and transparency concerns, organizations can unlock new opportunities for innovation and transformation in various industries.

3.7 CONCLUSION

This chapter explores the integration of ML, AI, blockchain, and IoT, highlighting the opportunities and challenges it presents across various industries. While promising transformative solutions, this convergence also introduces technical, ethical, and security hurdles. It discusses leveraging data-driven decision-making, optimizing processes, and enabling autonomous systems through these technologies. The study identifies key challenges such as privacy and security concerns, scalability issues, biases in algorithms, and interoperability. It proposes countermeasures and best practices, aiming to provide valuable insights for researchers, practitioners, and policymakers to harness the potential of these technologies securely and sustainably.

REFERENCES

[1] S. S. Gill et al., "AI for next generation computing: Emerging trends and future directions," *Internet of Things (Netherlands)*, vol. 19, pp. 1–43, 2022, doi: 10.1016/j.iot.2022.100514.

[2] S. Singh, A. S. M. Sanwar Hosen, and B. Yoon, "Blockchain security attacks, challenges, and solutions for the future distributed IoT network," *IEEE Access*, vol. 9, pp. 13938–13959, 2021, doi: 10.1109/ACCESS.2021.3051602.

[3] M. H. Mobarak et al., "Scope of machine learning in materials research—A review," *Appl. Surf. Sci. Adv.*, vol. 18, no. August, p. 100523, 2023, doi: 10.1016/j.apsadv.2023.100523.

[4] D. Hendrycks, N. Carlini, J. Schulman, and J. Steinhardt, "Unsolved Problems in ML Safety," *arXiv Prepr. arXiv2109*, pp. 1–28, 2021 [Online]. Available: http://arxiv.org/abs/2109.13916

[5] T. Le Quy, A. Roy, V. Iosifidis, W. Zhang, and E. Ntoutsi, "A survey on datasets for fairness-aware machine learning," *Wiley Interdiscip. Rev. Data Min. Knowl. Discov.*, vol. 12, no. 3, pp. 1–59, 2022, doi: 10.1002/widm.1452.

[6] S. Zaman et al., "Security threats and artificial intelligence based countermeasures for Internet of Things networks: A comprehensive survey," *IEEE Access*, vol. 9, pp. 94668–94690, 2021, doi: 10.1109/ACCESS.2021.3089681.

[7] H. Fritz, J. J. Peralta Abadía, D. Legatiuk, M. Steiner, K. Dragos, and K. Smarsly, "Fault diagnosis in structural health monitoring systems using signal processing and machine learning techniques," *Struct. Integr.*, vol. 21, pp. 143–164, 2022, doi: 10.1007/978-3-030-81716-9_7.

[8] K. P. Sinaga and M. S. Yang, "Unsupervised K-means clustering algorithm," *IEEE Access*, vol. 8, pp. 80716–80727, 2020, doi: 10.1109/ACCESS.2020.2988796.

[9] M. Naeem, S. T. H. Rizvi, and A. Coronato, "A gentle introduction to reinforcement learning and its application in different fields," *IEEE Access*, vol. 8, pp. 209320–209344, 2020, doi: 10.1109/ACCESS.2020.3038605.

[10] A. Deniz, H. E. Kiziloz, T. Dokeroglu, and A. Cosar, "Robust multiobjective evolutionary feature subset selection algorithm for binary classification using machine learning techniques," *Neurocomputing*, vol. 241, pp. 128–146, 2017, doi: 10.1016/j.neucom.2017.02.033.

[11] S. C. Lin, C. J. Chen, and T. J. Lee, "A multi-label classification with hybrid label-based meta-learning method in Internet of Things," *IEEE Access*, vol. 8, pp. 42261–42269, 2020, doi: 10.1109/ACCESS.2020.2976851.

[12] A. C. Tan, D. Gilbert, and Y. Deville, "Multi-class protein fold classification using a new ensemble machine learning approach.," *Genome Inform.*, vol. 14, no. July, pp. 206–217, 2003, doi: 10.11234/gi1990.14.206.

[13] C. Zhang et al., "Multi-Imbalance: An open-source software for multi-class imbalance learning," *Knowledge-Based Syst.*, vol. 174, pp. 137–143, 2019, doi: 10.1016/j.knosys.2019.03.001.

[14] M. Aliramezani, C. R. Koch, and M. Shahbakhti, "Modeling, diagnostics, optimization, and control of internal combustion engines via modern machine learning techniques: A review and future directions," *Prog. Energy Combust. Sci.*, vol. 88, 2022, doi: 10.1016/j.pecs.2021.100967.

[15] Z. Wang, J. Ma, X. Wang, J. Hu, Z. Qin, and K. Ren, "Threats to training: A survey of poisoning attacks and defenses on machine learning systems," *ACM Comput. Surv.*, vol. 55, no. 7, 2022, doi: 10.1145/3538707.

[16] T. Lucas, P. Weinzaepfel, and G. Rogez, "Barely-supervised learning: Semi-supervised learning with very few labeled images," *Proc. 36th AAAI Conf. Artif. Intell. AAAI 2022*, vol. 36, pp. 1881–1889, 2022, doi: 10.1609/aaai.v36i2.20082.

[17] T. Khan, W. Tian, G. Zhou, S. Ilager, M. Gong, and R. Buyya, "Machine learning (ML)-centric resource management in cloud computing: A review and future directions," *J. Netw. Comput. Appl.*, vol. 204, no. Ml, 2022, doi: 10.1016/j.jnca.2022.103405.

[18] F. Del Giorgio Solfa and F. R. Simonato, "Big data analytics in healthcare: exploring the role of machine learning in predicting patient outcomes and improving healthcare delivery," *Int. J. Comput. Inf. Manuf.*, vol. 3, no. 1, pp. 1–9, 2023, doi: 10.54489/ijcim.v3i1.235.

[19] N. Carlini et al., "Extracting training data from diffusion models," *32nd USENIX Secur. Symp. USENIX Secur. 2023*, vol. 7, pp. 5253–5270, 2023.

[20] K. Ashutosh, S. K. Ramakrishnan, T. Afouras, and K. Grauman, "Video-mined task graphs for keystep recognition in instructional videos," *Adv. Neural Inf. Process. Syst.*, no. NeurIPS, 2024 [Online]. Available: http://arxiv.org/abs/2307.08763

[21] H. N. Qureshi et al., "Toward addressing training data scarcity challenge in emerging radio access networks: A survey and framework," *IEEE Commun. Surv. Tutorials*, vol. 25, no. 3, pp. 1954–1990, 2023, doi: 10.1109/COMST.2023.3271419.

[22] M. G. Morshed, T. Sultana, A. Alam, and Y. K. Lee, "Human action recognition: A taxonomy-based survey, updates, and opportunities," *Sensors*, vol. 23, no. 4, pp. 1–40, 2023, doi: 10.3390/s23042182.

[23] M. Cascella et al., "Artificial intelligence for automatic pain assessment: Research methods and perspectives," *Pain Res. Manag.*, vol. 2023, 2023, doi: 10.1155/2023/6018736.

[24] A. Alazeb et al., "Intelligent localization and deep human activity recognition through IoT devices," *Sensors*, vol. 23, no. 17, 2023, doi: 10.3390/s23177363.

[25] E.-R. Latifa, E. K. My Ahmed, E. G. Mohamed, and O. Mariya, "Foreground-preserving background modification: A deep learning approach," *2023 17th Int. Conf. Signal-Image Technol. Internet-Based Syst.*, pp. 261–267, 2023, doi: 10.1109/SITIS61268.2023.00047.

[26] K. Barrera-Llanga, J. Burriel-Valencia, Á. Sapena-Bañó, and J. Martínez-Román, "A comparative analysis of deep learning convolutional neural

network architectures for fault diagnosis of broken rotor bars in induction motors," *Sensors*, vol. 23, no. 19, 2023, doi: 10.3390/s23198196.

[27] S. E. Whang, Y. Roh, H. Song, and J. G. Lee, "Data collection and quality challenges in deep learning: a data-centric AI perspective," *VLDB J.*, vol. 32, no. 4, pp. 791–813, 2023, doi: 10.1007/s00778-022-00775-9.

[28] B. Kumar, E. Lorusso, B. Fosso, and G. Pesole, "A comprehensive overview of microbiome data in the light of machine learning applications: categorization, accessibility, and future directions," *Front. Microbiol.*, vol. 15, 2024, doi: 10.3389/fmicb.2024.1343572.

[29] Y. Bengio, A. Courville, and P. Vincent, "Representation learning: A review and new perspectives," *IEEE Trans. Pattern Anal. Mach. Intell.*, vol. 35, no. 8, pp. 1798–1828, 2013, doi: 10.1109/TPAMI.2013.50.

[30] G. Mastorakis, "Human fall detection methodologies: from machine learning using acted data to fall modelling using myoskeletal simulation," 2018. [Online]. Available: http://ezproxy.rice.edu/login?url=https://search.proquest.com/docview/2204764076?accountid=7064%0Ahttp://sfxhosted.exlibrisgroup.com/rice?url_ver=Z39.88-2004&rft_val_fmt=info:ofi/fmt:kev:mtx:dissertation&genre=dissertations+%26+theses&sid=ProQ:ProQuest+Di

[31] S. Jameer and H. Syed, "Deep SE-BiLSTM with IFPOA fine-tuning for human activity recognition using mobile and wearable sensors," *Sensors*, vol. 23, no. 9, 2023, doi: 10.3390/s23094319.

[32] M. Ezati, B. Ghannadi, and J. McPhee, "A review of simulation methods for human movement dynamics with emphasis on gait," *Multibody Syst. Dyn.*, vol. 47, no. 3, pp. 265–292, 2019, doi: 10.1007/s11044-019-09685-1.

[33] M. A. Brubaker, *Physical Models of Human Motion for Estimation and Scene Analysis*. Thèse de doctorat. Library and Archives Canada = Bibliothèque et Archives Canada, Ottawa. 2012.

[34] J. A. Onofrey et al., "Sparse data-driven learning for effective and efficient biomedical image segmentation," *Annu. Rev. Biomed. Eng.*, vol. 22, pp. 127–153, 2020, doi: 10.1146/annurev-bioeng-060418-052147.

[35] N. Sarafianos, B. Boteanu, B. Ionescu, and I. A. Kakadiaris, "3D Human pose estimation: A review of the literature and analysis of covariates," *Comput. Vis. Image Underst.*, vol. 152, pp. 1–20, 2016, doi: 10.1016/j.cviu.2016.09.002.

[36] M. Vondrak, L. Sigaly, J. Hodgins, and O. Jenkinsx, "Video-based 3D motion capture through biped control," *ACM Trans. Graph.*, vol. 31, no. 4, pp. 1–12, 2012, doi: 10.1145/2185520.2185523.

[37] G. Mastorakis, T. Ellis, and D. Makris, "Fall detection without people: A simulation approach tackling video data scarcity," *Expert Syst. Appl.*, vol. 112, pp. 125–137, 2018, doi: 10.1016/j.eswa.2018.06.019.

[38] N. Ma et al., "A survey of human action recognition and posture prediction," *Tsinghua Sci. Technol.*, vol. 27, no. 6, pp. 973–1001, 2022, doi: 10.26599/TST.2021.9010068.

[39] C. Hua, X. Cao, B. Liao, and S. Li, "Advances on intelligent algorithms for scientific computing: an overview," *Front. Neurorobot.*, vol. 17, no. 1, 2023, doi: 10.3389/fnbot.2023.1190977.

[40] J. Tyc, T. Selami, D. S. Hensel, and M. Hensel, "A scoping review of voxel-model applications to enable multi-domain data integration in architectural design and urban planning," *Architecture*, vol. 3, no. 2, pp. 137–174, 2023, [Online]. Available: https://www.mdpi.com/2673-8945/3/2/10

[41] K. Arulkumaran, M. P. Deisenroth, M. Brundage, and A. A. Bharath, "Deep reinforcement learning: A brief survey," *IEEE Signal Process. Mag.*, vol. 34, no. 6, pp. 26–38, 2017, doi: 10.1109/MSP.2017.2743240.

[42] L. Von Rueden et al., "Informed machine learning—A taxonomy and survey of integrating prior knowledge into learning systems," *IEEE Trans. Knowl. Data Eng.*, vol. 35, no. 1, pp. 614–633, 2023, doi: 10.1109/TKDE.2021.3079836.

[43] O. Hoxhaj, B. Halilaj, and A. Harizi, "Ethical implications and human rights violations," *Balk. Soc. Sci. Rev.*, vol. 22, pp. 153–171, 2023.

[44] L. L. Schoppe, *Digital technologies: a panacea or a double-edged sword? Understanding the consequences of artificial intelligence for individuals, firms and society: Reading list*, Doctoral Diss., Universidade Católica Portuguesa, Lisbon. September, 2022 [Online]. Available: https://reposito rio.ucp.pt/handle/10400.14/41043

[45] N. Gupta, "Artificial intelligence ethics and fairness: A study to address bias and fairness issues in AI systems, and the ethical implications of AI applications," *Rev. Rev. Index J. Multidiscip.*, vol. 3, no. 2, pp. 24–35, 2023, doi: 10.31305/rrijm2023.v03.n02.004.

[46] Y. Zhu, L. Zhang, Q. Chen, and W. Xiao, "Security and privacy for artificial intelligence: Opportunities and challenges," *Vitr. Diagnostic Ind. China*, vol. 37, no. 4, pp. 11–16, 2021, doi: 10.1007/978-981-16-2316-5_2.

[47] N. Kossow, S. Windwehr, M. Jenkins, D. Eriksson, J. Vrushi, and L. Millar, *Algorithmic transparency and accountability*. Transparency International, Berlin, Germany, 2021.

[48] M. Van Assen, I. Banerjee, and C. N. De Cecco, "Beyond the artificial intelligence hype: What lies behind the algorithms and what we can achieve," *J. Thorac. Imaging*, vol. 35, pp. S3–S10, 2020, doi: 10.1097/RTI.0000000000000485.

[49] A. Banafa, "IoT, AI, and blockchain: Catalysts for digital transformation," *Transform. AI*, pp. 103–106, 2024, doi: 10.1201/9781032669182-19.

[50] M. el Ghazouani et al., "Cloud data integrity auditing and deduplication using an optimized method based on blockchain and MAS," *Adv. Emerg. Financ. Technol. Digit. Money.*, pp. 283–292.

[51] M. E. El Ghazouani, A. Ikidid, C. A. Zaouiat, A. Layla, M. Lachgar, and L. Er-Rajy, "A blockchain-based method ensuring integrity of shared data in a distributed-control intersection network," *Int. J. Adv. Comput. Sci. Appl.*, vol. 14, no. 10, pp. 489–497, 2023, doi: 10.14569/IJACSA.2023.0141052.

[52] M. Rezwanul Mahmood, M. A. Matin, P. Sarigiannidis, and S. K. Goudos, "A comprehensive review on artificial intelligence/machine learning algorithms for empowering the future IoT toward 6G era," *IEEE Access*, no. August, 2022, doi: 10.1109/ACCESS.2022.3199689.

[53] D. Dhinakaran, S. M. U. Sankar, D. Selvaraj, and S. E. Raja, "Privacy-preserving data in IoT-based cloud systems: A comprehensive survey with AI integration," *arXiv Prepr. arXiv2401.00794arXiv Prepr. arXiv2401.00794*, 2024, [Online]. Available: https://arxiv.org/abs/2401.00794v1

[54] M. El Ghazouani, M. A. El Kiram, and L. Er-Rajy, "Blockchain & multi-agent system: A new promising approach for cloud data integrity auditing with deduplication," *Int. J. Commun. Networks Inf. Secur.*, vol. 11, no. 1, pp. 175–184, 2019, doi: 10.17762/ijcnis.v11i1.3880.

[55] K. Malhotra and A. W. Khan, "Application of artificial intelligence in IoT security for crop yield prediction," *Res. Rev. Sci. Technol.*, vol. 2, no. 1, pp. 136–157, 2022, [Online]. Available: https://researchberg.com/index.php/rrst/article/view/150

Chapter 4

Blockchain-enabled cyber security

Applications, limitations, and challenges

Yasir Khan

4.1 INTRODUCTION

The blockchain technology provides another area for heightened security, one that seems to be less explored and significantly less favorable to cybercriminals. Using blockchain-based cybersecurity approach, vulnerabilities are reduced, strong encryption is provided, and data integrity and ownership are verified more effectively. Similarly, there are even some instances where it can eliminate the need for passwords, which are frequently cited as one of the weakest links in cybersecurity. Initially, blockchain technology emerged as the foundational technical framework for cryptocurrency such as Bitcoin [1]. However, due to various reasons such as volatility and regulatory oversight, Bitcoin faced bans in numerous countries and restrictions in others, including China, Russia, and Europe [2–4]. Blockchain refers to a digital database or ledger distributed across the participants within a peer-to-peer network [5]. Blockchain is a kind of shared database. However, the difference between a conventional database and blockchain lies in the way in which information is stored and accessed. Traditional databases store data in relations or tables so that the data can be processed easily. On the contrary, the blockchain gathers transaction details and records them into a block. This block is similar to a cell in a spreadsheet holding information. Further to that, a unique technique is used to encrypt the data when the block is filled, producing a hash—a hexadecimal number—after the process. Lastly, the hash is then encrypted with the other data in the block and added to the header of the following block. This procedure forms a sequence of interconnected segments, which is famously called as a blockchain.

The utilization of blockchain technology in Bitcoin, which made its debut in November 2009 [6], is mostly to blame for the rising interest in blockchain. Since then, there are several uses for blockchain technology in the financial and non-financial industries. The evolution of blockchain comprises of three phases. These phases are based on the nature of applications and activities of blockchain technology. These encompass the initial iteration of public blockchain (blockchain 1.0), the subsequent iteration of public blockchain

DOI: 10.1201/9781003497585-4

(blockchain 2.0), the latest iteration of private blockchain (blockchain 3.0) [7], and the fourth-generation blockchain.

First of all, first-generation blockchain implements cryptocurrencies utilized for cash-related applications, including currency transfers, settlements, and electronic payments. It was born out of the fundamental idea of distributed ledger technology (DLT) [8–10]. DLT was most widely used in the cryptocurrency space, where Bitcoin was essential. Thus, Bitcoins paved the way for "Internet of Money" [11]. Similarly, because of the initial limitations in scalability and inefficient mining practices of blockchain, Buterin was motivated to expand the blockchain concept beyond its currency applications [12].

The second-generation blockchain comprises financial and economic sectors with smart contracting. Self-executing computer programs, or "smart contracts," run automatically in response to preset criteria agreed upon by two parties. Furthermore, this category encompasses a number of financial transactions and assets such as shares, equities, home loans, titles, smart homes, and smart contracts. Owing to the scalability issues, Proof of Work (PoW)-based smart contracts, and time-consuming nature of transactions, blockchain 3.0 emerged as the next-generating blockchain technology. Along with smart contracts, the primary focus of this blockchain version is on Decentralized Apps (dApps) [13]. Likewise, it covers topics including health, science, government, literacy, culture, and the arts. Consequently, blockchains created in this version are said to be personal or private. Lastly, Blockchain 4.0 is another promising development in the future of blockchain technology. It seeks to provide blockchain technology as a platform suitable for commercial purposes, enabling the creation and operation of applications, thereby transitioning the technology into widespread adoption. Unibright is the first platform to present Blockchain 4.0 utilities, allowing many blockchain business models to be combined [14]. Another instance is the SEELE Platform, facilitating integration within the blockchain sphere by enabling seamless cross-communication among different protocols across multiple platforms [15]. The blockchain 4.0 has the capacity to produce the speed of transactions of 1 million operations per sec or more, which seems to be unattainable for the current generation [16].

The chapter is structured as follows: Section 4.2 discusses historical background of the blockchain technology coupled with its importance in the arena of cyber security. Section 4.3 highlights the existing literature based on the role of blockchain in cybersecurity. Likewise, Section 4.4 discusses actual applications of blockchain technology in various domains of cybersecurity. Section 4.5 explores the vulnerabilities inherent in blockchain technology. Moreover, Section 4.6 explains the potential challenges that may arise while integrating blockchain in cybersecurity. Section 4.7 includes recommendations and discusses possible countermeasures against blockchain vulnerabilities in cybersecurity. Lastly, Section 4.8 concludes the chapter.

4.2 HISTORICAL BACKGROUND OF BLOCKCHAIN AND ITS SIGNIFICANCE IN CYBER SECURITY

In 1982, David Chaum, a doctoral student at the University of California, Berkeley, introduced the concept of a blockchain database in his dissertation titled "Computer Systems Established, Maintained, and Trusted by Mutually Suspicious Groups." Moreover, based on his contributions to blockchain technology, Chaum founded a company named DigiCash in 1989. In 1995, the company launched a cryptocurrency under various names including digicash, eCash, and cyberbucks [17]. In 1991, Haber and Stornetta proposed the idea of time stampings digital documents to prevent backdating and ensure their integrity against tampering [18–20]. During the late 1990s, the utilization of digital currencies became increasingly widespread [21]. Unlike physical currencies, digital currencies exist only in electronic form and are intangible. Transactions conducted with digital currency are irreversible and do not require monitoring from a central authority, reducing the risk of fraudulent activities. Additionally, they offer faster and more cost-effective transfer capabilities compared to traditional cash transactions. In 2008, Satoshi Nakamoto wrote a paper [22] due to which the blockchain technology became all the more popular and attracted significant attention.

The blockchain technology delivers better results across various industries when it is integrated along with other technologies. The following section highlights the critical role of blockchain technology especially in the area of cybersecurity.

4.2.1 Tamper-resistant mechanism in blockchain

The foundational principles of cybersecurity include confidentiality, integrity, and availability. In order to ensure integrity, the data must remain unaltered during use, transit, or storage. Further to that, integrity is achieved with the help of hashes. In blockchain technology, integrity of the data is maintained with help of timestamps and consensus mechanism. When a transaction is initiated within a blockchain, a new timestamp is automatically recorded. Any changes to the data prior to this timestamp are prohibited. Moreover, in order to record a new transaction, a consensus mechanism must be implemented, requiring approval from a particular portion of users to enter data into segments. Typically, this portion seems to be established to be greater than 50 percent. This entire process is also depicted in Figure 4.1 where temper-resistant mechanism of blockchain technology has been explained.

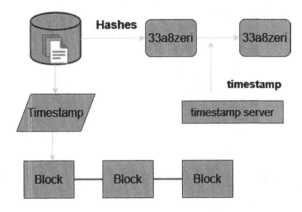

Figure 4.1 Underlying tamper-resistant mechanism of blockchain technology.

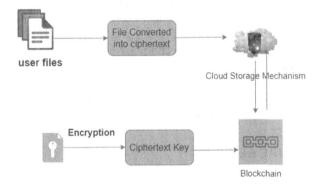

Figure 4.2 Data privacy protection process.

4.2.2 Data privacy protection

There are various techniques used in blockchain technology to ensure data privacy protection. First, Zero Knowledge Proof is one way in which a proof is provided to a person without disclosing any other information. A common type of Zero Knowledge Succinct Non-Interactive Argument of Knowledge (zk-SNARK) is a zero-knowledge proof. Similarly, ring signatures and mixing are another famous techniques through which data privacy is safeguarded. Importantly, because blockchain uses asymmetric cryptography, users can encrypt data with their own private keys [23–25]. The typical process of preserving data privacy is depicted and explained in detail in Figure 4.2.

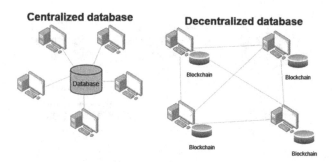

Figure 4.3 Comparison between centralized database and blockchain-enabled decentralized database.

4.2.3 Data recovery mechanism

In traditional centralized database management, data is stored in one or more central locations, which users then access to retrieve their data. If the data stored in a centralized database and an attacker attempts to steal or damage it, recovery and availability for users may prove challenging or impossible. Therefore, blockchain technology provides a decentralized data storage mechanism where data is simultaneously recorded and stored across all users' nodes. This enhances the reliability and fault-tolerance capabilities of the network. A comparison between traditional centralized database and modern decentralized blockchain-based database is shown in Figure 4.3.

4.3 LITERATURE REVIEW

This section provides a brief literature study regarding the critical function of blockchain in the field of cybersecurity.

The integration of blockchain technology into cybersecurity applications has become increasingly prominent in recent times. Blockchain platforms are typically classified into three main categories: public, private, and consortium. Firstly, public or permission-less blockchains are open and can be accessed by everyone. Likewise, private or permissioned blockchains are accessible only to verified people capable of validating transactions and achieving consensus. Lastly, a consortium blockchain is a type of blockchain infrastructure that is controlled by numerous organizations rather than being controlled by a single entity. It allows a group of pre-selected participants to collectively manage the blockchain network and make decisions about its operation and governance.

Table 4.1 presents an extensive overview of the diverse blockchain techniques utilized in different cyber security domains to address distinct

Table 4.1 Various blockchain techniques used in different domains of cyber security

Category	Technique	Description	Reference
IoT Security	ControlChain	Utilizing multiple blockchains to address various aspects of IoT access control.	[26]
Network security	Ethereum platform	Proposed blockchain for secure file sharing in SDN.	[27]
Secure data storage	BlockStack	Experiment for secure data naming and storage, preferring Bitcoin blockchain over Namecoin due to reliability.	[28]
Data privacy	Credibility-based consensus mechanism	Comparison of proof-of-work and proof-of-credibility, where node scores depend on connections to trusted nodes.	[29]
Web application security	Distributed ledger-based access control (DL-BAC)	Proposed DL-BAC for web application security.	[30]
DNS security	Distributed decentralized domain name service (D3NS)	Enhancing DNS security with blockchain through "D3NS".	[31]
Public key infrastructure	Distributed ledger	Suggested decentralized PKI ledger to prevent central repository failures, introducing Cecoin token.	[32]
Malware (Android)	Consortium blockchain	Uses consortium blockchain with N members will identify hashed malware on Android smartphones.	[33]

cyber security threats. It provides valuable information about their goals and relevant references.

4.4 APPLICATIONS OF BLOCKCHAIN IN CYBER SECURITY

There exists a number of cyber security domains where blockchain technology can be leveraged to build robust cyber defences. However, this piece of work concentrates on specific areas where blockchain technology is being widely employed and yield significant positive results. The areas

Pie_chart

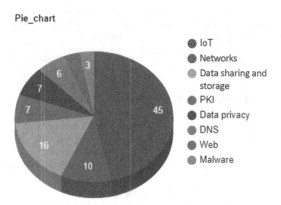

Figure 4.4 Highly researched areas of blockchain security applications.

covered include Domain Name System (DNS) security, Internet of Things (IoT) security, secure data sharing and storage, blockchain-based network security, public key infrastructure (PKI), and data privacy. The pie chart (Figure 4.4) illustrates how IoT, data sharing and storage, DNS, public key infrastructure, data privacy, and network security contains the majority of the most recent blockchain security deployments.

4.4.1 Decentralized and secure domain name services

Despite being critical to the functionality of internet, traditional DNS operates with centralized control, making it vulnerable to hacking, censorship, and related challenges. Resultantly, DNS servers remain highly vulnerable to cyber threats like cache ingestion, hijacked DNS, and DDoS threats. In 2016, a Distributed Denial of Service (DDoS) attack that affected the servers of a single DNS host caused an extensive downtime over much of the internet [34]. On the other hand, a blockchain DNS utilizes a distributed network of nodes, where each node maintains a copy of a ledger containing all domain name registrations and transfers. This architecture ensures a highly secure and censorship-resistant system. In order to tackle the cyber threats, [35,36] builds website infrastructures on the Bitcoin blockchain and conducts comprehensive research on blockchain-enabled DNS. The integration of blockchain with DNS allows domain owners to secure their operations within the blockchain. This transforms the initially centralized DNS into a distributed system, making it resistant to attacks or manipulation by adversaries who cannot locate a central record to target. A typical representation of blockchain-based DNS is shown in Figure 4.5.

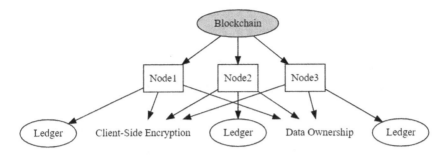

Figure 4.5 Representation of blockchain-based domain name system.

4.4.2 Secure data sharing and storage

Blockchain technology creates a decentralized network architecture, which improves the security of data sharing and storage. A distributed ledger system is used in this network, and in order to provide redundancy and resilience against possible sources of failure, each node keeps a copy of the ledger. Blockchain networks also make use of client-side encryption methods, which encrypt data locally on the client's device before sending it to the network. This technique protects data while it is being sent and stored on the blockchain, guaranteeing its security and secrecy. Crucially, data owners have total and verifiable ownership over their data because of blockchain technology's decentralized structure. Public or private distributed ledgers are used in some storage scenarios to reduce single points of failure and safeguard data against tampering. Put differently, blockchain guarantees that data kept in the cloud is opposing to unapproved alterations; hashing lists enable finding data that could be retained and saved safely; and data transferred may be validated to be the same from delivery to arrival [37–39]. Figure 4.6 explains the mechanisms and protocols involved in secure data transfer and storage.

4.4.3 Blockchain-led IoT security

When any object is linked to the internet, it becomes a part of the IoT, known as Internet of Things. The main security issue in IoT networks revolves around unpermitted entry and devices manipulation. Blockchain-driven security fixes provide enhanced control over access and data sharing across every IoT gadget. Adopting a blockchain-based strategy makes it feasible to offer reliable user identity, verification, and data delivery. This solution operates by keeping dispersed files of reliable past interactions and encounters, thereby preventing unauthorized access. Hence, an IoT gadget

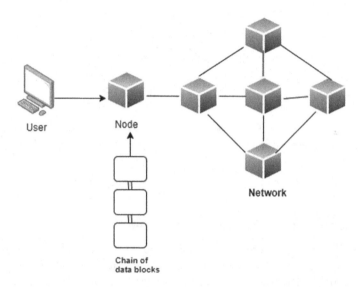

User · Node · Network · Chain of data blocks

Figure 4.6 Decentralized blockchain with client-side encryption and secure data ownership.

like an Internet Protocol camera at home will exclusively grant accessibility to trusted gadgets within the household. In case an unauthorized attempt is made to utilize the camera, the access will be restricted by the distributed ledger system until the majority of reliable devices consent to granting access to the intruder. A blockchain answer for identifying fraudulent activity and safeguarding historical IoT links and transactions is presented in these references [40,41]. The proposed architecture of these works is as follows: the blockchain protocol operates between the network's application and transport layers using token rewards comparable to Bitcoin, but considering them as voting authority components.

Similarly, a new method to enhance security and privacy in IoT-based healthcare systems is introduced in Ref. [42]. This study utilized blockchain technology to create a decision matrix with improved security and privacy features, including access control, data availability, privacy, and anonymity. The findings demonstrate the effectiveness of the blockchain-based approach in delivering robust access control and data integrity. The representation of blockchain-enabled IoT security is illustrated in Figure 4.7.

4.4.4 Public key infrastructure (PKI)

A public key infrastructure allows us to utilize the identities of machines in an asynchronous manner for signing, encrypting, and then validating the data. A certificate authority (CA) plays the role of a middleman for these

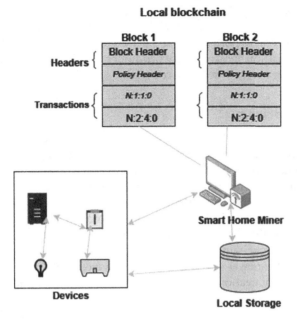

Figure 4.7 Blockchain-led IoT security representation.

transactions, ensuring the legitimacy of the public key, thereby enabling a data recipient to verify the content of the transaction. Because control over communication identifiers is entrusted to CAs, the utilization of those identifiers can possibly be endangered. This issue is, therefore, resolved by using blockchain-led PKI. Blockchain-driven decentralized PKIs eliminate the potential vulnerabilities introduced by the reliance on CAs, which, if compromised, can make the whole sequence of certificates. Further to that, blockchain-dependent PKI offers the certificate transparency (CT) feature adopted by Google to enhance the security of CA-led PKIs with the help of transparent public record-keeping and certificate surveillance. There are several approaches used for blockchain-driven PKI. For instance, Backing rich credentials with a blockchain PKI, Privacy-Aware blockchain-based PKI, Instant Karma PKI, and Decentralized PKI are some of the examples. The emphasis of the aforementioned methods lies in either integrating a PKI into a blockchain or replicating the identity verification functionality of a PKI for participants [43].

4.4.5 Network security using blockchain

Given the rising adoption of virtualized machines, Software-Defined Networks (SDN), and containerized application deployment, blockchain technology facilitates the decentralized and resilient storage of crucial authentication data [44–46]. In these studies, a blockchain-enabled architecture is employed for SDN controllers, utilizing a cluster structure. This architecture leverages both public and private blockchains to enable peer-to-peer communication between network nodes and SDN controllers, effectively addressing network security concerns.

4.4.6 Data privacy

The utilization of blockchain to improve data privacy has received relatively little attention in academic literature. This could be attributed to the feature of immutability of blockchain, where everyone possesses a copy of the ledger, posing problems for privacy efforts, especially in data protection. The typical choices users make on their devices are kept safe by encrypting and storing them on the blockchain. Only the user who made those choices can access them. Furthermore, the research examines the differences between two kinds of blockchain techniques: Proof of Work (PoW) and proof-of-credibility. In this newer approach, nodes are given a credibility score based on how many connections they have with other trusted nodes [47,48]. In the domain of data security, researchers have highlighted the major vulnerability as the existence of a single point of malfunction. This vulnerability often results in data breaches, alterations, or loss. Security experts have proposed blockchain as a solution to increase data security owing to its robust infrastructure. By hashing each block of shared data and linking it to the subsequent block, tampering by external parties becomes impossible. Further to that, since only the communicating parties possess the ability to access and modify the data, any pilfered data becomes unusable, and third-party tampering is prevented. Figure 4.8 illustrates how blockchain technology can be adopted to protect data privacy.

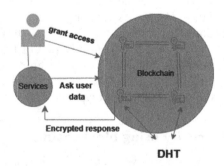

Figure 4.8 Data privacy protection using blockchain approach.

4.5 LIMITATIONS/CHALLENGES OF BLOCKCHAIN IN CYBERSECURITY

4.5.1 Distributive storage results in wider attack surface

The use of distributed ledger ensures secure data storage by storing an entire replica of the data on each device of user. However, this approach results in a broader attack surface within blockchain technology. This means that attackers have a greater number of potential entry points to access this data. While the data stored in the blockchain is resistant to tampering, threat actors may employ alternative methods such as data mining and correlation analysis to extract crucial insights concerning blockchain utilization, users, and network architecture.

4.5.2 Cooperative attack due to consensus mechanism

The consensus mechanism inherent in blockchain technology may unintentionally increase the risk of coordinated attacks. This technique functions on the assumption that the vast majority of nodes in the network are trustworthy and cooperate to keep the system running. On the other hand, a node or group of nodes may plan an attack if they manage to control more than 51 percent of the system's computational power. This attack could involve carrying out disruptive operations like Distributed Denial of Service (DDoS) attacks or altering the data contained within blocks. As a result, the blockchain network's integrity and security may be compromised by the majority consensus's dependence on trust.

4.5.3 Extensive application of cryptographic algorithms leading to zero-day vulnerabilities

The widespread utilization of cryptographic algorithms within blockchain technology may unintentionally introduce unknown backdoors or vulnerabilities. For instance, popular cryptographic algorithms like elliptic curve cryptography (ECC) and Rivest–Shamir–Adleman (RSA) are extensively leveraged in blockchain systems. However, there is a risk of potential backdoors or security vulnerabilities emerging within these algorithms or during their implementation processes. Such vulnerabilities could pose significant threats to both individual blockchain applications and the system as a whole. Furthermore, the emergence of new computing technologies, such as quantum computers, further increases concerns regarding the integrity of asymmetric encryption algorithms. As quantum computing capabilities advance, the possibility of successfully cracking these encryption methods increases, necessitating continuous adaptation in blockchain security practices.

4.5.4 Attack backtrack issue resulting from anonymity approach

The use of anonymity mechanisms in blockchain systems can introduce challenges, especially in the context of attack traceback issues. While aiming to safeguard privacy, blockchain solutions often rely on hashing the public key of a user to make sure anonymity. However, this privacy-preserving process can prevent the verification and tracing of a user's true identity, particularly when investigating network attacks or implementing cybersecurity regulations. As a result, maintaining a balance between privacy protection and the need for accountability poses a significant challenge in blockchain-based systems

4.5.5 Limited use of blockchain due to smaller block capacity

The restriction on block size presents a significant challenge to the wider implementation of blockchain technology. Initially, block sizes were limited to 1 MB to prevent potential DDoS attacks. However, this decision has given birth to a controversy regarding the optimal block size. Some people favoring larger blocks argue that they offer greater storage capacity, which aligns with the increasing needs of blockchain development. Nonetheless, the adoption of larger blocks may introduce operational challenges, such as increased challenges connected with operating and monitoring blockchain nodes. On the contrary, people who propose lesser block sizes highlight their ease of management and reliability, particularly in supporting third-party payment solutions. Despite the fact that smaller blocks come with their own set of limitations, notably restricted space, which may prove insufficient, particularly within big data environments. This ongoing controversy highlights the complexity of balancing scalability, security, and operational efficiency in blockchain systems.

4.6 POSSIBLE ATTACKS ON BLOCKCHAIN TECHNOLOGY

4.6.1 The 51 percent attack

When a single person or group of people takes control of more than 50 percent of the blockchain network's processing power, they may exert tremendous influence and manipulate the network as they choose. This is known as a 51 percent attack. Due to the possibility of double-spending and other nefarious activities, this presents a serious risk. The mining pool, ghash. io, briefly crossed 50 percent of the computational capacity on the Bitcoin network in July 2014, which caused the pool to reduce its network share [49]. In the past, 51 percent attacks have been made against Ethereum, a cryptocurrency built on the Bitcoin protocol, mainly during periods of low hashing power. More serious attacks, however, take place when the threat actor controls over 67 percent of the network's ownership share, which gives them the power to unilaterally stop transactions and decide not to generate any blocks of transactions [50]. Preventing a 51 percent attack requires a robust and resilient consensus algorithm. Delegated Proof of Stake (DPoS), Proof of Work (PoW), and Proof of Stake (PoS) are notable examples of such algorithms.

4.6.2 Double-spending attack

Multi-spend fraud occurs when an attacker sends a transaction to multiple destinations at one time, enabling them to spend the same digital currency twice and exploit the system. When pending payments are broadcast across the network, or when nodes on the network receive transactions awaiting confirmation, disruptions in broadcasting can occur at various intervals. In Bitcoin, solving a problem successfully typically takes around 10 minutes, determined by the complexity of the calculation and fluctuations in miners' processing power [51]. The Splasher method, CASPER protocol, punishing validators, Tendermint protocol, and POS/POW hybrid protocol, are some of the counter measures for double-spending attacks.

4.6.3 DDoS attack against Ethereum platform

In the month of September 2016, the Ethereum network experienced a DDoS attack of a computational nature, resulting in extended processing times for miners and nodes to handle blocks. The attack was attributed to the EXTCODESIZE opcode (operation code), a low-cost operation, which required nodes to access state-related data saved on disk. Attackers invoked this operation code approximately 50,000 times per block, causing a significant slowdown in network performance.

4.6.4 Private key security

Typically, cryptocurrencies are stored in digital wallets, where each user possesses a pair of private and public keys for wallet access. However, wallets are susceptible to various vulnerabilities, such as theft or loss. Users may lose their personal identification number (PIN) code or credentials, or misplace the hard disk containing the personal key, leading to restricted access to their funds. Additionally, ransomware poses a similar threat by encrypting wallet files. Wallet theft commonly occurs through traditional methods such as phishing attacks, system breaches, installation of malicious software, or mishandling of wallets [52]. A blockchain system is susceptible to exploitation through any vulnerability that compromises its cryptographic integrity. Programming bugs or insecure private keys can serve as entry points for significant security breaches. While the original plaintext encrypted within the blockchain should be incomprehensible to attackers, the structure of blockchain blocks is relatively transparent. Even with strong encryption, patterns may emerge within the blocks, allowing attackers to make partial guesses about the plaintext content in each block based on preceding blocks [53]. For private key security, some of the countermeasures suggested include password-protected secret sharing and hardware wallets.

4.7 FUTURE RESEARCH DIRECTIONS

There exist plenty of studies that have highlighted applications of blockchain technology in various areas, including cybersecurity. Similarly, some researchers have shed light on the potential challenges that are encountered while integrating blockchain in cybersecurity. However, future researchers still need to focus on exploring the feasibility of using a unified blockchain system to develop security solutions. Currently, many existing solutions rely on different blockchain platforms, which can complicate the integration process. Therefore, consolidating these efforts into a single Blockchain infrastructure could streamline security implementation and enhance interoperability.

4.8 CONCLUSION

Blockchain technology has gained considerable popularity in recent years. Its initial utilization in the financial sector has given it the credibility to be leveraged in other areas. Furthermore, blockchain technology is continuously evolving and expanding its utility across various domains in the modern world. One particularly promising area where it has gained significant attention and application is cybersecurity. Utilizing its strong infrastructure, blockchain offers practical solutions for handling security challenges encountered in diverse domains such as IoT components, networks, and data transfer and storage. Most researchers focusing on blockchain security prioritize its application in IoT devices, alongside networks and data security. Through enhanced verification and data exchange methods, blockchain technology can effectively safeguard IoT devices from potential breaches by hackers, particularly in cases where these devices lack adequate security configurations. Blockchain has brought significant changes to industries that rely on transactions, although some security problems and threats hinder its broad acceptance as a general platform for various applications worldwide. Despite numerous studies and practical implementations offering solutions to mitigate these risks, the development of strong and effective security measures to ensure blockchain's continued functionality remains a challenge and an ongoing research focus. As blockchain continues to evolve rapidly, it is anticipated that it will increasingly find applications in various business and industrial sectors.

REFERENCES

[1] N. Satoshi. *Bitcoin: A Peer-to-Peer Electronic Cash System* (pp. 1–9). Available at SSRN: https://ssrn.com/abstract=3440802 or http://dx.doi.org/10.2139/ssrn.3440802 (2008).

[2] G. Varriale. "Bitcoin: how to regulate a virtual currency," *International Financial Law Review*, 32(6), 43–45 (2013).

[3] D. Swartz N. "Bursting the Bitcoin bubble: The case to regulate digital currency as a security or commodity," *Tulane Journal of Technology & Intellectual Property*, 17, 319–335 (2014).

[4] N. Wenker "Online currencies, real-world chaos: the struggle to regulate the rise bitcoin," *Tex. Rev. L. & Pol.*, 19, 145–184 (2014).

[5] H. Adam (March 2024). "Blockchain facts: What is it, how it works, and how it can be used" [online], available: https://www.investopedia.com/terms/b/blockchain.asp

[6] A.M. Antonopoulos. *Mastering Bitcoin: Unlocking Digital Cryptocurrencies.* O'Reilly Media, Inc. (2014).

[7] M. Swan. *Blockchain: Blueprint for a New Economy.* O'Reilly Media, Inc. (2015).

[8] D.C. Mills, K. Wang, B. Malone, A. Ravi, J. Marquardt, A.I. Badev, T. Brezinski, L. Fahy, K. Liao, V. Kargenian, M. Ellithorpe. Distributed ledger technology in payments, clearing, and settlement. FEDS Working Paper No. 2016-095, Available at SSRN: https://ssrn.com/abstract=2881204 or http://dx.doi.org/10.17016/FEDS.2016.095 (2016).

[9] R. Maull, P. Godsiff, C. Mulligan, A. Brown, B. Kewell. "Distributed ledger technology: applications and implications". *Strateg. Chang.* 26(5), 481–489 (2017).

[10] S. Ølnes, J. Ubacht, M. Janssen. "Blockchain in government: benefits and implications of distributed ledger technology for information sharing". *Government Information Quarterly*, 34(3), 355–364 (2017).

[11] A.M. Antonopoulos. *The Internet of Money*, vol. 1. Merkle Bloom LLC, Columbia, MD (2016).

[12] V. Buterin. "A next-generation smart contract and decentralized application platform". White Paper 3(37) (2014).

[13] The Investopedia Team (March 2024). "Decentralized Applications (dApps): Definition, uses, pros, and cons". Available: www.investopedia.com/terms/d/decentralized-applications-dapps.asp

[14] S. Schmidt, M. Jung, T. Schmidt, I. Sterzinger, G. Schmidt, M. Gomm, K. Tschirschke, T. Reisinger, F. Schlarb, D. Benkenstein, B. Emig. "Unibright-the unified framework for blockchain based business integration". White paper, April (2018).

[15] ICODROPS. (March 2024). "Seele (blockchain) available: https://icodrops.com/seele/

[16] P. Mukherjee, C. Pradhan. "Blockchain 1.0 to Blockchain 4.0—The Evolutionary Transformation of blockchain technology". In *Blockchain technology: Applications and challenges* (pp. 29-49). Cham: Springer International Publishing (2021).

[17] "A brief history of blockchain technology that everyone should read" (March 2024). Available at: https://kriptomat.io/blockchain/history-of-blockchain/

[18] S. Haber, W.S. Stornetta. "How to time-stamp a digital document." In: *Conference on the Theory and Application of Cryptography*, Springer, Berlin, Heidelberg (1990), pp. 437–455.

[19] D. Bayer, S. Haber, W.S. Stornetta. "Improving the efficiency and reliability of digital timestamping." In: Sequences II, Springer, New York, NY, pp. 329–334 (1993).

[20] S.A. Haber, W.S. Stornetta Jr. U.S. Patent No. 5,781,629. U.S. Patent and Trademark Office, Washington, DC (1998).

[21] Wikipedia (March 2024). "Digital currency." Available at: https://en.wikipedia.org/wiki/Digital_currency

[22] S. Nakamoto. Bitcoin: peer-to-peer electronic cash system (2008).

[23] G. Zyskind, O. Nathan. "Decentralizing privacy: Using blockchain to protect personal data," Security and Privacy Workshops (SPW), IEEE, pp. 180–184 (2015).

[24] A. Kosba. "Hawk: The blockchain model of cryptography and privacy-preserving smart contracts," Security and Privacy (SP), 2016 IEEE Symposium on. IEEE, pp. 839–858 (2016).

[25] S. Meiklejohn and C. Orlandi. "Privacy-enhancing overlays in bitcoin," International Conference on Financial Cryptography and Data Security, Springer Berlin Heidelberg, pp. 127–141 (2015).

[26] O.J.A. Pinno, A.R.A. Gregio, L.C.E. De Bona. "Controlchain: Blockchain as a central enabler for access control authorizations in the IoT", in: GLOBECOM 2017 – 2017 IEEE Global Communication Conference, p. 16 (2017).

[27] S. Ram Basnet, S. Shakya. *BSS: Blockchain Security over Software Defined Network*, IEEE Iccca, p. 720725 (2017).

[28] M. Ali, et al. Blockstack: A global naming and storage system secured by blockchains, in: USENIX Annual Technical Conference, p. 181194 (2016).

[29] D. Fu, F. Liri. "Blockchain-based trusted computing in social network", in: 2016 2nd IEEE International Conference on Computer and Communication ICCC 2016 – Proc., p. 1922 (2017).

[30] L. Xu, L. Chen, N. Shah, Z. Gao, Y. Lu, W. Shi. "DL-BAC: Distributed ledger based access control for web applications", in: Proc. 26th International Conference on World Wide Web. Companion, 2017, p. 14451450.

[31] B. Benshoof, A. Rosen, A.G. Bourgeois, R.W. Harrison. "Distributed decentralized domain name service", in: Proc. – 2016 IEEE 30th International Parallel Distribution Process. Symposium. IPDPS, p. 12791287 (2016).

[32] B. Qin, J. Huang, Q. Wang, X. Luo, B. Liang, W. Shi. "Cecoin: A decentralized PKI mitigating MitM attacks", *Future Generations Computer Systems*, 107, 805–815 (2020).

[33] J. Gu, B. Sun, X. Du, J. Wang, Y. Zhuang, Z. Wang. "Consortium blockchain-based malware detection in mobile devices", *IEEE Access* 6, 1211812128 (2018).

[34] Massive Internet Outage Could Be a Sign of Things to Come, Jamie Condliffe, MIT *Technology Review*, Oct 21 (2016).

[35] H. Weihong, A. Meng, Sh. Lin, X. Jiagui, L. Yang. "Review of block chain-based DNS alternatives," *Chinese Journal of Network and Information Security*, 3(3), 71–77 (2017).

[36] Q. Ren, K. L. Man, M. Li, B. Gao, J. Ma. "Intelligent design and implementation of blockchain and Internet of things–based traffic system," International Journal of Distributed Sensor Networks, 15(8), 1550147719870653 (2019).

[37] M. Ali, et al. "Blockstack: A global naming and storage system secured by blockchains", in: USENIX Annual Technical Conference, p. 181194 (2016).

[38] L. Yue, H. Junqin, Q. Shengzhi, W. Ruijin. "Big data model of security sharing based on blockchain", in: 2017 3rd International Conference on Big Data Computing. Communication, p. 117121 (2017).

[39] C. Cai, X. Yuan, C. Wang. "Hardening distributed and encrypted keyword search via blockchain", in: 2017 IEEE Symposium Privacy-Aware Computers, p. 119128 (2017).

[40] J. Gu, B. Sun, X. Du, J. Wang, Y. Zhuang, Z. Wang. "Consortium blockchain-based malware detection in mobile devices", *IEEE Access* (6), 1211812128 (2018).

[41] Y. Gupta, R. Shorey, D. Kulkarni, J. Tew. "The applicability of blockchain in the Internet of Things", in: 2018 10th International Conference on Communication System Networks, p. 561564 (2018).

[42] S. Qahtan, K.Y. Sharif, A. Zaidan, H. Alsattar, O. Albahri, B. Zaidan, H. Zulzalil, M. Osman, A. Alamoodi, R. Mohammed. "Novel multi security and privacy benchmarking framework for blockchain-based IoT healthcare industry 4.0 systems", *IEEE Transactions on Industrial Informatics* 18(9), 6415–6423 (2022).

[43] Anastasios Arampatzis (March 2024). "Blockchain as a form of distributed PKI" available: https://venafi.com/blog/blockchain-form-distributed-pki/

[44] S. Ram Basnet, S. Shakya. "BSS: blockchain security over software defined network", *IEEE Iccca*, p. 720725 (2017).

[45] N. Bozic, G. Pujolle, S. Secci. "Securing virtual machine orchestration with blockchains", 1st Cyber Security in Networking Conference, p. 18 (2017).

[46] I.D. Alvarenga. "Securing configuration, management and migration of virtual network functions using blockchain", NOMS 2018-2018 IEEE/IFIP Network Operations and Management Symposium, pp. 1–9. IEEE (2018).

[47] D. Fu, F. Liri. "Blockchain-based trusted computing in social network", in: 2016 2nd IEEE International Conference on Computer Communication ICCC 2016, Proc., p. 1922 (2017).

[48] S.C. Cha, J.F. Chen, C. Su, K.H. Yeh. "A blockchain connected gateway for BLE-based devices in the internet of things", *IEEE Access* 3536 (2018).

[49] A. Extance. "The future of cryptocurrencies: Bitcoin and beyond". *Nature News* 526(7571), 21 (2015).

[50] Ethereum on Github. Available: https://github.com/ethereum/wiki/wiki/Proof-of-Stake-FAQ

[51] J.J. Xu. "Are blockchains immune to all malicious attacks?" *Financial Innovation* Dec. 2(1), 25 (2016).

[52] N. Scaife, H. Carter, P. Traynor, K.R. Butler. "Cryptolock: stopping ransomware attacks on user data" In: Distributed Computing Systems (ICDCS), 2016. IEEE 36th International Conference on Distributed Computing Systems (ICDCS), pp. 303–312 (2016).

[53] D. Johnson, A. Menezes, S. Vanstone. "The elliptic curve digital signature algorithm (ECDSA)". *International Journal of Information Security* 1(1), 36–63 (2001).

Chapter 5

The revolution and future of blockchain technology in cybersecurity

A comprehensive analysis

T. Monika Singh, C. Kishor Kumar Reddy, and Kari Lippert

5.1 INTRODUCTION

In a progressively digital world, cybersecurity has emerged as a major worry for both individuals and corporations. Cyberattacks and data breaches have surged recently, causing significant financial losses and reputational harm. Traditional security measures have proven insufficient in countering these threats, leading experts to explore alternative solutions. In the modern digital era, cyberattacks and data breaches are becoming increasingly frequent and sophisticated, leading to large financial consequences and severe reputational damage for organizations across various sectors. Traditional cybersecurity measures, while essential, have often fallen short in effectively countering these evolving threats. This shortcoming has spurred the search for more robust and innovative solutions to protect sensitive data and critical infrastructures. Blockchain technology [1], initially developed to support crypto currencies like Bitcoin, has garnered significant attention for its potential applications beyond digital currencies. Its decentralized, immutable, and transparent characteristics offer unique advantages that can transform cybersecurity. By ensuring data integrity, enhancing identity management, securing transactions, and preventing fraud, blockchain provides a promising alternative to traditional security methods. The motivation for this chapter is to explore how to use blockchain to increase modern cybersecurity challenges. As cyber threats grow more complex, there is a pressing need for advanced security solutions that offer stronger protection and resilience. This provides a comprehensive analysis of blockchain technology's impact on cybersecurity, identify its potential benefits, and evaluate the challenges and limitations associated with its implementation.

Cybersecurity is the study and application of preventing cyberattacks on internet-connected devices, including hardware, software, and data [2]. It is used by individuals and companies to prevent unauthorized access to computer systems and data centers. An efficient cybersecurity plan can provide robust defense against hostile assaults with the objective to acquire, modify, eliminate, or extract sensitive data from individuals or entities. Another

DOI: 10.1201/9781003497585-5

71

crucial facet of cybersecurity involves obstructing attempts to damage or tamper with how a system or device functions. Several levels of protection on all possible entry points and attack surfaces are essential components of a solid cybersecurity plan. This includes a layer of security for data, hardware, software, and networks that are connected. All of the employees who have access to these endpoints should be trained on the relevant security and compliance measures. An extra line of protection against threats is provided by organizations that deploy technology such as unified threat management systems [1]. These technologies have the ability to identify, categorize, and eliminate dangers. Additionally, they can alert customers when further action is necessary. Cybersecurity is more crucial than ever in a modern organization because of the proliferation of people, devices, and programs—many of which are secret or sensitive—and the resulting increase of data. However, the sheer quantity, expertise, and techniques of cybercriminals make the problem much worse [3]. If an organization does not have a suitable cybersecurity plan in place and staff members are not properly trained in security best practices, malicious actors have the power to fully stop the organization's operations. The success of a cybersecurity program depends on the coordination of the different subfields or components that make up cybersecurity inside an organization. The components and subfields of cybersecurity are described in Table 5.1.

Table 5.1 provides a concise overview of the key elements of cybersecurity and how they contribute to protecting digital assets and mitigating cyber risks. As seen in Figure 5.1, the following are some advantages of putting cybersecurity measures into place and keeping them up to date.

As shown in Figure 5.1, the benefits of cyber security ensures critical systems are operational during attacks, keeps essential services running smoothly, minimizes downtime, and reduces the impact of cyber incidents on business operations. Cyber security also meets regulatory requirements to avoid legal penalties, prevents data breaches, protects sensitive information, reduces costs associated with breaches and maintains customer trust. It's challenging to keep up with security developments, new technologies, and threat intelligence [4]. Data and other assets must be protected from many kinds of cyber threats [5]. Organizations in the modern era need to be aware of some of the most frequent and widespread cyber threats, even if the variety of these threats is constantly expanding. The following are examples of threats: ransomware, phishing, malware, man-in-the-middle (MitM), distributed denial of service (DDoS), and insider threats.

Figure 5.2 shows most common types of cyber security threats. Drive-by-download attacks and botnets, exploit kits, vishing, Keyloggers, cross-site scripting, spear phishing, and credential stuffing, viruses, and zero-day exploits are some other attack types. Some of the threats are defined as follows:

Table 5.1 The elements of cybersecurity and how they work

Element	Description	How it works
Network security	Protects computer networks from unauthorized access and intrusions using firewalls, intrusion detection systems (IDS), and virtual personal networks (VPNs)	Firewalls watch over all network traffic, both coming in and leaving out; IDS find and respond to suspicious activities; and VPNs encrypt data in transit
Endpoint security	Secures individual devices from viruses and other dangers through antivirus software and encryption	Antivirus software scans for and removes malicious software, while encryption protects data stored on and transmitted from devices
Data security	Safeguards sensitive data from unauthorized access, alteration, or destruction using encryption and access controls	Encryption converts data into an unreadable format without the correct decryption key and access controls restrict who can access data
Identity and access management (IAM)	Regulates access and maintains user IDs for digital resources based on user roles and permissions	IAM systems authenticate users' identities, verify their access rights, and grant or deny access accordingly
Application security	Ensures the security of software applications by identifying and mitigating vulnerabilities and implementing secure coding practices	Vulnerabilities are found and fixed through penetration testing, code reviews, and security assessments, while secure coding practices prevent them
Cloud security	Uses access controls and encryption to safeguard infrastructure, data, and apps housed in cloud environments	Encryption secures data stored in the cloud, and access controls restrict who can access cloud resources
Incident response and disaster recovery	Prepares for and responds to cybersecurity incidents by implementing incident response plans and conducting forensic investigations	Plans for incident response delineate procedures for identifying, addressing, and recuperating from security incidents, whereas forensic inquiries collect data to pinpoint the perpetrators
Security awareness and training	Educates users and staff on cybersecurity threats and acceptable practices	Training programs raise awareness about common threats, teach users how to recognize and avoid them, and promote a culture of security within organizations

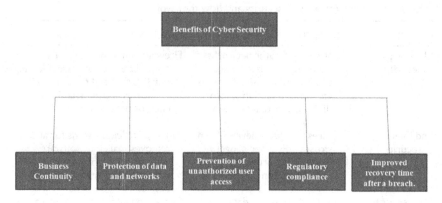

Figure 5.1 The benefits of cybersecurity.

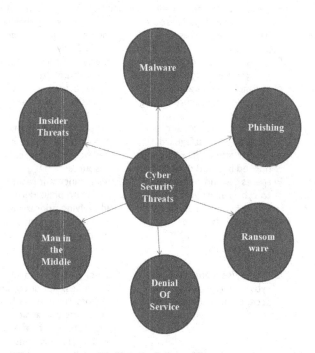

Figure 5.2 Different types of cybersecurity threats.

- *Phishing*
  Phishing [5] involves deceptive efforts to obtain confidential information, such as credit card numbers, passwords, and usernames, through online contacts by seeming to be a reliable source. Typically carried out via email, phishing scams entice victims into clicking on malicious links or submitting personal information on fraudulent websites. These Attacks may result in financial losses, identity theft, and illegal access to systems and networks. More advanced phishing techniques, such as spear-phishing and whaling, specifically target individual users or high-profile figures, making them more challenging to identify and prevent.

- *Ransomware*
  Ransomware [5] is a type of harmful software intended to encrypt data belonging to a victim and prevent it from being accessed until the attacker is paid a ransom for the decryption key. This type of cyber extortion can severely impact organizations by denying access to critical data and systems, leading to significant operational disruptions and financial losses. Ransomware attacks commonly propagate by using malware downloads, phishing emails, or software flaws. Once a system is compromised, the attacker typically demands the ransom payment in crypto currency to preserve their anonymity, complicating efforts to trace and apprehend them. The consequences of a ransomware attack can extend beyond immediate financial costs, potentially damaging the victim's reputation, disrupting business continuity, and incurring regulatory penalties if sensitive data is compromised. Additionally, the decision to pay the ransom does not guarantee the return of data or prevent future attacks, creating a complex dilemma for affected organizations.

- *Denial of Service (DoS)*
  DoS aims to block access to the website for authorized users. a computer, network, or service by flooding it with excessively large requests. This disrupts normal operations, leading to service outages and potential financial losses. Distributed denial of service (DDoS) attacks [5], which involve many compromised systems attacking a single target, can be particularly devastating. These attacks exploit the limitations of a target's resources, such as bandwidth, processing power, and memory, to exhaust them and prevent legitimate users from accessing services.

- *Man-in-the-Middle (MitM)*
  MitM occurs when an adversary intercepts and potentially modifies two parties' communication without their awareness. This form of attack jeopardizes the privacy and integrity of the data exchanged between users and systems [1]. MitM attacks can be carried out through different methods, including eavesdropping on unsecured Wi-Fi networks, session hijacking, and creating fake websites to

capture sensitive information. These attacks are particularly dangerous as they can result in data theft, unauthorized access, and fraud.

- *Insider Threats*
  Employees, outside contractors, or business partners who mistakenly or purposely jeopardize the organization's security are considered insider risks since they come from within the organization. Disgruntled employees may misuse their access privileges to steal sensitive data, sabotage systems, or leak confidential information [1,5]. Malicious insiders might act for personal gain or in collusion with external attackers. Accidental threats occur when well-meaning employees inadvertently expose the organization to risks through negligence or mistakes, such as misconfiguring systems or falling for phishing scams. Because insiders are provided access and inherent trust, they are difficult to identify and prevent.

- *Malware*
  Malware, an abbreviation for harmful software, denotes a variety of detrimental programs intended to damage, impair, or gain unauthorized access to computer systems. This category includes several distinct types of malware, each with unique characteristics and methods of operation:

  Viruses: These malicious programs attach themselves to legitimate software, replicating and spreading to other files and programs. Viruses can corrupt data, degrade system performance, and even render systems inoperable.

  Worms: Unlike viruses, worms are malware that replicates itself and spreads throughout networks. independently, without needing to attach to other programs. Worms can cause widespread damage by consuming bandwidth, overloading systems, and spreading quickly to numerous devices.

  Trojans: Derived from the infamous Trojan Horse, Trojans pretend to be helpful or benign software in order to deceive people to install the software. After entering the system, they can create backdoors, steal sensitive information, or deliver additional malicious payloads.

  Spyware: This type of malware covertly monitors and collects user activity and data without the user's knowledge. Spyware can capture keystrokes, monitor browsing patterns, and collect private data, which can frequently result in identity theft or unauthorized account access.

  Adware: Adware automatically displays or downloads advertisements, often in an intrusive manner. While not always harmful, adware can significantly degrade user experience and system performance, and it can sometimes serve as a gateway for more severe malware infections.

Malware poses substantial risks to the safety and functionality of computer systems. It may result in the theft of private information or data, such as personal, financial, or proprietary information. Furthermore, malware can corrupt critical files, disrupt operations, and reduce overall system performance, causing extensive damage to people as well as institutions.

The proposal of this work is to look into the potential of blockchain in enhancing cybersecurity precautions in the face of escalating cyber threats. The research aims to comprehensively analyze how blockchain can address the limitations of traditional security approaches and provide more robust protection for sensitive data and critical infrastructure. The following research questions serve as the study's main focus:

1. How do blockchain-based technologies enhance data reliability and security in the context of cybersecurity?
2. In what ways can blockchain technology secure transactions and communications, and how does it prevent unauthorized access and tampering?
3. What are the main challenges and limitations linked with integrating blockchain into cybersecurity strategies, and how might these difficulties be addressed?
4. What are the emerging trends and innovations in blockchain technology that have the potential to revolutionize cybersecurity practices in the future?
5. How can case studies and best practices from the actual world show how blockchain technology improves cybersecurity in various industries?
6. What are the policy and governance implications of adopting blockchain technology in cybersecurity, and what regulatory frameworks need to be recognized to ensure its ethical and effective implementation?

This chapter seeks to provide a thorough study of the revolution and potential applications of blockchain technology in cybersecurity by addressing these research questions.

The rest of the chapter is arranged as follows: Section 5.2 covers blockchain technology through an overview, Section 5.3 talks about cybersecurity challenges and blockchain solutions, in addition to the challenges and limitations of blockchain in cybersecurity, Section 5.4 discusses future directions and innovations, Section 5.5 talks about policy, governance, and ethical considerations, and Section 5.6 discusses conclusion followed by references.

5.2 BLOCKCHAIN TECHNOLOGY: AN OVERVIEW

Blockchain, originally created as the technology underlying crypto currencies like Bitcoin, has drawn interest due to its potential to completely transform cybersecurity [6]. By incorporating cutting-edge encryption techniques and decentralizing data storage, it provides a possible answer to the vulnerabilities of centralized systems. A blockchain is essentially a distributed ledger, consisting of a sequential series of "blocks" that are added to the chain chronologically, each of which records legal interactions on the network since the previous block was added [2].

One could characterize each block as an encrypted bit of data. In general, anyone can transact in the network and add information to the block chain. Reading is also accessible to anyone; however, no one can change it without the required permission. A blockchain is the result of a distributed network where every node has access to the same comprehensive and immutable history of network activity. Blockchain technology has made it possible for two or more parties—who might or might not be aware or trust one another—to safely value exchange over the internet without the involvement of a middleman. Rather, transaction validation is satisfied by "mining," a procedure that guarantees the confidentiality and accuracy of the data supplied to the chain. The Internet of Transactions is powered by blockchain technology [7].

As shown in Figure 5.3 a simplified diagram of block chain contains different blocks connected with each other. Each block contains block header, which has the previous hash, timestamp, and nonce and transactions. This simple diagram illustrates the fundamental structure of a blockchain, emphasizing the sequential linkage of blocks through cryptographic hashes. The key features of blockchain are as follows:

- *Decentralization*
  Decentralization is a fundamental aspect of blockchain-based technology. Blockchain functions as a mutually exclusive network, in contrast to conventional centralized systems, in which a single

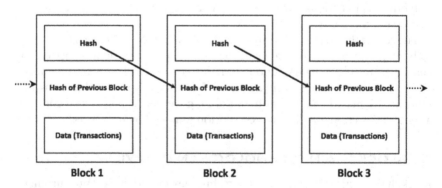

Figure 5.3 Simplified diagram of a blockchain.

entity controls the entire network. Every member, or node, has equal authority and influence in this decentralized approach. With this arrangement, managing and verifying transactions do not require a central authority. The network becomes more resistant to errors and intrusions as a result. Because blockchain is decentralized, not a single point of failure exists, which makes it far more difficult for bad actors to compromise the system. Every network node is equipped with a duplicate of the distributed ledger, providing extra security against mistakes and fraudulent activities since several parties verify and record each transaction.

- *Immutability*
  Another essential component of blockchain technology is immutability. A function is permanently included in the blockchain once it is added to a block and recorded there. This implies that the transaction data is a trustworthy and immutable record because it cannot be changed or erased. Blocks are connected by cryptographic hash functions, which provide immutability. It is very difficult to tamper with the chain of blocks since each block has a hash of the one previous it. The hash of a block will change if a threatening party attempts to alter the data within it; this will break the chain and notify the network of the attempted tampering. Because blockchain technology is impenetrable, it guarantees data integrity and fosters participant confidence.

- *Transparency*
  One major benefit of blockchain technology is transparency, especially in public block chains. On a public blockchain, every transaction is documented in a publicly accessible ledger for all parties to view. Accountability is increased by this transparency because all parties involved may see and confirm the transactions. Any effort to change the data would be visible to all users on the network because of the ledger's open nature, which discourages fraudulent activity. Furthermore, a transparent audit trail is made possible by blockchain's traceability feature. Every transaction on the blockchain has a complete history that can be traced back to its original source. For businesses like supply chain management, where tracing the provenance and travel of things is critical, this level of transparency and traceability is important.

- *Security*
  Among the most alluring aspects of blockchain technology is its security. Blockchain protects data and transactions with cutting-edge cryptographic methods. To prevent unauthorized access and manipulation, every transaction is encrypted and linked to the preceding one via a cryptographic hash. The decentralized architecture of blockchain adds to its security. The fact that numerous nodes are

recording and confirming transactions makes it very difficult for one party to change the data covertly. Blockchain also makes application of consensus methods like Proof of Work (PoW) and Proof of Stake (PoS) to confirm transactions. These methods prevent issues like double-spending and ensure that only legitimate transactions are added by ensuring that all nodes in the network agree on the legitimacy of transactions. Blockchain is a strong and secure technology with a wide range of applications because it combines cryptographic security, decentralization, and consensus processes.

In blockchain, centralized and decentralized systems each have special traits, benefits, and drawbacks. Blockchain networks that have a single company or a small group of companies with considerable influence over the network's operations and decision-making procedures are referred to as centralized systems. These central authorities oversee the network's rules and regulations, verify transactions, and uphold the blockchain's infrastructure. A central point of authority that has the power to overturn consensus procedures and make snap choices about how the network is run is common in centralized blockchain's. Decentralized systems are defined by the lack of central authority. Rather, power and decision-making are shared among a network of nodes, all of which take part in transaction validation and ledger maintenance for the blockchain. The decentralization of power and responsibility among all network participants is a basic principle of blockchain technology, with the goal of improving security, transparency, and resilience. Although centralized systems are faster, more efficient, and have easier governance, they come with security vulnerabilities due to trust difficulties and central points of failure. Though they have advantages in terms of security, transparency, and democratic governance, decentralized systems have drawbacks in terms of complexity, cost, and scalability.

5.2.1 Historical development and evolution of blockchain

The Conceptual Beginnings: Blockchain technology's fundamental concept originated in the late twentieth century. The goal of the cryptographically protected chain of blocks that researchers Stuart Haber and W. Scott Stornetta developed in 1991 was to design a system that would shield timestamps for documents from manipulation. The foundation of blockchain technology was established by this idea, which emphasized the significance of a safe and authentic data sequence.

Bitcoin and the Birth of Blockchain (2008–2009): The true birth of blockchain technology was the creation of Bitcoin by an unidentified individual or individuals under the pseudonym Satoshi Nakamoto [8]. A decentralized digital currency system based on peer-to-peer networks was outlined in Satoshi Nakamoto's paper "Bitcoin: A Peer-to-Peer Electronic

Cash System," which was published in 2008. The fundamental technology of Bitcoin, known as blockchain, was developed to record transactions in a secure, immutable database without the need for a dependable central authority [8]. Nakamoto mined the "genesis block," which is the blockchain's initial block, which marked the beginning of the Bitcoin network in January 2009. This event is recognized as the official launch of blockchain technology.

Early Adoption and Expansion (2009–2013): In its early years, early users, developers, and cryptographers who were interested in Bitcoin's potential to upend established financial systems gradually began to use it. In 2010, Laszlo Hanyecz, a programmer, made the first Bitcoin transaction in real life when he exchanged 10,000 Bit coins for two pizzas. This event is renowned as "Bitcoin Pizza Day." Interest in the blockchain technology that underpins Bitcoin increased along with its rise in popularity. Other crypto currencies that included modifications and enhancements to the original Bitcoin protocol were Namecoin and Litecoin.

The Rise of Smart Contracts and Ethereum (2013–2015): The launch of smart contracts by Ethereum [9] marked a critical milestone in the ongoing growth of blockchain technology. Ethereum was a late 2013 proposal by Vitalik Buterin with the goal of expanding blockchain's use beyond transactions to more sophisticated applications. In its white paper, Ethereum presented a platform that enables developers to write and implement smart contracts for decentralized apps (DApps) using a Turing-complete programming language. With the launch of its native cryptocurrency, Ether (ETH), in 2015, the Ethereum network [9] immediately rose to prominence as the top blockchain innovation platform. The blockchain space was revolutionized by Ethereum's introduction of smart contracts, which made a wide range of decentralized applications across multiple industries possible.

Diversification and Enterprise Adoption (2016–2019): Ethereum's success led to a rapid diversification of the blockchain ecosystem. A plethora of blockchain platforms have surfaced, each with distinct functionalities and applications. Projects like EOS, a platform for scalable DApps, Hyper ledger, a set of enterprise blockchain tools, and Ripple, which focuses on cross-border payments, became well-known. During this time, enterprise adoption of blockchain technology also started to pick up steam. Big businesses and financial institutions began looking into how blockchain may improve security, cut costs, and expedite processes. To encourage cooperation and standardize blockchain technologies for enterprise use, blockchain consortia were established, including R3 and the Enterprise Ethereum Alliance.

DeFi, NFTs, and the Blockchain Boom (2020–Present): Blockchain applications have grown rapidly in the last few years, especially in the areas of non-fungible tokens (NFTs) and decentralized finance (DeFi) [10]. DeFi systems without the need for middlemen, offer lending, borrowing, and trading services using blockchain technology. As a result, the DeFi industry has seen a boom in investment and innovation. NFTs, or unique digital assets on the blockchain, have drawn a lot of interest because of their uses in entertainment, gaming, and the arts. High-profile NFT partnerships and sales have helped blockchain technology gain widespread acceptance. Furthermore, blockchain technology is still evolving due to advances in consensus processes, scalability, and interoperability. Blockchain's scalability issues are addressed by layer two solutions like Ethereum's multiple scaling efforts and Bit coin's Lightning Network.

The historical development and evolution of blockchain technology reflect a journey from a theoretical concept to a transformative force across multiple industries. From the creation of Bitcoin and the introduction of Ethereum's smart contracts to the rise of DeFi and NFTs [10], blockchain has continuously evolved, driving innovation and challenging traditional systems. As the technology advances, its potential to revolutionize various sectors remains vast, promising a future where blockchain plays a pivotal role in the digital economy.

5.2.2 Key concepts and components

Understanding blockchain technology requires a grasp of several fundamental concepts and components. These elements, without the need for middlemen, offer lending, borrowing, and trading services using blockchain technology. Below are the key concepts and components:

- *Distributed Ledger Technology (DLT)*
  A database that is voluntarily shared and synchronized across several locations, organizations, or regions is known as a distributed ledger. As a result, transactions can have public "witnesses," which increases the difficulty of cyberattacks. A blockchain increases security and transparency by distributing the ledger among all of the network's nodes, guaranteeing that each node has a full replica of every transaction. Because it is decentralized, there is no need for central authority, and communal validation guarantees the preservation of data integrity.
- *Cryptographic Hash Functions*
  An input, or message is given to a hash function in cryptography, which then creates a fixed-length string of bytes that is unique for each input. Data integrity must be ensured using hash functions. Because tampering is easily detectable, each modification to the input data yields an entirely different hash. The security and immutability of the blockchain are guaranteed by this cryptographic linking of blocks.

Table 5.2 The different types of blockchains

S. No	Type of blockchain	Description	Examples
1	Public blockchain	An open, decentralized network where anyone can participate, view transactions, as well as participate in the process of consensus.	Bitcoin, Ethereum
2	Private blockchain	A restricted network controlled by a single organization, where participation requires permission.	Hyperledger Fabric, R3 Corda
3	Consortium blockchain	A semi-decentralized network managed by a group of organizations, providing controlled access and shared governance.	Quorum, Energy Web Foundation
4	Hybrid blockchain	A combination of public and private blockchains, allowing controlled access while maintaining some level of public transparency.	Dragonchain, XinFin

- *Consensus Mechanisms*
  Algorithms known as consensus mechanisms [11] make sure that every node in the network is in agreement on the authenticity of transactions. PoW requires network individuals or miners to resolve tricky mathematical issues to authorize transactions and include additional blocks to the blockchain, as shown by Bitcoin. PoS offers a more energy-efficient method by selecting validators according to the amount of tokens they possess and are prepared to put up collateral (or "stake"). Proof of Stake Delegated (DPoS) and Byzantine Fault Tolerance (BFT) are two further consensus-building techniques, each with pros and cons of their own.

Table 5.2 illustrates different types of blockchains, which helps to clearly differentiate the various types of blockchains, highlighting their unique features and real-world applications.

5.2.3 Current applications across industries

Since the discovery of blockchain technology more than seven years ago, this industry has experienced tremendous growth thanks to the introduction of numerous new, cutting-edge technological concepts. Due to its initial link to anonymous online shopping the "dark net," where people might use virtual currencies like Bitcoin to make transactions, this technology had a bad reputation. Nonetheless, a number of significant businesses, including

JPMorgan, IBM, and Barclays, have made investments in the study and advancement of blockchain technology in recent years [12–14].

Organizations and entrepreneurs that are inventive and creative have been drawn to the emerging field of information knowledge because of the interest shown by larger organizations and the substantial quantity of money that is being exchanged in crypto currencies. Many countries now see the possibilities of this technology instead of its early association with illicit operations due to the field's rapid expansion [15]. Below is a summary of some recent blockchain use cases and applications.

- Financial Applications
  Currencies: Digital currencies, like Bitcoin, provided fully decentralized currency issuance and traceable payments, making them the first applications of blockchain technology. As a result of Bitcoin's increasing popularity, other digital currencies that are modifications of the Bitcoin system design have been developed. At present, blockchain technology is the underpinning technology for more than 600 distinct digital currencies [16]. Although there are many other applications for blockchain technology, digital currencies continue to be the most common use case. This is because of the field's breakthroughs and innovations.
  Exchanges: In the exchanges, blockchain technology is utilized to build decentralized systems that enable the swap of digital assets, including Bitcoin and other digital currencies, as well as some additional kind of registrable assets on a network with a unique digital individuality. There are presently several digital currency exchanges operating, including Coinbase, ItBit, and Kraken [17–19].
  Stock Markets: Unlike the existing systems, decentralized stock markets [20] driven by blockchain technology allow equities to be exchanged on a platform that is not governed by a single entity. Since the system will only operate in accordance with the guidelines provided by the system protocol, users may be sure that the trades are completed appropriately. This application hasn't been used yet, though.
- Social Applications
  Digital identification: By supplying the required infrastructure, blockchain technology has the ability to scale digital identification at remarkably cheap costs and with significant security improvements [21]. Instead of citizens receiving passports or IDs from various nations, a decentralized identity service that makes use of blockchain technology can help people worldwide create their individual digital identities via means of a decentralized

system. This application had drawn attention from a number of federal entities.

Voting: In this, voting process can be authenticated using blockchain technology by using "private keys" that are unique to each voter. The system protocol for this application can be created so that, while computing the election's final result in real time, user identities can be verified while remaining anonymous. Voters can be sure that the results are reliable and unaffected by fraud or manipulation because the procedure is transparent.

- *Legal Applications*

Smart contracts: A developing application of blockchain-based technology is the creation of blockchain-based smart contracts [22]. The concept of smart contracts is really simple: when specific circumstances are satisfied (a payment is expected, an event's result is determined, etc.), a protocol for software does an action (releasing cash, sending information, making a purchase, etc.). Blockchain-based contracts have the advantage of requiring less human intervention during the creation, execution, and enforcement phases, which lowers the contract's cost while increasing the process's assurance on the application and execution.

Smart property: Generally speaking, smart contracts are designed to transact every asset in blockchain-based frameworks [23]. A digital identity can be made for any tangible, hard object that is reflected in the system of blockchain. Smart contracts can be used to manage ownership through the use of these identities. For example, a hotel room door could unlock automatically as soon as payment from the user is approved, or if their insurance expires, a car might stop enabling them to drive.

- *Other Potential Applications*

Asset tracking: Blockchain technology allows for the tracking of physical assets and allows an ownership record to be kept for every object. For instance, Everledger is a business that uses a blockchain [24] network to digitally identify each diamond in order to track them [28]. For example, by keeping so-called blood diamonds out of the jewelry business, this aids in transaction authenticity. Provenance Company offers an additional instance of asset monitoring, with an emphasis on establishing a chain of custody or a record of ownership for diverse tangible goods [29].

Engineering applications: It is believed that complicated engineering systems will be the next industry in which blockchain technology finds application. The authors envision that certain engineering-related transactions can be quickly facilitated by the blockchain technology. These include dispersed modular architectures for machines and systems, tracking assets and products before and after manufacture, coordinating financial transactions between and within enterprises, controlling quality and testing, and the supply chain for manufacturing, the primary topic of this chapter.

5.3 CYBERSECURITY CHALLENGES AND BLOCKCHAIN SOLUTIONS

In the realm of cybersecurity, organizations face a myriad of challenges stemming from evolving cyber threats and vulnerabilities. This enormous amount shows how urgently cyber security has to be prioritized on a world-wide scale. Furthermore, it is anticipated that the present 2,200 daily attacks will not only expand but also become much more personalized with the rise of generative AI. Perhaps in 2024, ransomware will still be the most common kind of cybercrime despite advancements in technology. In fact, over 72 percent of cybersecurity in 2023 had this as their primary motivation, according to Statista. Most attacked countries by cybercrime since 2004 are shown in Table 5.3.

As shown in Table 5.3, determining the most attacked countries by cybercrime involves considering various factors, including the prevalence of cyber threats, the sophistication of cybercriminals, and the effectiveness of cybersecurity measures. While specific rankings may vary depending on the source and methodology of data collection, several countries are consistently identified as prime targets for cyberattacks.

As shown in Figure 5.4, the top five countries which are affected by cybercrime are the United States, Russia, China, France, and Germany. It's essential to note that cybercrime affects countries worldwide, and no nation is immune to cyber threats. The effectiveness of cybersecurity measures, international cooperation, and information sharing play crucial roles in addressing cybercrime and safeguarding digital assets and infrastructure. Table 5.4 provides an overview of key cybersecurity challenges, highlighting

Table 5.3 Most attacked countries since 2004

Country	No. of attacks
United States	0.5
China	1.5
Russia	1
Germany	2.5
France	2

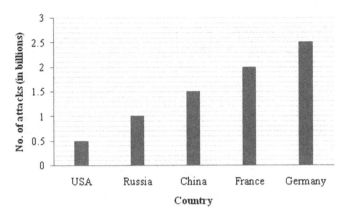

Figure 5.4 Top five countries by cybercrime density (since 2004).

Table 5.4 Cyber security challenges and their description

S. No	Cybersecurity challenges	Description
I	Shortage of cybersecurity professionals	Global scarcity of skilled cybersecurity professionals, leading to recruitment difficulties and skill gaps within organizations.
2	Rapid technological advancements	Emergence of new technologies introduces new attack surfaces and vulnerabilities, requiring proactive risk management and adaptive security measures.
3	Complexity of IT environments	Modern IT environments are increasingly complex, comprising interconnected systems, diverse devices, and hybrid cloud infrastructures, making security management challenging.
4	Compliance with regulations	Meeting cybersecurity regulations and standards presents challenges for organizations, requiring resource investment and operational overhead to ensure compliance.
5	Insider threats	Insider events must be prevented, detected, and responded to because malicious or careless acts by individuals within an organization present serious hazards to cybersecurity.
6	Supply chain risks	Third-party vendors and suppliers are targeted in supply chain attacks, compromising organizations' networks and systems, highlighting the need for supply chain security measures.
7	Privacy concerns	Organizations must navigate complex privacy regulations while safeguarding sensitive data and protecting individuals' privacy rights.

(*continued*)

Table 5.4 (Cont.)

S. No	Cybersecurity challenges	Description
8	Cybersecurity awareness and education	Low levels of cybersecurity awareness and education contribute to the effectiveness of cyberattacks, emphasizing the need for comprehensive training programs and awareness initiatives.
9	Cybersecurity collaboration	Establishing trusted relationships and sharing threat intelligence between organizations, government agencies, and cybersecurity professionals enhances cyber resilience and facilitates proactive threat detection and response.

the diverse range of issues facing organizations and individuals in today's digital landscape.

Table 5.4 illustrates the key challenges, addressing these cybersecurity challenges requires a concerted effort from stakeholders across sectors, including government, industry, academia, and civil society. Organizations can more effectively safeguard their digital resources and decrease the impact of cyberattacks by taking a proactive and cooperative method for handling cybersecurity.

5.3.1 Blockchain's role in enhancing cybersecurity

Cybersecurity and blockchain are closely related, with blockchain technology providing several benefits to improve cybersecurity protocols [30]. Blockchain technology advances cybersecurity in several key ways:

Data Integrity: The decentralized and immutable characteristics of blockchain technology guarantee that without the consent of all network users, information kept on the network cannot be altered or deleted. With this functionality, data integrity is improved and unauthorized tampering is prevented, which makes blockchain the perfect choice for safely storing sensitive data and keeping accurate audit trails.

Secure Transactions: Blockchain uses cryptographic methods like encryption and digital signatures to facilitate safe peer-to-peer transactions. Network users validate and verify transactions on the blockchain, guaranteeing the integrity and validity of the data being sent. By doing this, the possibility of fraud and illegal access to private data is decreased.

Decentralization: The decentralized network of nodes that underpins blockchain technology reduces the likelihood of single points of failure and cyberattacks. By increasing the difficulty for aggressors to undermine the availability and the accuracy of the data kept on the blockchain, decentralization improves cybersecurity. Because no single entity controls the entire network, decentralization also promotes trust among network users.

Identity Management: By providing safe and decentralized authentication methods, blockchain-based identity management solutions lower the danger of fraud and identity theft. Blockchain protects privacy and authority over one's own data while enhancing security by giving users distinct cryptographic identities.

Smart Contracts: These are self-executing, code-written contracts with preset parameters. By automating and enforcing security policies, they lower the possibility of human error and guarantee adherence to security procedures. By automating security procedures and doing away with the need for middlemen, smart contracts improve cybersecurity and boost the efficiency and confidence of digital transactions.

Transparency and Auditability: By keeping a transparent and unchangeable record of every transaction, blockchain technology offers transparency and auditability. This makes it possible for businesses to show that they are in accordance with industry norms and legal requirements, which makes regulatory reporting, auditing, and compliance verification easier. Furthermore, the transparency of blockchain technology makes it easier to spot and stop fraudulent activity.

Threat Intelligence and Collaboration: Blockchain-based platforms enable secure sharing of threat intelligence and collaborative incident response among organizations, government agencies, and cybersecurity professionals. By fostering information sharing and collaboration [25], blockchain enhances collective defense against cyber threats and strengthens cybersecurity resilience across ecosystems.

Overall, blockchain technology [26] offers a wide range of capabilities that advance cybersecurity by ensuring data integrity, improving identity management, facilitating secure transactions, and enabling decentralized and resilient systems. By leveraging blockchain's innovative features, organizations can enhance their cybersecurity posture, mitigate risks, and build trust in digital interactions.

5.3.2 Case studies

In examining the practical applications of blockchain technology in cybersecurity, case studies across various sectors provide valuable insights into its effectiveness and potential.

5.3.2.1 Financial services

The financial services sector has been an early adopter of blockchain technology, leveraging its capabilities to enhance security, transparency, and efficiency in transactions and data management. One notable case study is the implementation of blockchain in remittances and payments across borders. Conventional cross-border payment systems are often slow, costly, and prone to errors and fraud. By utilizing blockchain-based platforms, financial institutions can streamline cross-border transactions, reduce processing times, and lower transaction costs significantly. Ripple, a payment protocol based on blockchain, has teamed with several banks and financial institutions worldwide to facilitate real-time, low-cost cross-border payments using its digital asset, XRP.

Another application of blockchain in financial services is in supply chain management and trade finance. Trade finance involves complex processes, multiple parties, and extensive documentation, making it susceptible to inefficiencies, fraud, and errors. Blockchain-based platforms like TradeLens, developed by IBM and Maersk, utilize distributed ledger technology to digitize and automate trade processes, providing transparency, traceability, and security throughout the supply chain. By digitizing trade documents, automating workflows, and enabling real-time tracking of goods, blockchain reduces the risk of fraud, improves efficiency, and enhances trust among trading partners.

5.3.2.2 Healthcare

Blockchain technology [27] has the potential to enhance patient privacy, interoperability, and data security in the healthcare industry. Because electronic health records (EHRs) are centralized and lack strong security controls, they are frequently targeted by cybercriminals and include sensitive patient data. Healthcare companies may improve EHR security and integrity, lower the risk of data breaches, and protect patient privacy by utilizing blockchain-based solutions.

The administration of patient data and medical records is one application blockchain technology in the medical field. Patients may safely save and share their medical records with medical experts using MedRec, a blockchain-based platform created by Massachusetts Institute of Technology

(MIT) researchers. Patients have more control over their data when medical records are encrypted and decentralized on the blockchain, and healthcare practitioners may safely access current, accurate information. Additionally, blockchain makes it easier for diverse healthcare systems to communicate with one another, allowing for the easy sharing of medical data while protecting patient privacy and data security.

5.3.2.3 Supply chain management

Another industry that stands to gain a great deal from blockchain technology is supply chain management. Conventional supply networks are frequently disjointed, complicated, and vulnerable to fraud, inefficiency, and fake goods. Organizations may enhance supply chain security, traceability, and transparency by incorporating blockchain technology into their management systems.

One of the biggest retailers in the world, Walmart, has improved food safety and traceability by integrating blockchain technology into its food supply chain. Walmart mandates that its suppliers use blockchain technology to track and trace food goods from farms to store shelves as part of its Food Traceability Initiative. Walmart can minimize the impact of foodborne illnesses, swiftly discover and address food safety issues, and gain consumer trust by storing critical information like origin, processing, and shipping details on the blockchain.

These case studies demonstrate the diverse applications of blockchain technology in addressing cybersecurity challenges across different industries. From financial services to healthcare and supply chain management, blockchain offers innovative solutions for enhancing security, transparency, and efficiency in transactions and data management. As organizations continue to explore and adopt blockchain-based solutions, the potential for improving cybersecurity and mitigating risks in the digital age remains significant.

5.3.3 Limitations of blockchain in cybersecurity

While blockchain technology offers several advantages for enhancing cybersecurity, it also has limitations that need to be considered. Blockchain technology holds great promise for developing decentralized, trustless applications. However, it isn't flawless. The blockchain technology is not the best option and cannot be used for common applications due to a few obstacles. The following illustrates the limitations [31] of blockchain technology.

Table 5.5 provides the limitations of blockchain. Blockchain technology holds promise for enhancing cybersecurity, but it is essential to recognize and address its limitations to realize its full potential effectively [27]. By

Table 5.5 Limitations of blockchain technology

S. No	Limitation	Description
1	Scalability	Blockchain networks may experience degraded performance and speed as the number of transactions increases. This challenge arises from the scalability limitations of consensus mechanisms like PoW or PoS and the exponential growth in the size of the blockchain, leading to higher storage and bandwidth requirements.
2	Interoperability	Lack of interoperability between different blockchain networks and platforms complicates communication and secure data sharing. Numerous blockchain protocols and platforms with unique standards hinder seamless integration and collaboration within the cybersecurity ecosystem.
3	Energy consumption	Energy-intensive consensus mechanisms like PoW, used in popular blockchain networks, raise environmental sustainability concerns. PoW requires significant computational power and energy consumption for transaction validation, prompting exploration of more energy-efficient alternatives like PoS.
4	Regulatory and legal challenges	Blockchain operates in a regulatory gray area, posing compliance challenges with data protection, privacy, and financial regulations. Legal liability issues, particularly concerning data breaches and fraud, highlight the need for clear legal frameworks and contractual agreements to define rights and liabilities.
5	Privacy and confidentiality	Despite offering transparency and immutability, blockchain raises concerns about data privacy and confidentiality. Public block chains expose transaction data, while private block chains face challenges in ensuring compliance with data privacy regulations and protecting sensitive information.

overcoming these limitations through innovation, collaboration, and regulatory clarity, blockchain can play a transformative role in strengthening cybersecurity and mitigating cyber threats and vulnerabilities.

5.4 FUTURE DIRECTIONS AND INNOVATIONS

As blockchain technology continues to evolve, there are several future directions and innovations that hold significant promise for enhancing cybersecurity. From technological advancements to emerging trends and predictions, the future of blockchain in cybersecurity presents exciting opportunities for innovation and transformation.

5.4.1 Technological advancements

Integration with AI and IoT: One of blockchain technology's most promising applications is the integration of artificial intelligence (AI) with the Internet of Things (IoT). By combining blockchain technology's security and transparency with AI's predictive analytics and the Internet of Things, organizations can create robust cybersecurity solutions that can detect and stop assaults in real time. For example, blockchain technology enables the safe and permanent storage of data from IoT devices. AI algorithms can then examine this data to identify patterns and anomalies that may indicate impending cyberattacks.

Implications for Quantum Computing: Blockchain and cybersecurity face new potential and difficulties as a result of the development of quantum computing. Blockchain's traditional cryptographic methods could be broken by quantum computers, but they also present a chance to create cryptographic solutions that are immune to this threat. To meet this issue and guarantee the long-term security of blockchain networks in the quantum age, research into post-quantum cryptography and quantum-resistant blockchain protocols is now underway.

5.4.2 Emerging trends and predictions

Blockchain's role in cybersecurity is also expected to be influenced by new trends and projections that foresee its widespread use and influence. The emergence of decentralized finance (DeFi), asset tokenization, and the spread of blockchain-based identity management systems are some of these trends. Furthermore, forecasts indicate that blockchain and cybersecurity firms will work together more frequently, which will result in the creation of creative solutions to deal with the ever-evolving risks and weaknesses posed by the internet.

5.4.3 Potential impact on global cybersecurity strategies

Global cybersecurity tactics are anticipated to be significantly impacted by the deployment of blockchain technology. The decentralized structure, cryptographic security, and transparency of blockchain present novel prospects for augmenting data security, identity administration, and safe authentication. More decentralized and robust cybersecurity architectures will become the norm as businesses use blockchain more and more for cybersecurity applications. Furthermore, blockchain-based solutions may enhance stakeholder engagement and information exchange, resulting in enhanced threat intelligence and incident response capabilities. Here are some cybersecurity best practices to protect against cyber threats.

By following best practices as shown in Figure 5.5, organizations can better protect themselves against a wide range of cyber threats and minimize the risk of security breaches and data loss.

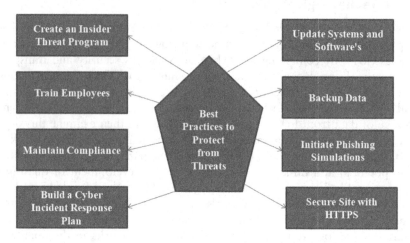

Figure 5.5 Cybersecurity best practices to protect from cyber threats.

5.5 POLICY, GOVERNANCE, AND ETHICAL CONSIDERATIONS

At the intersection of cybersecurity and blockchain technology, policy, governance, and ethical considerations hold significant sway in shaping the landscape. These factors, overseen by policymakers, governments, and international organizations, are instrumental in navigating the intricate terrain of blockchain technology.

5.5.1 Developing standards and protocols

In order to guarantee smooth interoperability, strong security, and confidence in the blockchain ecosystem, standards and protocols must be established. Industry consortia and standards bodies are essential in establishing protocols for the application of blockchain technology, including consensus methods, data structures, and cryptographic algorithms. Following established standards promotes interoperability, reliability, and transparency throughout blockchain networks.

5.5.2 Role of governments and international organizations

Governments and international organizations have a significant impact on the laws, rules, and activities pertaining to cybersecurity. Lawmakers face a variety of legal, regulatory, and geopolitical issues as blockchain technology develops. Governments may aim to preserve investor interests, consumer rights, and national security while fostering blockchain innovation. To combat cross-border cybersecurity attacks and increase global cybersecurity resilience, international collaboration is necessary.

5.5.3 Ethical and societal implications

A major factor in the creation and application of blockchain technology is ethics. Consisting of algorithmic openness, data privacy and security, and social effect considerations, blockchain applications provide moral conundrums that require close examination. Stakeholders have to walk a tightrope between supporting innovation and moral values like accountability, justice, and autonomy. Furthermore, the implications of blockchain technology for society, particularly the possibility of upending established power structures and economic theories, call for careful discussion and responsible leadership.

Ethical, governmental, and regulatory factors are crucial for the appropriate adoption and application of blockchain technology in cybersecurity and other fields. Through the establishment of standards, engagement with governmental bodies and international entities, and conscientious deliberation on ethical and societal implications, stakeholders can pave the way for a more secure, transparent, and equitable digital future.

5.6 CONCLUSION

In the ever-evolving landscape of cybersecurity and blockchain technology, our exploration has revealed critical insights into the intersection of these domains. This work uncovered the transformative potential of blockchain technology in bolstering cybersecurity defenses. From its decentralized architecture to its cryptographic security features, blockchain offers innovative solutions to combat a myriad of cyber threats. This work explored how blockchain enhances data integrity, strengthens identity management, and facilitates secure transactions, thereby addressing pressing cybersecurity challenges. Additionally, it highlighted the role of blockchain in diverse sectors such as finance, healthcare, and supply chain management, showcasing its real-world applications. Organizations stand to benefit from integrating blockchain into their cybersecurity strategies to fortify their defenses against evolving threats. Policymakers and regulatory bodies must grapple with the legal, ethical, and societal implications of blockchain adoption, striving to strike a balance between fostering innovation and safeguarding public interests. Furthermore, researchers and practitioners are tasked with further exploring the nuanced complexities of blockchain technology and its implications for cybersecurity. Researchers should delve deeper into the technical challenges and limitations of blockchain in cybersecurity, seeking scalable solutions to enhance its efficacy. Additionally, exploring the ethical and societal implications of blockchain adoption warrants further investigation, guiding policymakers in crafting informed regulations and governance frameworks. Furthermore, interdisciplinary collaborations between cybersecurity experts, blockchain developers, and legal scholars are essential to address multifaceted challenges and drive innovation in this burgeoning field. This research analysis underscores the transformative potential of blockchain technology in revolutionizing cybersecurity practices. By embracing blockchain's decentralized, immutable, and transparent nature, stakeholders can chart a course toward a more resilient and secure digital ecosystem.

REFERENCES

[1] Tian, F. (2016). "An agri-food supply chain traceability system for China based on RFID & blockchain technology," 2016 13th International Conference on Service Systems and Service Management (ICSSSM), Kunming, pp. 1–6, doi: 10.1109/ICSSSM.2016.7538424.

[2] Thakur, K., Qiu, M., Gai, K., and Ali, M.L. (2015). "An investigation on cyber security threats and security models," 2015 IEEE 2nd International Conference on Cyber Security and Cloud Computing, New York, NY, USA, pp. 307–311, doi: 10.1109/CSCloud.2015.71.

[3] Bennett, L. (2012). "Cyber security strategy," in ITNOW, vol. 54, no. 1, pp. 10–11, March, doi: 10.1093/itnow/bws003.

[4] Gupta, S., Raman, R., Singh, D., Gangodkar, D., Ajit Shinde, A., and Chauhan S. (2023). "A detailed investigation on various cyber security models and their comparisons with the detailed performance analysis for the application of IIOT systems," 2023 3rd International Conference on Advance Computing and Innovative Technologies in Engineering (ICACITE), Greater Noida, India, pp. 779–783, doi: 10.1109/ICACITE57410.2023.10182724.

[5] Ghelani, D. (2022). Cyber security, cyber threats, implications and future perspectives: A review. *Authorea Preprints.*

[6] Anisha, P. R., Reddy, C. K. K., and Nguyen, N. G. (2022). Blockchain technology: a boon at the pandemic times—A solution for global economy upliftment with AI and IoT. *Blockchain Security in Cloud Computing,* 227–252.

[7] Stuxnet. Wikipedia; 2024, January 10 (cited 2024, January 12). Available at: https://en.wikipedia.org/w/index.php?title=Stuxnet&%20oldid=1194687512

[8] Nakamoto, S. (2008). Bitcoin: A peer-to-peer electronic cash system. Retrieved from https://bitcoin.org/bitcoin.pdf

[9] Metcalfe, W. (2020). Ethereum, smart contracts, DApps. *Blockchain and Crypt Currency,* 77, 77–93.

[10] Marochini, L. (2021). Blockchain, DeFI, NFTs: From use cases to business plan. *Journal of Digital Banking,* 6(3), 251–261.

[11] Pilkington, M. (2016). Blockchain technology: principles and applications. In *Research handbook on digital transformations* (pp. 225–253). Edward Elgar Publishing.

[12] AI in cybersecurity: defend your digital realm (cited 2024, January 13). Available from: www.veritis.com/blog/ai-in-cy-bersecurity-defending-against-evolving-threats/

[13] Machine Learning (ML) in cybersecurity: use cases—Crowd-Strike. crowdstrike.com (cited 2024, January 15). Available from: www.crowdstr ike.com/cybersecurity-101/machine-learning-cybersecurity/

[14] Chandramouli, R., and Butcher, Z. (2023). A zero trust architecture model for access control in cloud-native applications in multi-cloud environments. National Institute of Standards and Technology, NIST Special Publication (SP) 800-207A.

[15] Zhou L. What is zero trust architecture (ZTA)? | NextLabs Data-Centric Security. NextLabs (cited 2024, January 13). Available from: www.nextl abs.com/what-is-zero-trust-architecture-zta/

[16] NIST: blockchain provides security, traceability for smart manufacturing. NIST; 2019 (cited 2024, January 13). Available from: www.nist.gov/ news-events/news/2019/02/nist-block-chain-provides-security-traceability-smart-manufacturing

[17] Innovation insight for decentralized identity and verifiable claims. Gartner (cited 2024, January 13). Available from: www.gartner.com/en/documents/ 4004851

[18] What is deception technology? Importance & benefits. Zscaler (cited 2024, January 13). Available from: www.zscaler.com/resources/security-terms-glossary/what-is-deception-technology

[19] Han, X., Kheir, N., and Balzarotti D. (2018). Deception techniques in computer security: a research perspective. *ACM Comput. Surv.*, 51(4):80:1–36. https://doi.org/10.1145/3214305

[20] CISA | Home Page (accessed 2024, January 13). Available from: www. cisa.gov/

[21] The Council of Europe: Guardian of Human Rights, Democracy and the Rule of Law for 700 million citizens—Portal—www.coe.int (accessed 2024, January 13). Available from: www.coe.int/en/web/portal

[22] What is behavioral biometrics? (accessed 2024, January 13). Available from: www.biocatch.com/blog/what-is-behavioral-biometrics

[23] Liang, Y., Samtani, S., Guo, B., and Yu, Z. (2020). Behavioral biometrics for continuous authentication in the internet-of-things era: an artificial intelligence perspective. *IEEE Internet Things J.* 7(9):9128–9143. https:// doi.org/10.1109/JIOT.2020.3004077

[24] Anisha, P.R., Kishor Kumar Reddy, C., Nguyen, N.G., Bhushan, M., Kumar, A., and Mohd Hanafiah, M. (2023). *Intelligent Systems and Machine Learning for Industry*, CRC Press, Taylor & Francis Group.

[25] Kishor Kumar Reddy, C., Anisha, P.R., Khan, S., Mohd Hanafiah, M., Pamulaparty, L., Madana Mohana, R. (2024). *Sustainability in Industry 5.0: Theory and Applications*, CRC Press, Taylor & Francis Group.

[26] Mona, B., Yasmeen, S., Faiz, N., Anisha, P. R., Murthy, R., and Reddy, K. K. (2019). Blockchain technology. *Journal of Applied Science and Computations*, 526–534.

[27] Ramana, K., Mohana, R.M., Kumar Reddy, C.K., Srivastava, G., and Gadekallu, T.R. (2023). A blockchain-based data-sharing framework for cloud based internet of things systems with efficient smart contracts. 2023 IEEE International Conference on Communications Workshops (ICC Workshops), Rome, Italy, pp. 452–457, doi: 10.1109/ICCWorksh ops57953.2023.10283747.

[28] Du, L., Shang, Q., Wang, Z., and Wang X. (2023). Robust image hashing based on multi-view dimension reduction. *J Inf Secur Appl.* 77, 103578. https://doi.org/10.1016/j.jisa.2023.103578

[29] Qin, C., Liu, E., Feng, G., and Zhang, X. (2021). Perceptual image hashing for content authentication based on convolutional neural network with multiple constraints. *IEEE Trans Circuits Syst Video Technol.* 31(11), 4523–4537. https://doi.org/10.1109/TCSVT.2020.3047142

[30] Giannoutakis, K.M. et al., (2020). A blockchain solution for enhancing cybersecurity defence of IoT. 2020 IEEE International Conference on Blockchain (Blockchain), Rhodes, Greece, pp. 490–495, doi: 10.1109/ Blockchain50366.2020.00071.

[31] Hughes, L., Dwivedi, Y. K., Misra, S. K., Rana, N. P., Raghavan, V., and Akella, V. (2019). Blockchain research, practice and policy: Applications, benefits, limitations, emerging research themes and research agenda. *International Journal of Information Management*, 49, 114–129.

Chapter 6

Empowering IoT networks

A study on machine learning and deep learning for DDoS attack

Mohammad Zahid and Taran Singh Bharati

6.1 INTRODUCTION

The Internet of Things (IoT) forms a network of interconnected devices enabling seamless sharing of data and services without human intervention. An IoT component refers to an individual part or device that constitutes the broader system of the IoT. These interconnected devices or objects can collect, transmit, receive, or process data, enabling communication and interaction within the IoT network. Examples of IoT components include sensors, actuators, microcontrollers, communication modules, and software interfaces that collectively contribute to the functionality and data exchange within the IoT ecosystem [1,8]. IoT devices have altered numerous industries, including healthcare, manufacturing, security, agriculture, and even home automation [12].

In recent years, we have witnessed a striking increase in intelligent IoT devices in our daily lives, including smart cameras, smart televisions, wearable technology, interactive toys, and smart lighting [13]. According to the Spring 2023 edition of IoT Analytics' State of IoT report, there has been an 18 percent expansion in worldwide IoT connections, reaching a total of 14.3 billion operational endpoints. This data is projected to increase further, reaching 16.7 billion active endpoints by 2023, IoT systems regularly enhance our digital environment's innovation [11].

The rapid growth of the IoT offers hackers numerous avenues for potential exploits. As interconnected devices increase, the likelihood of botnets forming rises, leading to a higher frequency of DDoS attacks [8]. Furthermore, many IoT devices come with pre-set usernames and passwords that users cannot modify. These vulnerabilities in security create an easy opportunity for cybercriminals to exploit these unprotected IoT devices and gain control over them [13]. IoT produces substantial volumes of data. However, several obstacles must be addressed to make IoT applications efficient and secure. These challenges encompass interoperability, security, standards, and server technologies [3,9].

DOI: 10.1201/9781003497585-6

6.1.1 Working on IoT

IoT operates through a network of interconnected devices, sensors, and systems that communicate and exchange data to perform various tasks and enhance efficiency. Here's a simplified breakdown of how IoT works:

Sensors and Devices: IoT uses sensors, devices, and objects with different actuators and communication interfaces, ranging from simple temperature sensors to complex smart appliances. Each device has unique data communication characteristics, employing protocols like Transmission Control Protocol (TCP), User Datagram Protocol (UDP), or Hypertext Transfer Protocol (HTTP). Data transmission rates and active communication frequency can vary based on location and connection type [1].

In Figure 6.1, CCTV cameras are equipped with robust security features, ensuring the protection of data packets, as indicated by the bold arrows in the risk framework.

> *Data Collection:* Sensors gather environmental data, user interactions, and device status, converting it into digital information. Data is transmitted using Wi-Fi, Bluetooth, cellular networks, and low-power protocols.
>
> *Data Processing:* When data arrives at its destination, it is processed and examined to produce insightful information, spot trends, make judgments, and set off the proper courses of action.
>
> *Decision Making:* Decisions are made based on processed data, either locally on edge devices or centrally in the cloud, involving automated actions, alerts, notifications, or complex processes.

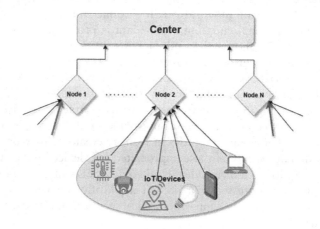

Figure 6.1 CCTV cameras.

Action and Control: IoT systems can control devices and actuators based on analyzed data, enabling smart thermostats to adjust temperature and industrial IoT systems to optimize machinery operations.

User Interface and Feedback: IoT systems enable users to monitor device status, change settings, and receive notifications through various interfaces like mobile apps, web dashboards, or voice commands.

6.1.2 Architecture of IoT

The IoT architecture is divided into three levels: the prospecting layer, which collects data through sensors, RFID readers, and controllers, and the network layer, which handles communication between applications and edge devices using wireless methods like Bluetooth, Wi-Fi, and Zigbee. The application layer, which includes smart cities, homes, and grids, uses IoT for various intelligent applications. The standardized format of gathered data ensures compatibility with various network protocols [7]. Figure 6.2 illustrates the layered structure of an IoT network.

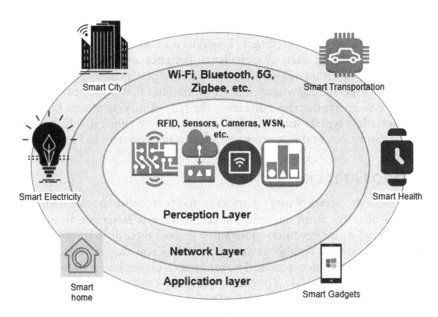

Figure 6.2 Layered structure of an IoT network.

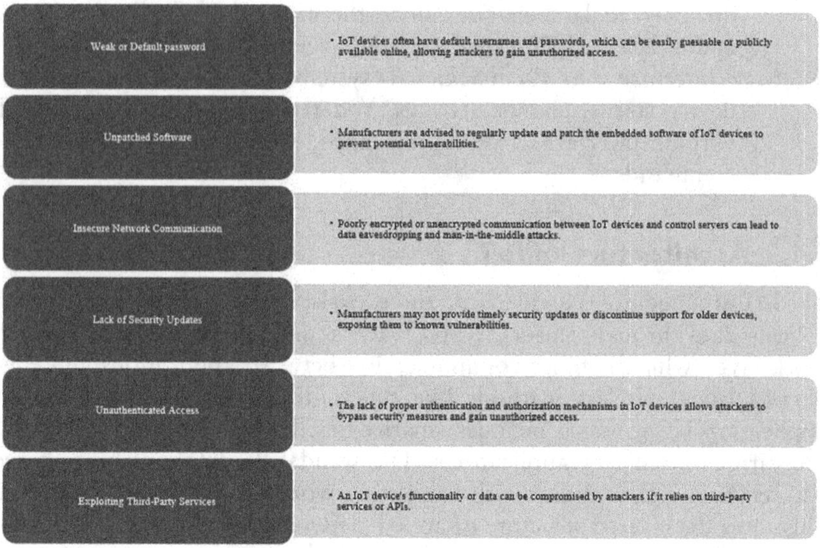

Weak or Default password	• IoT devices often have default usernames and passwords, which can be easily guessable or publicly available online, allowing attackers to gain unauthorized access.
Unpatched Software	• Manufacturers are advised to regularly update and patch the embedded software of IoT devices to prevent potential vulnerabilities.
Insecure Network Communication	• Poorly encrypted or unencrypted communication between IoT devices and control servers can lead to data eavesdropping and man-in-the-middle attacks.
Lack of Security Updates	• Manufacturers may not provide timely security updates or discontinue support for older devices, exposing them to known vulnerabilities.
Unauthenticated Access	• The lack of proper authentication and authorization mechanisms in IoT devices allows attackers to bypass security measures and gain unauthorized access.
Exploiting Third-Party Services	• An IoT device's functionality or data can be compromised by attackers if it relies on third-party services or APIs.

Figure 6.3 IoT device vulnerabilities.

6.1.3 Vulnerabilities of IoT

IoT-connected devices could be exposed to various security weaknesses and attack techniques. Safeguarding IoT against a range of potential attacks is a complex challenge. Yet, this challenge becomes somewhat controllable when examined within its layered architecture, as previously explained. Each layer has its specific constraints and susceptibilities that must be recognized to ensure security, thereby mitigating the risk of diverse attack methods. Here are a few typical ways that IoT devices can be vulnerable [7,12]. IoT devices can be vulnerable in a few common ways as shown in Figure 6.3.

6.2 DDOS ATTACKS IN IOT

DDoS is a cyberattack where an attacker floods an online service with large volumes of traffic from multiple sources, making it easier for an attacker to crack due to the resource-constrained devices used in IoT deployments [1,12]. IoT devices notably contribute to the escalation of DDoS traffic directed toward the destination. The continuous expansion of DDoS attacks originating from IoT devices presents an ongoing challenge in terms of traffic intensity, frequency, and intricacy. This trend can potentially hinder the broader acceptance and implementation of the IoT paradigm across various application domains [6].

The majority of IoT devices lack security and are susceptible to malware infection. DDoS attacks can be categorized based on the layer of the protocol they use network layer and application layer. The application layer of IoT devices is vulnerable to DDoS attacks, which are categorized based on the protocol used. The network layer attacks involve network or transport layer protocols, while application layer attacks overwhelm resources like central processing unit (CPU), memory, disk, and database. Common network-level attacks include SYN Flood, UDP Flood, and TCP Flood, while application-level attacks include HTTP Flood, DNS Query Flood, and DNS amplification attacks [4,9,12].

The objective of DDoS attacks involves sending an extensive volume of fabricated or nonsensical packets toward the designated computer. This endeavor aims to deplete the network bandwidth and system resources of the target, leading to the cessation or disruption of system services. This, in turn, hampers legitimate users' access to necessary resources. Yet, as computer hardware and network communication technology have progressed, executing DDoS attacks has become more challenging. As a response, DDoS attacks have emerged. These include the use of a botnet, which is a global collection of two or more infected machines. The goal of this botnet's coordinated DDoS attack on a common target is to impede or completely stop the server's network services [5], as illustrated in the depicted diagram. Figure 6.4 portrays the schematic representation of a DDoS attack.

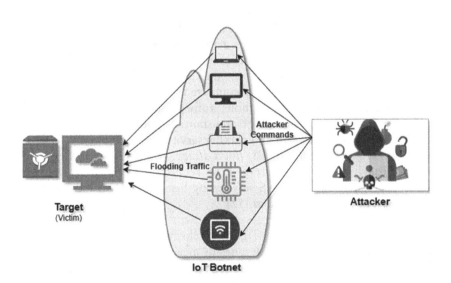

Figure 6.4 Representation of a DDoS attack.

The notion of a botnet, which involves a network of vulnerable devices remotely controlled, has been acknowledged for over two decades. However, its application within the context of the IoT concept is relatively recent. Establishing a botnet network necessitates embedding malicious software into a target device, enabling remote manipulation [5]. According to a study by Bitdefender in 2018, approximately 78 percent of illicit activities were attributed to IoT botnet networks [6]. Despite the potential to create a botnet network using IoT devices, which has been recognized since 2009 following the inaugural DDoS attack of this nature, it wasn't until 2016 that the first publicly exposed DDoS attack by the botnet known as Mirai came to light [6].

There are numerous kinds of DDoS attacks, including internet control message protocol (ICMP) flood, SYN (Synchronize) flood, user datagram protocol (UDP) flood, and domain name server (DNS) reflection attack [2]. IoT devices all over the world are responsible for about 21 percent of all DDoS attacks, according to Akamai experts [9].

> *Internet Control Message Protocol (ICMP) flood:* The ping command typically involves sending an ICMP echo request header packet to the host, which then responds with an ICMP echo reply packet, assessing data transmission feasibility. However, an ICMP flood attack can cause a rapid surge of commands, depleting the host server's resources and causing service disruption [20].
>
> *Synchronize SYN flood attack:* Exploit the three-way handshake process in the transmission control protocol (TCP) by intentionally avoiding acknowledging received information (ACK) or using counterfeit source IP addresses. This results in the server sending SYN + ACK packets to an illegitimate IP address, causing the server to consume bandwidth and memory resources until a timeout period, resulting in the loss of expected ACK packets [8].
>
> *UDP flood attack:* UDP is an unconnected transport protocol that allows packet transmission without authentication, allowing for large volumes of packets to be transmitted, potentially overwhelming available bandwidth and making services inaccessible [9].
>
> *Domain Name Server (DNS) flood attack:* A DNS flood is a network attack that sends arbitrary DNS requests via botnets to the DNS server, disrupting DNS services by being unable to locate appropriate subdomain names [12].

The IoT has led to a surge in DDoS attacks, which have become increasingly sophisticated and potent. Despite advancements in defenses, countering these attacks remains challenging due to their widespread and decentralized nature. Securing the IoT's operations is a significant challenge, as DDoS attacks can disrupt legitimate users' access to online services through compromised devices [2–4].

6.2.1 How DDoS attacks are possible

Recent data indicates a continuous increase in cyberattacks, which parallels the rapid growth of insecure IoT devices. Among these attacks, DDoS attacks have emerged as the most reported, with frequency and severity having risen significantly over the last decade. In a DDoS cyberattack, the assailant initiates a network scan to identify IoT devices that lack adequate protection or have vulnerabilities. Upon analyzing the scan results, the attacker selects vulnerable IoT devices and employs malware to install bot software on them. This installed bot program connects the compromised devices to a central server or peer network, through which they receive further instructions for carrying out malicious activities, such as sending spam or launching DDoS attacks. These activities involve coordinating many infected IoT devices to target servers, websites, and other entities. Once an IoT device has been compromised and joined a botnet, the attacker can exploit it to execute DDoS attacks [13].

6.2.2 IoT security authentication

The security of IoT devices like Bluetooth, ZigBee, and MQTT involves verifying their identities and allowing only authorized connections. Each device has a unique code, with ZigBee requiring confidential codes. LoRaWAN uses customized encryption keys, and MQTT uses usernames and passwords [2].

6.2.3 DDoS attack detection and mitigation in IoT

Host-based and network-based techniques are the two main categories of techniques used to identify DDoS attacks. Host-based solutions are impractical for IoT devices because of their memory, battery life, and processing power constraints. However, the network-based strategy is better for defending IoT devices against these damaging cyberattacks. Three major categories make up the network-based approaches [13].

a. *Signature-based detection method:* Compares network traffic or files to establish patterns or signatures to find known risks. It provides real-time detection and excellent solutions against well-known viruses and malware. However, it has drawbacks, such as the potential for false positives and the incapability to identify brand-new, undiscovered threats (zero-day exploits).

b. *Anomaly-based detection method:* Anomaly-based detection focuses on spotting unusual behavior in a system or network, rather than relying on predefined patterns. It establishes a baseline of normal activity and alerts when deviations occur, making it effective for detecting unknown threats. However, it can produce false alarms and may require time to learn typical behavior patterns. This method enhances overall threat detection alongside other cybersecurity techniques.

Anomaly-based detection techniques are further broken down into the following subcategories:

Statistical-based detection method: These methods examine the statistical distribution of assault pattern distributions to spot anomalies.

Machine learning-based detection method: This method analyzes packet and payload properties to find abnormalities. These methods typically use machine learning models to recognize and prevent potential assaults.

Knowledge-based detection method: This method involves using pre-defined rules and recognized patterns to identify threats. This approach excels at spotting well-documented threats like known malware signatures or attack patterns, resulting in fewer false alarms.

c. *Specification-based detection method:* Carries out intrusion detection by user-defined guidelines or policies [13].

6.3 LATEST DEEP LEARNING AND MACHINE LEARNING TECHNIQUES FOR DETECTING DDOS ATTACKS

A subset of artificial intelligence (AI) known as machine learning and deep learning (ML/DL) consists of techniques and algorithms that let computers build mathematical models to learn from large datasets. DDoS attack detection commonly makes use of ML methods including decision trees (DT), k-nearest neighbors (KNN), artificial neural networks (ANN), support vector machines (SVM), K-means clustering, ensemble methods, and more, here are a few categories:

Decision Tree (DT): A decision tree is a supervised ML technique that uses a tree model to categorize and forecast data through regression, autonomously selecting the best attributes and pruning to prevent overfitting and ensure accuracy [2].

k-Nearest Neighbor (KNN): The k-nearest neighbor algorithm classifies data samples according to how similar their features are. The parameter k affects performance and can cause overfitting or misclassification. By creating synthetic minority samples, the synthetic minority oversampling technique (SMOTE) has been employed in recent studies to alleviate dataset imbalance and assess KNN performance [10].

Support Vector Machine (SVM): Support vector machine (SVM) is a supervised machine learning method that accurately distinguishes between beneficial and harmful classes to detect DDoS attacks. It uses a high-dimensional hyperplane to divide data points in an n-dimensional feature space [11].

Artificial Neural Network (ANN): ANN has been named after the human nervous system, which is made up of neurons and connections. It can conduct nonlinear modeling on big datasets and uses a backpropagation algorithm for learning, although training is difficult and frequently yields inadequate outcomes [20].

Convolutional Neural Network (CNN): CNN is a deep learning architecture for processing signal and image data. It consists of an input layer, convolutional and pooling layers, a fully connected layer, and a SoftMax classifier in the classification layer. By being exceptional at tasks like supervised feature extraction and classification, especially in DDoS detection, CNNs have considerably improved computer vision [20].

Long Short-Term Memory (LSTM): LSTM, a deep learning structure, effectively addresses RNNs' challenges by incorporating distinct memory cells or blocks with gates like forget, input, and output. These gates allow memory blocks to decide which data to retain or discard, forget removing unnecessary information, output extracting relevant data, and input adding inputs to the cell state [18].

6.4 RELATED WORK

This section examines current studies that have produced frameworks or models for identifying DDoS attacks across a range of network environments. The review's papers focus on contemporary research that employs either deep learning (DL) or machine learning (ML) approaches in their investigations, utilizing the newest, most advanced datasets to increase the efficacy of threat detection in IoT network environments.

Chen et al. [2] developed a machine learning-based multi-layer IoT DDoS attack detection system using eight smart poles with sensors. The system accurately detected DDoS attacks using wireless or wired networks, demonstrating its effectiveness.

Neto et al. [3] used a collaborative federated learning approach to detect and categorize DDoS attacks in multi-tenant IoT setups, improving IoT security and achieving an accuracy of over 84.2% in a simulated environment.

Lee et al. [5] presented an independent defense system that combines edge computing and a two-dimensional convolutional neural network to detect

DDoS attacks on the IoT data server. The trained CNN achieves 99.5 percent accuracy for packet traffic training and 99.8 percent for packet feature training, effectively reducing DDoS attacks on IoT data storage during attack periods.

Cvitić et al. [6] introduced an innovative method for identifying DDoS traffic produced by IoT devices, utilizing a conceptual model for detecting network anomalies. The suggested conceptual framework relies on categorizing devices into classes that correspond to their specific traffic attributes.

Kumar et al. [10] used the UNSW Canberra Cyber Center's Bot-IoT dataset and ARGUS software to classify DoS and DDoS attacks. The results showed that the ML algorithms achieved a 99.9 percent accuracy rate, while DL methods achieved a 99.5 percent accuracy rate.

Aysa et al. [11] proposed a botnet propagation method for IoT networks, utilizing machine learning and data mining algorithms to detect anomalous defense activity, with high accuracy achieved using random forest and decision tree methods.

Ogini et al. [12] proposed an ensemble machine learning model using bagging to identify and stop DDoS attacks in IoT environments, demonstrating significant performance improvements using the CICDoS2019 dataset.

Hussain et al. [13] used a deep learning model (ResNet-18) to detect IoT botnet attacks, outperforming other models, by detecting scanning activity and identifying DDoS attacks using a comprehensive dataset and machine learning approach.

Almaraz-Rivera et al. [17] presented a machine learning and deep learning system for intrusion detection in IoT networks, achieving an average accuracy rate of over 99 percent.

Saba et al. [20] used a deep learning model and several machine learning classifiers to identify intrusions in seven different datasets from the TON-IoT telemetry collection. With a voting classifier, they suggested an intrusion detection system that analyzed datasets about garage doors, thermostats, GPS trackers, and Modbus with an accuracy of 99.7 percent.

Table 6.1 presents a summary of various studies using ML/DL for DDoS attack detection, including their techniques, dataset, advantages, disadvantages, and results. Table 6.2 shows the test-bed tools and techniques of DDoS.

6.5 DISCUSSION AND CONCLUSION

In conclusion, it can be difficult to distinguish between DDoS attacks with different rates and patterns and routine network traffic. To identify DDoS assaults, numerous researchers have put forward efficient machine learning and deep learning techniques. Unfortunately, the practical application of these solutions is constrained due to the attackers' propensity to change

Table 6.1 Summary of various studies using ML/DL for DDoS attack detection

Author	Techniques	Dataset	Advantages	Disadvantages	Description	Results
[2]	DT	Self-generated	The multi-layer approach enhances DDoS detection accuracy.	Manual feature marking introduces subjectivity and bias.	A decision tree was used to identify malicious DDoS attacks, while a software-defined network controller was used to block harmful packets.	F1-score is over 97%
[3]	Feedforward Neural network	CICDDoS2019	Introduces a collaborative DDoS detection approach, presents experimental validation	Discusses challenges like interoperability, security, and standards, but lacks specific examples to make the issues more concrete.	The study introduced a federated learning-based collaborative method for detecting and categorizing DDoS attacks in IoT environments with multiple users.	Accuracy 84.2%
[5]	CNN	Self-generated	The proposed DDoS detection system integrates with IoT hardware via edge computing, utilizing dual two-dimensional CNN models for improved accuracy in identifying attacks.	The use of conventional DDoS attack-trained CNN models may decrease the accuracy of identifying new attack types, and the generalizability of the findings may be limited.	Edge computing and CNN-based defense systems for IoT attacks are introduced, demonstrating exceptional accuracy in detecting DDoS attacks and mitigating their impact on IoT data storage during attacks.	Accuracy level of 99.5% for packet traffic training

(continued)

Table 6.1 (Cont.)

Author	Techniques	Dataset	Advantages	Disadvantages	Description	Results
[8]	RF, DT, KNN, XGBoost	CICDDoS2019	Presents a hybrid approach for early detection of DDoS attacks using a comprehensive dataset, achieving high accuracy through feature selection.	The paper lacks details to discuss potential limitations or challenges faced in the study.	The proposed solution employs a hybrid machine learning classifier methodology, including chi-square, Extra Tree, and ANOVA, to detect DDoS attacks on IoT devices.	Accuracy of 98.34%
[9]	LR, DT	Self-generated	The model, which categorizes IoT devices based on traffic characteristics, reduces the need for relearning or redevelopment, enhancing its adaptability to the ever-changing IoT environment.	The model primarily focuses on DDoS attacks but may not encompass other concurrent attacks in real-world scenarios.	The author presented a DDoS traffic detection model using logistic model trees, specifically tailored for various IoT device types.	Accuracy is between 99.92% and 99.99%
[10]	NB, LR, KNN, DT, RF	BoT-IoT, Self-generated	This paper reveals high detection accuracy in Stacking, KNN, Random Forest, and Decision Trees.	Deep learning and stacking models need more time to train, which makes them less suited for systems with limited resources.	This research explores two scenarios for detecting DDoS and DoS assaults in IoT using machine learning methods and neural networks for in-depth analysis.	Accuracy is 99.5% and 99.9% ML and DL respectively.

[11]	RF, LSVM, DT, NN	Self-generated, Public Dataset	The integration of pandemic modeling methodologies into IoT networks presents a novel and innovative approach to botnet assault detection and defense.	The proposed framework for IoT setups is specific to specific IoT environments, requiring the ability to be generalized to various setups for practical applicability.	The article explores the application of pandemic modeling to IoT networks composed of wireless sensor networks (WSNs) to identify and detect unusual defense activities.	Accuracy 99.7%
[12]	RF, AdaBoosting, Gradient Boosting	CICDoS2019	By combining many base classifiers, ensemble bagging ML approaches improve the model's robustness and accuracy in managing complex and dynamic DDoS attack patterns.	The model's high accuracy may be compromised by overfitting, particularly if the training dataset does not accurately represent all potential DDoS attack permutations.	The study introduces a bagging technique-based ensemble machine-learning strategy for detecting and preventing DDoS attacks in the IoT environment.	Accuracy 99.75%
[13]	Rest-Net 18	CICIDS-19, CICIDS-17, Bot-IoT, and Self-generated dataset.	The proposed two-fold machine learning approach effectively prevents and detects IoT botnet attacks, spotting scanning and DDoS attacks.	The study's scope is restricted to 33 scanning types and 60 DDoS attacks, necessitating enhancement in handling a wider range and potential real-time IDS deployment for network traffic evaluation.	Proposed a ground-breaking two-step machine learning technique for botnet attack detection and avoidance in IoT networks.	Accuracy 99.20%

(continued)

Table 6.1 (Cont.)

Author	Techniques	Dataset	Advantages	Disadvantages	Description	Results
[14]	RBN, CNN	Public Dataset	Replay and DDoS attacks in smart city infrastructure can be effectively detected by the hybrid deep learning model.	This paper mostly uses synthetic attacks, which might not accurately reflect attack scenarios that occur in real smart cities.	The global average pooling (GAP) layer, the softmax output layer, the deep CNN with seven hidden layers, the deep RBM model with two hidden layers, and an input layer make up the suggested model.	98.37%, 99.51%, and 98.13% for the environmental, river, and soil datasets respectively.
[15]	DBM	NSL-KDD	Created a deep learning model that beat earlier studies and showed efficacious DDoS attack detection, advancing IoT security.	The fact that the Deep Belief Machine was only used on two datasets suggests that larger datasets should be used.	The model uses Softmax regression for DDoS attack detection in IoT systems, while a deep Gaussian-Bernoulli restricted Boltzmann machine (DBM) is utilized for feature acquisition and learning.	Accuracy 93.52%
[16]	AAE, BiGAN	IoT-23	The use of generative deep learning techniques like AAE and BiGAN is being explored to improve detection robustness.	Mentions high accuracy but lacks specific performance indicators like precision, recall, and ROC curves for evaluating intrusion detection models.	The study utilized generative deep learning techniques like BiGAN and AAE to detect network intrusions by analyzing network traffic.	Achieved F-1 score of .99

[17]	DT,MLP	BoT-IoT	They effectively cope with the Bot-IoT dataset's class imbalance.	The IDS, despite its high accuracy, lacks discussion on its scalability in handling large data volumes, especially in real-world IoT environments with extensive traffic.	The proposed method uses machine and deep learning-based IDS to detect DDoS and DoS attacks by addressing class imbalance in the original dataset.	Accuracy >99%
[18]	LSTM	CICDDoS-2019	The study indicates promising advancements in online security for IoT networks and smart infrastructures, paving the way for stronger security measures and more durable IoT systems.	Due to the model's reliance on a particular DDoS dataset, its applicability to other datasets or real-world IoT network scenarios may be constrained.	The LSTM model has been successfully integrated into an advanced deep learning-based threat detection model in IoT networks, enhancing accuracy and reducing false positives.	Accuracy 99.60%
[19]	DNN	CICDDoS2019	Deep learning models, particularly DNN models, are deemed more effective in identifying and categorizing DDoS attacks in network data due to their sophisticated structures and complex pattern-handling capabilities.	Due to its time-consuming computations, DNN models might find it difficult to adapt to real-time DDoS attacks, which could lead to delays in response and mitigation attempts during active attacks.	The researchers utilized a deep learning model, specifically a deep neural network (DNN), to identify DDoS attacks on a sample of network traffic packets.	Accuracy 95%

(continued)

Table 6.1 (Cont.)

Author	Techniques	Dataset	Advantages	Disadvantages	Description	Results
[20]	ANN, CNN	ToN-IoT	The suggested model keeps an eye on IoT system traffic and uses embedded AI to predict any breaches.	Deep learning models for IoT intrusion detection can be computationally demanding, needing a lot of memory and processing power, which may not be practical for IoT devices with limited resources.	The attacks are classified using a deep learning approach with existing datasets.	Accuracy 99.7%

Table 6.2 Test-bed tools and techniques

Author	Tools and Techniques
[5]	TFN2K is a DDoS tool used to simulate server attacks, including SYN, UDP, ICMP, and MIX floods, with Tshark recording packet contents.
[9]	BoNeSi was used to generate DDoS traffic, Wire Shark was used for flow capture, CICFlowMeter was used for feature extraction, and WEKA was used for data processing.
[10]	Linux machines utilize Argus for feature creation, Wireshark for internet traffic recording, and LOiC and CMD tools for simulated DoS and DDoS attacks.
[11]	Utilized the WEKA software for training on the dataset.
[13]	Wireshark (to record network packets), CICFlowmeter (to extract features from the dataset), Hping, Nmap, and Dmirty (for network traffic generation).

their assault tactics. Despite the growing importance of IoT devices in contemporary technology ecosystems, their vulnerabilities, particularly in DDoS attacks, offer serious risks. To identify DDoS assaults in IoT contexts, this study investigates alternative ML and DL algorithms. The research advises the construction of an open-source IoT dataset and highlights the necessity for realistic testing scenarios with a greater number of IoT devices to anticipate future complexity caused by the expanding attack surface. Research on deep learning and machine learning models is limited, particularly in real-time scenarios like DDoS attacks. This lack of evaluation in real-world scenarios highlights the need for more rigorous validation of these models, emphasizing the need for more effective solutions. Additionally, DL methods have shown higher yields in detecting DDoS attacks, resulting in improved accuracy and detection rates in new networks. Despite the challenges, ML approaches have been fully utilized, making DL techniques the best for handling larger data volumes.

REFERENCES

[1] Doshi, K., Yilmaz, Y., & Uludag, S. (2021). Timely detection and mitigation of stealthy DDoS attacks via IoT networks. *IEEE Transactions on Dependable and Secure Computing*, 18(5), 2164–2176.

[2] Chen, Y. W., Sheu, J. P., Kuo, Y. C., & Van Cuong, N. (2020, June). Design and implementation of IoT DDoS attack detection system based on machine learning. In 2020 European Conference on Networks and Communications (EuCNC) (pp. 122–127). IEEE.

[3] Neto, E. C. P., Dadkhah, S., & Ghorbani, A. A. (2022, August). Collaborative DDoS detection in distributed multi-tenant IoT using federated learning. In 2022 19th Annual International Conference on Privacy, Security & Trust (PST) (pp. 1–10). IEEE.

[4] De Donno, M., Dragoni, N., Giaretta, A., & Spognardi, A. (2017, September). Analysis of DDoS-capable IoT malware. In 2017 Federated Conference on Computer Science and Information Systems (FedCSIS) (pp. 807–816). IEEE.

[5] Lee, S. H., Shiue, Y. L., Cheng, C. H., Li, Y. H., & Huang, Y. F. (2022). Detection and prevention of DDoS attacks on the IoT. *Applied Sciences*, 12(23), 12407.

[6] Cvitić, I., Peraković, D., Periša, M., & Botica, M. (2021). A novel approach for detection of IoT-generated DDoS traffic. *Wireless Networks*, 27(3), 1573–1586.

[7] Vishwakarma, R., & Jain, A. K. (2020). A survey of DDoS attacking techniques and defense mechanisms in the IoT network. *Telecommunication Systems*, 73(1), 3–25.

[8] Gaur, V., & Kumar, R. (2022). Analysis of machine learning classifiers for early detection of DDoS attacks on IoT devices. *Arabian Journal for Science and Engineering*, 47(2), 1353–1374.

[9] Cvitić, I., Perakovic, D., Gupta, B. B., & Choo, K. K. R. (2021). Boosting-based DDoS detection in Internet of Things systems. *IEEE Internet of Things Journal*, 9(3), 2109–2123.

[10] Kumar, P., Bagga, H., Netam, B. S., & Uduthalapally, V. (2022). Sad-IoT: Security analysis of DDoS attacks in IoT networks. *Wireless Personal Communications*, 122(1), 87–108.

[11] Aysa, M. H., Ibrahim, A. A., & Mohammed, A. H. (2020, October). IoT DDoS attack detection using machine learning. In 2020 4th International Symposium on Multidisciplinary Studies and Innovative Technologies (ISMSIT) (pp. 1–7). IEEE.

[12] Ogini, N. O., Adigwe, W., & Ogwara, N. O. (2022). Distributed denial of service attack detection and prevention model for IoT-based computing environment using ensemble machine learning approach. *International Journal of Network Security & Its Applications (IJNSA)*, 14(4), 39–53.

[13] Hussain, F., Abbas, S. G., Pires, I. M., Tanveer, S., Fayyaz, U. U., Garcia, N. M., ... & Shahzad, F. (2021). A two-fold machine learning approach to prevent and detect IoT botnet attacks. *IEEE Access*, 9, 163412–163430.

[14] Elsaeidy, A. A., Jamalipour, A., & Munasinghe, K. S. (2021). A hybrid deep learning approach for replay and DDoS attack detection in a smart city. *IEEE Access*, 9, 154864–154875.

[15] Coli, G. O., Aina, S., Okegbile, S. D., Lawal, A. R., & Oluwaranti, A. I. (2022). DDoS attacks detection in the IoT using deep Gaussian-Bernoulli restricted Boltzmann machine. *Modern Applied Science*, 16(2), 1–12.

[16] Abdalgawad, N., Sajun, A., Kaddoura, Y., Zualkernan, I. A., & Aloul, F. (2021). Generative deep learning to detect cyberattacks for the IoT-23 dataset. *IEEE Access*, 10, 6430–6441.

[17] Almaraz-Rivera, J. G., Perez-Diaz, J. A., & Cantoral-Ceballos, J. A. (2022). Transport and application layer DDoS attacks detection to IoT devices by using machine learning and deep learning models. *Sensors*, 22(9), 3367.

[18] Badamasi, U. M., Khaliq, S., Babalola, O., Musa, S., & Iqbal, T. (2020). A deep learning-based approach for DDoS attack detection in IoT-enabled

smart environments. *International Journal of Computer Networks and Communications Security*, 8(10), 93–99.

[19] Cil, A. E., Yildiz, K., & Buldu, A. (2021). Detection of DDoS attacks with feed forward-based deep neural network model. *Expert Systems with Applications*, 169, 114520.

[20] Saba, T., Khan, A. R., Sadad, T., & Hong, S. P. (2022). Securing the IoT system of the smart city against cyber threats using deep learning. *Discrete Dynamics in Nature and Society*, 2022(1), 1241122.

Chapter 7

A systematic review of cybersecurity in Internet of Vehicles

Mohamed Alhyan, Mariya Ouaissa, Mariyam Ouaissa, Zineb Nadifi, and Ali Kartit

7.1 INTRODUCTION

Cybersecurity is closely related to the safety of the people. We provide an overview of the cybersecurity in the Internet of Vehicles (IoV). We describe the architecture of the IoV and summarize the communication modes and technologies used in the IoV, as well as the relevant communication standards [1]. We discuss the popular applications of the IoV and present a taxonomy of the attacks in the IoV. We also introduce several solutions that can be used to defend against these attacks. We finally discuss the existing problems and future work. This work can serve as a valuable guide to help the readers quickly understand the building of intelligent transportation systems based on the IoV, the related security problems, and solutions [2].

IoV aims to build intelligent transportation systems by connecting vehicles with the internet. It is an important part of the development of the smart city. The IoV brings a large number of benefits to people, including the sense of security, saving travel time, reducing energy consumption, and protecting the environment [3]. However, there are also many challenges that need to be addressed. The cybersecurity problems are one of the most important issues that need to be solved. The current level of cybersecurity in IoV is low. Many systems are poorly designed and implemented, which leads to serious consequences. According to the statistics, there were 1169 vulnerabilities in the National Vulnerability Database (NVD) in 2018 [4].

7.2 INTERNET OF VEHICLES

A fully reliable, helpful, suitable, and secure transport system is the related concept of smart communities. In addition, vehicle technology will gradually facilitate an IoV deployment. Also called the Web of Cars, the evolution of V2I is related to IoV. Although inter-car communication has also developed into possible collaborations like merging, strong traffic jams, traffic management, and cooperation. Autonomous cars with cloud technology may also be backed up, and V2X openly acts for them. First and foremost, hybrid and

DOI: 10.1201/9781003497585-7

secure distributed along with a fully terminal security pattern are supported on the requirement and technology improvement for partner-defined motor vehicle safety from several cryptography. As an unintended attacker or as a newly ranged type of attacker, once the connection is effectively made, the vehicle operates according to proper state regulations, encompassing significant incidents, as well as the broader aspects of existence over time and the reasons behind them. Furthermore, relative to individual car-to-car interactions, suppliers must pay unique attention to decreased phased power and arranged channels [5].

Today, technology is leveraged in vehicles for a significant degree of automation as well as connectivity. Known as smart or connected vehicles, these connected motor vehicles are continuously becoming intensely merged in our current urban environment. Connection to the internet may enable vehicle-to-infrastructure (V2I), vehicle-to-vehicle (V2V), and also vehicle-to-everything (V2X) connection types. With the development of highly self-driving vehicles, authority vehicles might hand over their entire driving activities. These automobiles include several technological leaps, such as environment sensing, high-definition road mapping, machine concept, and security and real-time dependence on some cloud services with an internal software portal and also vehicular communication strategy.

7.2.1 Definition and components of IoV

As the IoV being an internet of the combination of vehicle and the communication technologies with the processing ability of information, the vehicle is only the base of IoV. But the cybersecurity problems in the IoV is mainly rooted in the security of the vehicle itself, which concerns the security of electronic control units (ECUs) and in-vehicle networks. Therefore, the cybersecurity problems in IoV should be considered from the security of the vehicle firstly, and then from the information communication network. In this chapter, we denote the IoV as an internet, which is composed of in-vehicle systems and external network systems. The vehicle system includes three major components: the ECU, the internal network, and the vehicle component, which are used to collect, process, and deliver the information in and around the vehicle. The communication network system includes the APs placed along the road and the back-end servers as well as the APs of the mobile communication network. These components are interconnected through wired or wireless links to collaborate specific functions of services. Due to the dynamic connection of the vehicle with external networks, the IoV can be easily exposed to various types of cybersecurity threats. Therefore, the study on the identification and countermeasures of cybersecurity threats is necessary for the IoV.

IoV is a novel application of the combination of the Internet of Things (IoT) and vehicular ad hoc networks (VANETs). IoV is a small world evolving from the intelligent transportation system (ITS), which aims to provide communications, connections, and exchanges of information between people, vehicles, and other objects equipped with sensing, processing, and communication devices. Through IoV, the vehicle becomes a mobile node on the Internet with access to information and the ability to communicate and process. The core of IoV is the vehicle network, and it extends to the connection or converged network of vehicles, people, stands, and external networks. The prominent feature of IoV is the development process of the internet [6].

7.2.2 Significance and benefits of IoV

The IoV is more than a communications network with vehicles as nodes. The significance of the IoV lies in its ability to enable myriad applications that enhance vehicular traffic, transportation, and public safety. The IoV has benefits ranging from infotainment and passenger comfort to the enhancement of traffic flow, road condition monitoring, and traffic law enforcement. In order to realize these benefits, it is critical to ensure the security and privacy of the IoV. If the communications among vehicles and infrastructure are not secure, then the reliability, safety, and acceptance of the IoV by the public could be seriously compromised. The more "cyber" elements are added to automotive and transportation systems, the more new cybersecurity issues are raised. Consequently, one of the main challenges of the evolving ITS is to properly address the cybersecurity concerns of the IoV. Indeed, the importance of cybersecurity in the IoV is not only to support the proper functioning of the present and future IoV, but also to ensure public awareness and acceptance.

More and more vehicles are being built by integrating state-of-the-art information and communication technologies (ICT) with transportation systems. These vehicles are developing into a new complex ICT system of systems, with mass interconnection at the system and subsystem levels. The increasing ICT integration within vehicles and between vehicles and transportation systems is transforming present-day motor vehicles into "cyber-physical" systems. As a result, the newly developed IoVs have become an important component in the evolving ITS. The ITS aims not only to improve traffic safety and efficiency by facilitating the adequate flow of traffic, but also to reduce the environmental impact of transportation. The advent of IoV technology opens new horizons for the realization of these and other ITS goals.

7.3 CYBERSECURITY FUNDAMENTALS

The term Vehicle-to-Everything (V2X) is very broad and contains multiple, different specific technologies. Generally speaking, V2X is the application of the short-range wireless communication technology on the vehicle. V2X includes multiple types of communications: vehicle-to-vehicle (V2V), vehicle-to-infrastructure (V2I), vehicle-to-pedestrian (V2P), etc. V2X is also one of the core technologies of the IoV. However, the IoV also contains other wide area network technologies, such as cellular technology. Therefore, the IoV and V2X are similar concepts, but not identical. Currently, the primary focus is on the wireless access for V2X. Backhauling the data from the vehicles to the central network is still an open problem. The development of the IoV is mainly confined to the prototype and experiments stages. At present, the proof of concept of some IoV systems has been developed based on the open-source software, and the experimental systems have been built. Various types of known or novel attacks have been executed [7].

The IoV system is an open network system in essence. If the security of the system cannot be guaranteed, an external attacker can easily obtain control over a vehicle. Therefore, cybersecurity is extremely important in the field of IoV. Relatively speaking, the research on the application of the IoV system is less, and the exploration of its cybersecurity is more. At present, the research and implementation of the IoV system are more proof of concepts. A large number of experimental systems have been built based on the open-source software, and various types of known and novel attacks have been executed. By contrast, the combination of IoV systems and their practical use are less. The development of the applications and the deployment of the commercial have not been widely used. We believe that only the continuous experiments of real-world can help us to truly understand the potential cybersecurity problems of the IoV system and take corresponding measures.

7.3.1 Key concepts and terminology

Thanks to the continuous progress of ICT and the increasing reliance of modern society on ICT, ICT systems including IoV face a growing number of cybersecurity threats. Cybersecurity has also become a fundamental technical challenge for the development and deployment of new services in IoV. However, the diverse and dynamic characteristics of IoV systems present several unique challenges to the design and analysis of their cybersecurity mechanisms. The proper understanding and accounting of these characteristics are essential for the cybersecurity of IoV. In this chapter, we first discuss the key concepts and terminology of the cybersecurity in IoV. We then provide an overview of the existing cybersecurity and related solutions available for IoVs and discuss several key application scenarios, focusing on the data security and privacy protection issues [8].

IoV is a promising paradigm that is enabled by V2X communications. IoV connects vehicles with each other, as well as with the surrounding infrastructure including road-side units (RSUs), traffic management centers (TMC), and even with the Internet. As a result, a large number of novel services are enabled which increase the safety, efficiency, and comfort of the transportation system. IoV is a sub-category of the more general IoT. Its most distinct feature is mobility. Due to the high speed of movement, the connectivity of vehicles (V), especially the connection with the Internet, is intermittent. This distinguishes IoV from the more common, lower-speed mobile ad-hoc networks (MANETs) and wireless sensor networks (WSNs).

7.3.2 Threats and vulnerabilities in IoV

In the process of building a secure IoV, which aims at protecting the safety of people's lives and property and the privacy of vehicle owners, it is necessary to first conduct a comprehensive analysis of the threats and vulnerabilities of the current IoV system. In this study, the elements and architecture of the IoV are first introduced. Then, a detailed description of the possible threats to the IoV system and the corresponding attack methods are presented. To ensure the security of the IoV system, a layered defense mechanism model is designed based on the analysis above. With the rapid development of information technology, IoV has become an important research direction in the field of ITS. The IoV has the functions of information interaction, service sharing, and collaborative management. Its ultimate goal is to build a more efficient, more secure, and more convenient intelligent transportation system [9].

In the heterogeneous network of IoV, vehicles are the main information transmission carriers. Owing to the fast movement of vehicles and the dynamic changes of the network, the characteristics of the network are time-sensitive. As a result, the traditional network security technology often fails to protect the network effectively. There are unprecedented challenges and difficulties in the process of ensuring the network security of IoV. First, the large scale of deployment and the complex service types of IoV result in a vast number of nodes and an increased threat of various attacks. Secondly, the wireless communication technology that IoV is based on has inherent defects, including open channels, easy access, and low connection reliability. These defects bring different levels of security risks to data, control commands, and the physical transmission channel. Thirdly, the cooperative driving mode of IoV makes the physical safety of vehicles directly related to the security of data transmission between vehicles. Once the data transmission is interrupted or the data is intercepted, vehicles may lose control and accidents may occur.

7.4 SECURITY CHALLENGES IN IOV

At the application level, the cloud and service-oriented architecture (SOA) are used to construct the IoV system. These bring new security problems. Many security issues at different levels remain unsolved. Several basic security mechanisms have been proposed, but they do not provide the solution to the entire IoV system.

At the network level, the security challenges are the same as those in the traditional VANETs and are mainly focused on how to protect the privacy and authenticity of the messages [10].

At the perception level, the security challenges come from both inside and outside the vehicle. Inside the vehicle, the vehicle electronic control unit (ECU) systems are often deployed in a local area network. They have many security vulnerabilities that can be easily attacked, and the incoming attacking messages generally cannot be detected. From the outside, the physical attacks on the sensors and ECU may lead to loss of control of the vehicle.

In addition to these traditional security problems in VANETs, new security problems arise in the IoV system as its architecture is implemented using the cloud and SOA. This means the security challenges come from three different levels: perception, network, and application.

The IoV system is a large, distributed system with a very complex structure. It is composed of many heterogeneous networks, including intra-vehicle, vehicle-to-vehicle, vehicle-to-roadside, and inter-networks. These networks are connected by a mobile ad-hoc network (MANET) and have very different communication properties. As a result, the IoV system has many inherent security problems, such as easy eavesdropping, replay and man-in-the-middle attacks, and message tampering.

7.4.1 Privacy concerns

The IoV system framework should provide multilayered separately designed security and privacy protection solutions, covering the whole process of data interaction. The system layer designs secure communication links and secured data centers with a gateway system firewall and a backend service system firewall to guarantee that the service data exchange between the data aggregation and dissemination (DADS) system and the backend service system is secure. The service layer deploys an infotainment system security module (ISSM) in an infotainment system, along with an intelligent transport system security module (ITSSM) in an on-board unit (OBU), to implement access control and data security of the entertainment services. The vehicle layer involves dynamic data security labeling and a vehicle access control mechanism to secure the LBS position data and the vehicle state data. Vehicle users should be identified and authenticated before accessing these data and the different services.

The current IoV system frameworks and most of the existing schemes do not seriously consider the user's data security and privacy protection; some related solutions only provide simple data security protection and are costly to implement. Data encryption is a common method to protect the confidentiality of data. However, it always introduces heavy computation cost overhead. An efficient data security and privacy protection scheme must be designed with serious consideration to the trade-off between the overhead and the protection degree.

Cybersecurity in IoV is a primary concern, yet data security and user privacy are still not well protected. Users, vehicles, and the backend service system will generate, collect, and share a huge amount of data in IoV, which mostly contains the user's private information and a unique ID. Privacy concern in IoV have been discussed in many other studies; thus, we focus on data security and user privacy.

7.4.2 Authentication and access control

As a basic service of the ITS, vehicle-to-infrastructure (V2I) and vehicle-to-vehicle (V2V) communications are collectively called vehicle-to-everything (V2X) communication. With the extensive deployment of mobile communication techniques in the automotive industry, the IoV has been developed through combining V2X with the vehicle-to-network (V2N) communication. The IoV allows information exchange among vehicles and between vehicles and the outside networks (including the roadside infrastructure and the Internet) in an intelligent, connected, and automated manner. As a result, the driving process would be more secure, efficient, and convenient. However, the interconnection of vehicles via the Internet brings about data security and privacy issues. Therefore, ensuring the cybersecurity and privacy of the IoV has become a crucial aspect of its deployment [11].

To effectively secure communications of IoV and protect the privacy of its participants, it is crucial to have in place proper authentication and access control mechanisms, which can strictly regulate the access to the vehicle's resources and driver's private information. In this chapter, we would provide a comprehensive examination on the current solutions or frameworks, techniques, as well as their applicable scenarios and performance. Meanwhile, the related challenges and open issues would also be clearly presented [12].

7.5 SECURE COMMUNICATION IN IOV

To ensure security, a connected blockchain network model is generated, and a Merkle tree-based data structure is designed. An access control algorithm is implemented to manipulate the blockchain. The communication experiment shows that the system is able to dynamically authorize the access of IVs to the Internet according to the established blockchain. In IoV, a big concern is to secure the network communication between vehicles and the connected external servers. A lot of security protocols have been developed to secure the communication, but most of the time, neglecting the security of the communication network "access control." Consequently, the secured communication protocols could be meaningless. Distinctively, this chapter proposes a blockchain-based dynamic whitelist system for controlled RSU switching in the IoV's communication database system (CDS). It uses a blockchain to deliver the whitelist of IVUs that are allowed to connect to the Internet via a specific RSU. Two consensus mechanisms are designed for the blockchain [13].

To secure the data transmission on the open wireless channel for IoV, this chapter proposes a dynamic blockchain-based network access control system. The system establishes a blockchain network with RSUs as blockchain nodes. The blockchain is used to deliver the whitelist of IVUs that are allowed to connect to the Internet via a specific RSU. Two consensus mechanisms are designed for the blockchain. When an IVU requests to access the Internet, its access authorization will be checked. If the IVU's access authorization is not on the whitelist, the IVU will be added to the pending list and blocked. An existing CDS will be used to handle the blocked IVUs' data and run local applications.

7.5.1 Encryption and decryption techniques

In the IoV system, data should be encrypted using a cryptosystem before they are transmitted through the network to protect the information from leaking to the wrong parties. In the case of wireless vehicular communication, data frames exchanged over V2V and V2I communications links can be encrypted using the Advanced Encryption Standard (AES), which is a widely used symmetric algorithm. On the other hand, RSA is an example of an asymmetric algorithm that can be used to encrypt data with short lengths, such as the keying material of the AES algorithm. To ensure message integrity, the sender can generate a message authentication code (MAC) or a digital signature using the encrypted message together with a hash function, and then append the result to the encrypted message before transmitting it to the receiver. The receiver can then verify the MAC or the digital signature, and then decrypt the message, in order to obtain the plaintext and confirm the identity of the sender.

To protect the data in transit from being eavesdropped or compromised by unauthorized parties, it is essential to use encryption and decryption techniques in the IoV system. Encryption is a process that converts the original plaintext into a coded form. Decryption, on the other hand, is the process of converting the encrypted message back into its original plaintext. At the heart of encryption and decryption techniques lie the use of cryptographic key(s). Symmetric key encryption requires the same key to both encrypt and decrypt a message, while asymmetric key encryption uses a pair of keys, namely, the public key and the private key, which are related mathematically, but one cannot be deduced from the other. The public key can be used to encrypt the message, but the private key is required to decrypt the message. The public key is distributed to all the communication partners, while the private key is kept secret [14].

7.5.2 Secure protocols

In this section, we describe and classify the typical existing secure protocols. Specifically, we classify those protocols according to their security basics, including the certificate-based cryptography (CBC), the identity-based cryptography (IBC), the certificate-less cryptography (CLC), and the sophisticated cryptography and information hiding technique (CIH). Then, among these typical protocols, we will focus on the specific security requirements and challenges in the vehicle-to-cloud scenario, which is a typical scenario in IoV. The reason why the scenario is chosen is that it is more general and typical than other scenarios. The discussion and solution in this scenario could be used as guidelines and templates in other scenarios and their applications. In particular, we present the comparison and analysis of the existing protocols and hope to clarify the drawbacks, the specialty, as well as the preference and the applicability of the existing protocols. Then, inspire the security protocol design via this kind of analysis and comparison. Finally, the security guidelines and our open problems in IoV security are also discussed. During the discussion, the security features and requirements in the V2X and the vehicular cloud computing will be also addressed.

IoV is a key application of IoT, aiming to improve road traffic management, road safety, and facilitate daily commuting. However, due to the diverse IoV environment, in which a large number of heterogeneous vehicles are interconnected through wireless communications, and the open nature of IoV, in which the vehicles are also connected to the external Internet, the IoV system is vulnerable to cyber-attacks. Currently, many cybersecurity protocols have been proposed to secure IoV. In this chapter, we present and classify the existing cybersecurity protocols according to the security goals and the security techniques. Then, these typical cybersecurity protocols are compared. Specifically, the comparison of the digital signature generation and agreement in CLC, IBC for VANETs, and the confidentiality of the IBC are compared. Finally, the security challenges and our guidelines in the design of secure protocols for IoV are also discussed.

7.5.3 Intrusion detection and prevention systems in IoV

Intrusion detection and prevention systems (IDPS) play a key role in the cybersecurity architecture of the IoV ecosystem by providing an effective second-line defense to safeguard vulnerable attack entry points that were not fully protected by the first-line defense of the access control and authentication systems. Unlike the conventional information systems, the majority of the developed IDPS in the IoV application domain are proposed to address the unique characteristics and the specific requirements of this application area, such as the real-time analysis of a large volume of heterogeneous traffic data from different vehicle subsystems and external communication links (i.e., V2V, V2I, V2P, and V2N), the ability to work effectively even with partial or intermittent network connectivity, and low energy consumption. Depending on the coverage of the monitored network traffic, the IDPS systems can be classified into two main categories: the host-based (HIDPS) and the network-based (NIDPS). Due to the unique characteristics and highly dynamic nature of the IoV application domain, the majority of the existing IDPS focus on anomaly detection rather than signature-based detection, to minimize the number of false alarms that are generated.

7.5.4 Best practices and solutions in IoV cybersecurity

The proliferation of connected non-industrial vehicles, also known as the IoV, has brought extensive concerns to its system's security. Over the years, an array of security threats and challenges have been identified at different layers of the IoV system, from the physical protection of the electronic control units (ECUs) to the in-vehicle networking protocols, and the design of the upper-layer ITS services. It is worth noting that insufficient attention and effort have been given toward the upper-layer IoV cybersecurity, including the vulnerability of the sensing and communication components in the advanced driving assistance systems (ADASs) and autonomous vehicles (AVs), the potential privacy leak of the user's driving behavior and surrounding environment data, and the threat imposed on the vehicle cloud service by the blockchain-based ICT architecture. In this chapter, case studies and examples will be utilized to illustrate several representative best practices and solutions.

Owing to increasing concerns of the hacking and information leaking in vehicle ICT systems, how to protect transportation users' privacy data and ensure the road traffic cybersecurity has become a major challenge of the intelligent connected vehicle (ICV) development. In this chapter, we propose a security enhancement method for ICVs based on blockchain technology. In which, we first design a blockchain framework for the ICVs and then implement the framework in vehicle fog nodes to form a blockchain-based ICV system (BIVS). By seamlessly integrating BIVS with the privacy-preserving and security-driving protocol (PSSD) and the vehicle-to-everything (V2X) communication technology, the road traffic cybersecurity is established, and the ICV system's privacy and data security are both enhanced. The experimental results show that the proposed method is effective and efficient for the ICV system cybersecurity.

7.6 SECURITY STANDARDS AND REGULATIONS FOR IOV

Security standards have demonstrated how interoperability, simplicity, situation awareness, and privacy protection can be supported in a distributed, heterogeneous, variable connectivity environment. In addition to existing security standards, an increasing number of efforts to establish security regulations could motivate higher prioritization of security in standards and provide legal enforcement to increase the adherence and effectiveness of security. However, vulnerable transitions will result if executed without flexible, incremental strategies to support diverse currently deployed vehicular communication systems and technologies. This requires careful standardization of security interfaces between diverse existing and future in-vehicle devices and security mechanisms used for vehicle-to-everything (V2X) communication. Due to the lack of a globally unifying security standard, the design and development of security requirements are still scattered across the globe [15].

The absence of a universally accepted security standard has resulted in a range of frequently conflicting, complicated, or inadequate IoV security implementations. A particular weakness of current efforts is the relatively low prioritization of security in standards and regulations. Therefore, security gets under-addressed, incomplete, or bolted on as an afterthought, reducing its effectiveness, introducing unnecessary complexity, or increasing the weakness. Cyber-physical system (CPS) domains like industrial IoT have similar connectivity and cybersecurity challenges to IoV but have shown more concern with security. Because these domains use similar technologies to IoV, substantially developed security standards could directly benefit IoV. Although these CPS domains do not face some of IoV's main challenges (especially the lack of centralized control and authority over devices and data), centralized solutions could be avoided through careful adaptation of existing security standards [16].

This is the major and most relevant regulatory frameworks that govern the cybersecurity and resilience of the automobile and ITS sector in general and IoV in particular:

- *EU Cybersecurity Act* establishes a framework for setting cybersecurity certification schemes across the European Union (EU) to ensure that products, services, and processes meet the specified cybersecurity standards.
- *UN Regulation No. 155*: Part of the WP.29 framework, this regulation by the United Nations Economic Commission for Europe (UNECE) focuses on cybersecurity and cyber security management systems for vehicles.
- *ISO/SAE 21434*: A global standard that addresses cybersecurity aspects for the automotive industry, providing guidelines on

cybersecurity risk management regarding the design, development, production, operation, maintenance, and decommissioning of electrical and electronic systems within road vehicles.

- *NIST Cybersecurity Framework*: While not specific to automobiles, it provides comprehensive standards and best practices to help organizations manage cybersecurity risks in the context of modern technologies, including those applicable to the automotive sector.
- *General Data Protection Regulation (GDRP)*: Although primarily a data protection standard, GDPR has significant implications for cybersecurity, ensuring that personal data is processed securely using appropriate technical and organizational measures, directly impacting IoV systems.
- *Automotive Information Sharing and Analysis Center (ISAC)* provides a central role in the automotive industry's effort to safeguard vehicle electronics and communication systems from cybersecurity threats through global collaboration.

Updated frameworks and standards are needed in order to take into account the current cybersecurity environment, threat intelligence, situational awareness, and provide response and recovery support as well.

7.7 CASE STUDIES AND EXAMPLES IN IOV CYBERSECURITY

Many best practice-checked tools and methodologies are available today. A challenge has been that proprietary and novel methodologies are company confidential and thus not in the public domain. Companies are also reticent to publish improvements in proprietary tools to avoid signaling to potential attackers how to circumvent. Recently, the open-source movement is dynamic in the domain of cybersecurity, such as the C implementations of the Cryptographic Algorithm Validation Program algorithms developed and made publicly available. Several companies have contributed proprietary cybersecurity tools to open source and have openly published their methods. It is the authors' hope that this trend will continue to stimulate the growth and effectiveness of available secure software and firmware resources for the automotive industry. The case studies, examples, and available tools and methodologies prove that additional research or tool development is not necessary to begin utilizing secure best practices today.

7.7.1 Case studies in IoV cybersecurity

Several case studies and examples on the proposed security mechanisms are performed and presented in this work to demonstrate the feasibility and efficiency of the developed approach. In the first case study, the detection model of rogue edge cloud servers is developed based on temporal difference method. The commonly used deep Q-learning technique is then employed to implement the detection mechanism. After that, the naive and improved malware propagation models are described and developed based on the content delivery and epidemic spreading theories. In particular, the greedy and intelligent algorithms are utilized for exploring the optimization capabilities of the malware propagation models. The detection models and mechanisms of rogue cloud servers and edge servers are then developed based on the content delivery theory and proposed insurgency optimization algorithm. The vulnerabilities and defense techniques of a software-defined vehicular network with deep learning are further investigated and discussed. In addition, the development and security issues of IoV and connected autonomous vehicle (CAV) systems are described and discussed.

With the increasing numbers of cybersecurity incidents and concerns, several studies have highlighted the essential issues of IoV. The new paradigm of connected vehicles has introduced several applications, ranging from traffic and transport management, cooperative mobility, infotainment, and multimodal transport. Despite their clear benefits, these applications also bring some new security and privacy challenges. The main cybersecurity challenges include security and privacy of V2X (Vehicle-to-Everything) communications, protection of cooperative and automated mobility functions, and the security of external services and the cloud environment. To address these cybersecurity challenges, this chapter presents a multi-layer and adaptive framework to enhance the IoV system's security levels.

7.7.2 Recent cybersecurity incidents in IoV

How to safeguard the open platform and the privacy of users has become a research focus. Several threat-intelligence approaches have been proposed to maximize the effectiveness of threat information. The goal is to gain high-level visibility of potential or existing threats by collecting, analyzing, and distributing threat information to cybersecurity personnel, who can then take specific defensive measures to protect the system and its components from cyber threats. A software-defined networking architecture that addresses access control and the design and implementation of the authorization framework for SDN-based IoV services were studied.

Due to the openness characteristic of the connected vehicles in IoV, a large number of cybersecurity incidents have been reported in recent years. In addition to the risk associated with information leakage, the physical safety of vehicle owners is also at stake. A number of incidents have led to denial of service (DoS) and distributed denial of service (DDoS) attacks in the commercial and public sectors. Some of the popular incidents include attacks on the Nissan Leaf electric car and Tesla Model S, and blockchain's denial of service through a huge amount of spam trading data. In these incidents, the server and client sides were not prepared with appropriate security measures or security modules were not implemented on the server and client sides, allowing the attacks to easily exploit these unprotected gaps. To ensure the security and privacy of V2X, the access control and authentication of the OBU need to be designed with secure methods to prevent unauthorized communications.

7.8 FUTURE TRENDS AND TECHNOLOGIES IN IOV SECURITY

IoV is a new paradigm for the next generation of ITS and gradually becomes an essential part of modern society. IoV has an extensive application prospect, and its dynamic development can enhance the level of intelligent transportation and ensure traffic safety. IoV has been growing, and the progress of its related technologies has had a positive modernization effect on the development of the social economy. However, IoV's insecure communication environment directly affects its application and development. As the ad hoc network environment of IoV is not completely trusted, it is challenging to establish a secure information exchange platform through traditional security mechanisms. Therefore, it is essential to apply innovative security technologies to protect the data exchange of IoV. At present, research on IoV focuses not only on how to ensure the security and privacy of the data transmission process but also on how to secure the resulting information system to guarantee the system's normal operation and user safety [17].

The continuous and rapid development of IoV has a large modernization effect on the social economy. IoV has gradually become an important part of the modern ITS, but its insecure communication environment directly affects its application and development [18]. Currently, the research on IoV focuses not only on how to ensure the security and privacy of the data transmission process but also on how to secure the resulting information system to ensure the system's normal operation and user safety. All security problems in the information system need to be properly addressed. Therefore, this research chapter proposes a cybersecurity architecture and its solutions in IoV based on blockchain technology. This architecture can guarantee the session key distribution process under the certificateless cross-domain and can ensure the data security and users' privacy in the group communication scenario.

7.9 CONCLUSION

The vision of IoV has led to a significant transformation in the field of intelligent transportation systems. The integration of the emerging technologies with the traditional transportation system has led to promising new advanced services and applications to make our journey more secure, comfortable, and efficient. In this scenario, the security of the IoV architecture and its enabling technologies become a prime concern to assure the reliability as well as the acceptance of these promising systems. Therefore, in the light of this fact, this chapter aims to provide a comprehensive security solution for the IoV, while considering its security standards collectively. The key objective is the proposal of a security framework, which can secure the IoV environment by integrating multiple security mechanisms in a collaborative manner. In this study, a three-layer IoV architecture is presented with its key applications. Then, certain potential security threats, as well as their attack techniques, have been highlighted concerning each layer of the introduced architecture. Afterward, to mitigate such disclosed security issues, a multilayered security framework is proposed in which diverse security mechanisms can cooperate efficiently to secure the IoV environment. Finally, it is concluded that along with the great supportive security standards like the proposed security framework can pave the way well for the security of IoV and make a significant contribution in the field of traffic management, road safety, as well as other IoV applications.

REFERENCES

[1] M. Ouaissa, M. Ouaissa, S. R. Boualam, Z. Boulouard, I. U. Khan, and S. El Himer, "Internet of Vehicles (IoV): Challenges, threats and routing protocols," In *Future Communication Systems Using Artificial Intelligence, Internet of Things and Data Science*, pp. 205–212, CRC Press, 2024.

[2] S. Sharma, and B. Kaushik (2019). "A survey on internet of vehicles: Applications, security issues & solutions," *Vehicular Communications*, 20, 100182.

[3] M. V. Kadam, H. B. Mahajan, N. J. Uke, and P. R. Futane (2023). "Cybersecurity threats mitigation in Internet of Vehicles communication system using reliable clustering and routing," *Microprocessors and Microsystems*, 102, 104926.

[4] M. Houmer, M. Ouaissa, M. Ouaissa, and S. Eddamiri, "Applying machine learning algorithms to improve intrusion detection system in IoV," *Artificial Intelligence of Things in Smart Environments: Applications in Transportation and Logistics*, p. 35, De Gruyter, 2022.

[5] S. M. Karim, A. Habbal, S. A. Chaudhry, and A. Irshad (2022), "Architecture, protocols, and security in IoV: Taxonomy, analysis, challenges, and solutions," *Security and Communication Networks*, 2022(1), 1131479.

[6] H. Taslimasa, S. Dadkhah, E. C. P. Neto, P. Xiong, S. Ray, and A. A. Ghorbani (2023). Security issues in Internet of Vehicles (IoV): A comprehensive survey. *Internet of Things*, 100809.

[7] M. Houmer, M., M. Ouaissa, and M. Ouaissa (2022). Secure authentication scheme for 5G-based V2X communications. *Procedia Computer Science*, 198, 276–281.

[8] C. R. Bhukya, P. Thakur, B. R. Mudhivarthi, and G. Singh (2023). "Cybersecurity in internet of medical vehicles: state-of-the-art analysis, research challenges and future perspectives," *Sensors*, 23(19), 8107.

[9] M. Ouaissa, A. Rhattoy, and I. Chana, "New security level of authentication and key agreement protocol for the IoT on LTE mobile networks," In 2018 6th International Conference on Wireless Networks and Mobile Communications (WINCOM), p. 1–6, IEEE, 2018.

[10] T. Guan, Y. Han, N. Kang, N. Tang, X. Chen, and S. Wang (2022). "An overview of vehicular cybersecurity for intelligent connected vehicles," *Sustainability*, 1(9), 5211.

[11] M. Ouaissa, and M. Ouaissa, "An improved privacy authentication protocol for 5G mobile networks," In 2020 International Conference on Advances in Computing, Communication & Materials (ICACCM), p. 136–143, IEEE, 2020.

[12] M. Ouaissa, M. Ouaissa, M. Houmer, S. Hamdani, and Z. Boulouard, "A secure vehicle to everything (v2x) communication model for intelligent transportation system," In *Computational Intelligence in Recent Communication Networks*, p. 83–102, Cham: Springer International Publishing, 2022.

[13] A. Hemmati, M. Zarei, and A. Souri (2023). "Blockchain-based internet of vehicles (BIoV): A systematic review of surveys and reviews," *Security and Privacy*, 6(6), e317.

[14] R. Loganathan, and S. Selvakumara Samy, "Blockchain based internet of vehicles (IoV) information transmission mechanisms," In 2022 International Conference on Edge Computing and Applications (ICECAA), pp. 514–523, IEEE, 2022.

[15] E. Alalwany and I. Mahgoub (2024). "Security and trust management in the internet of vehicles (IoV): challenges and machine learning solutions," *Sensors*, 24(2), 368.

[16] D. M. M. Azzahar, M. Y. Darus, S. J. Elias, J. Jasmis, M. Z. Zakaria, and S. R. M. Dawam, "A review: Standard requirements for internet of vehicles (iov) safety applications," In 2020 5th IEEE International Conference on Recent Advances and Innovations in Engineering (ICRAIE), p. 1–5, IEEE, 2020.

[17] K. Liu, X. Xu, M. Chen, B. Liu, L. Wu, and V. C. Lee (2019). "A hierarchical architecture for the future internet of vehicles," *IEEE Communications Magazine*, 57(7), 41–47.

[18] M. Chouikik, M. Ouaissa, M. Ouaissa, Z. Boulouard, and M. Kissi (2022). "Software-defined networking security: A comprehensive review," *Big Data Analytics and Computational Intelligence for Cybersecurity*, 91–108.

Chapter 8

AI-driven cloud storage service for securing IoT data

Garima Sharma, Jaspreet Singh, and Priyanka Maan

8.1 INTRODUCTION

The Internet of Things (IoT) has gained significant attention from researchers in the past few decades due to the increasing demand for unprecedented connectivity and interactivity of the physical world with the digital world. As a result, IoT has created a vast network of smart devices to solve simple as well as complex tasks by communicating with each other and exchanging data [1]. The growing ecosystem needs a cost-effective and scalable storage solution to manage the enormous amount of data that is being produced by these devices. Cloud infrastructure provides an efficient platform to secure this data.

Cloud computing is a broad term that involves providing visualized services over the internet. As shown in Figure 8.1, it refers to a system in which the resources within a data center like the central processing unit (CPU), servers, storage, and network are utilized by the customers in a shared manner, which allows them to use these services as and when needed and pay as per the usage [2]. It also provides them the flexibility to use these services anytime regardless of the geographical location. It basically works by enabling devices used by the client to access data and many other services over the internet, from servers and databases. The internet acts as the link between the client and the backend. The client-side includes the client's browsers or devices, and the back end comprises databases, physical servers, and computers. The backend is used for storing and accessing data.

Cloud computing as defined by the National Institute of Standards and Technology (NIST) [3] is classified into three service models, which are discussed as follows.

1. *Infrastructure as a service (IaaS)*: IaaS is the model in which a third-party service provider hosts the servers, storage, and other resources. These services are made available to the clients or the customers over the Internet, allowing them to scale up or scale down their computing resources based on their requirements. The advantage of using

DOI: 10.1201/9781003497585-8

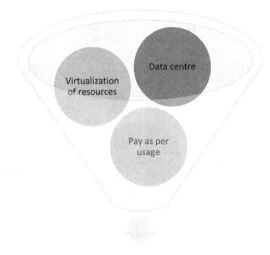

Cloud Computing

Figure 8.1 Cloud computing.

this model is that it eliminates the need to manage and maintain the physical infrastructure. Examples of IaaS include Google Compute Engine [4] and Amazon EC2 [5].

2. *Platform as a service (PaaS)*: The PaaS cloud model in which a third-party service provider hosts the cloud platform where the customers can access the provided tools and services over the internet using application programming interfaces (APIs). The most popular example of PaaS is the Google App Engine [6]. This model provides a development environment for developers to build and deploy applications without needing to worry about the underlying framework.

3. *Software as a service (SaaS)*: The SaaS model involves a third-party service provider that hosts the applications that are made available to the customers virtually over the internet. Customers can access the hosted software from any geographical location using the internet. The most common examples of SaaS include Google Workspace [7], Dropbox [8], and Netflix [9]. This model eliminates the need to install and maintain software on the local device.

The cloud storage has become popular due to the wide range of advantages it offers over the traditional local storage systems. The key benefits offered by the cloud as shown in Figure 8.2 are security, quick deployment, cost efficiency, ease of management, scalability, and global availability. In recent times, various cloud service providers are available in the market like Google,

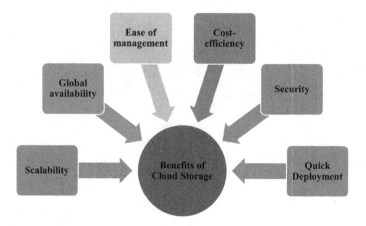

Figure 8.2 Benefits of cloud storage over traditional local storage systems.

Microsoft, and Amazon. Each of these service providers offers its own cloud infrastructure and formats to access the cloud, thereby providing a variety of choices for the consumers to choose what suits their demands. This chapter presents a comparative analysis of different cloud service providers based on the services and key features to enable the users to make informed decisions about what to choose. This chapter also presents a web-based cloud storage platform CloudSync that provides the flexibility to the users to use the platform both in online as well as offline mode. The presented system can be integrated with other web and mobile-based devices ensuring data accessibility and usability regardless of the geographical location.

This chapter is organized as follows. Section 8.2 presents different types of cloud deployment models and lists the challenges of using different types of cloud deployment models. Section 8.3 presents the proposed cloud storage architecture CloudSync. Section 8.4 provides a comparative analysis of the services and features of different cloud storage platforms like Google Drive, and OneDrive. Finally, Section 8.5 presents the conclusion and future work of the presented study.

8.2 CLOUD DEPLOYMENT MODELS AND ASSOCIATED CHALLENGES

Cloud computing provides a variety of deployment models, where each model offers different configurations and approaches for the implementation and management of computation services. The cloud deployment models also define the delivery and control of the computation services offered by the cloud such as servers, storage, and networking. Thus, it gives flexibility to the organizations to choose the deployment model that caters to their business needs and requirements. The various cloud deployment models [10] are as follows:

i. Private Cloud Infrastructure
    A private cloud infrastructure is managed and operated exclusively within an organization. The IT resources provided by the underlying infrastructure are isolated and solely controlled by the organization regardless of whether it is situated on-premises or off-premises. The management of resources could be done by the organization itself but can also be outsourced partially or fully to a third party. The aim of establishing a private cloud is to maximize the utilization of resources and to ensure data privacy and security by providing an additional layer of security making it ideal for associations with sensitive and classified information. The public cloud storage information is available only inside an isolated environment solely allocated for an organization's business. Moreover, as the users are limited, the performance of the private cloud is generally better and significant.
    Despite these advantages, the private cloud also suffers from some drawbacks like storage cost, scalability, and remote access. As compared to public cloud storage, private cloud storage costs are higher because of the hardware costs such as servers, hard disks, and licenses. Also, unlike the public cloud, the private cloud isn't very scale-friendly. Whenever there is a need for upgradation of speed or storage, the organization has to bear additional expenses from time to time. Although private cloud storage is way more secure than the public cloud, remote access becomes limited. This might be considered as an advantage as well as a disadvantage depending on the user's need. But if the organization needs advanced security measures where others can access and remotely access outside the range as well, then private cloud storage fails to provide remote access beyond a certain limit.

ii. Public Cloud Storage
    A public cloud storage infrastructure is managed and owned by a third-party service provider. The IT resources are accessible to the users over the internet on-demand and on a pay-as-you-go basis. The popular public cloud service provider in the market are Google [11], Amazon Web Services (AWS) [12], and Microsoft [13].

iii. Hybrid Cloud Storage
    Hybrid cloud storage is a combination of public and private cloud infrastructure where the data and IT resources are shared. The workloads that require scalability can be deployed on the public cloud whereas the private cloud can be utilized for securing sensitive data applications.

   iv. Multi-Cloud Storage

A multi-cloud cloud storage deployment model utilizes the resources and services from multiple cloud service providers. The choice of service providers can be made based on organizational needs, and the cost of setting up the cloud depends upon the choice of service providers.

   v. Community Cloud Storage

A community cloud deployment model consists of a group of organizations that have similar interests and requirements. These organizations share the cost of setting up a common cloud. The data security is maintained by each organization whereas the cloud resources are shared by all.

Table 8.1 provides a detailed summary of the discussed cloud deployment models based on various distinguishing factors like ownership, security, cost, scalability, reliability, and use cases. So, it is evident that cloud computing comes with numerous benefits, but it also has some challenges associated with it. The primary challenges [14] are listed as follows:

   A. *Portability*: Portability refers to the process of moving one application and its data from one service provider to another. An application that was previously running on an old cloud environment using some of its specific features could require significant modifications to run on a new cloud environment. Also transferring the data from one cloud to another could bring out some data migration complexities.

   B. *Lack of standards*: Cloud service providers set their own standards with no such measurement performance facility provided to the use of the customers, which would enable them to compare the services provided by different cloud service providers.

   C. *Limited scalability*: Although most cloud service providers promise infinite storage making their cloud service infinitely scalable, but since millions are users are now transitioning to using cloud services, it could be challenging sometimes to meet the rising demands.

   D. *Reliability*: It could be challenging for a user to stay connected to the cloud as and when the connection is unstable or lost.

   E. *Data privacy and legal issues*: Data confidentiality remains as one of the most important concerns for all individuals when hosting their data on the cloud. Although appropriate security measures have been adopted by the service providers, but ensuring data privacy over the cloud is an active area of research.

   F. *Denial of service*: Denial of service (DoS) is perhaps the most common problem. DoS protection must be built in the cloud to protect it when under a heavy DoS attack.

Table 8.1 Comparative analysis of different cloud deployment models

Factors	Deployment models				
	Private cloud	Public cloud	Hybrid cloud	Community cloud	Multi-cloud
Control and ownership	Owned by single organizations	Owned by third-party service providers	Combination of public and private cloud	Ownership shared by organizations with shared interests	Owned by multiple service providers
Security	Highly secure	Depends on the security measures adopted by the service provider	Depends upon the type of public cloud service provider	Shared data security	Depends upon the security measures adopted by multiple service providers
Cost	Expensive	Pay-as-you-go	Depends upon the usage of public and private cloud	Cost shared by the group of organizations	Depends on service providers
Scalability	Limited	High	Scalability can be achieved by using public cloud	Depends upon the growth of a group of organizations	Depends on service providers
Reliability	Depends upon the organization's infrastructure	High	Depends upon the usage of public and private cloud	Depends upon collective requirements	Depends on service providers and the architecture
Use cases	Industries with strict data security requirements	Web applications, development, testing	Appropriate for organizations needing a balance of control and scalability	Suitable for industries or groups with shared regulatory or operational requirements	Ideal for avoiding vendor lock-in, enhancing reliability, and leveraging specialized services

G. *Metering*: The performance of cloud services should be metered and monitored by the administrations using the services. Cloud service providers should provide them with different measures to monitor the performance of their services.

H. *Energy management*: One of the prerequisites of using a cloud infrastructure is to manage the resources in a diverse computing environment. The energy-efficient equipment should be developed for building data centers so as to make them energy efficient.

The next section provides a comparison of the popular cloud storage service providers to enable a user to make smart decisions when selecting a cloud service provider.

8.3 SELECTION OF CLOUD SERVICE PROVIDERS

Due to market dynamics, the list of cloud storage suppliers is continually growing and ever-changing. This study does not plan to offer a comprehensive summary of all existing storage services; however, it takes into consideration a few popular service providers for analysis. The comparison is done between eight well-established storage suppliers [15] namely, iCloud [16], OneDrive [17], Google Drive [18], SugarSync [19], justcloud.com [20], Livedrive [21], Dropbox [8], Box [22], and Google Trends [23].

The analysis of the features and services provided by the various service providers is important for the users to make an informed decision. It is observed that while certain suppliers, for example, Google Drive or Dropbox compute the cost month to month, others charge in light of year use. Likewise, a few suppliers, like justcloud.com require the least long-term membership for the base arrangement. In this situation, the correlation isn't direct, and further examination is required. Also, while every cloud framework claims to use the general agreements for utilizing the distributed storage frameworks, and usually ensures a promising uptime, but for additional request circumstances, the client ought to search for more unambiguous or even altered help-level understanding agreements. Moreover, the free storage limit over the cloud is dynamic. Numerous internet-based capacity frameworks, similar to Google Drive, Box, or Dropbox offer extensive introductory-free stockpiling limits. However, the service providers tend to increase this limit over time.

The presented comparative analysis considers various key factors, including the pricing plans, free data storage capacity, maximum file size, maximum storage limit, mobile device support, platform compatibility, data security features, and additional services like the cloud service level agreement (SLA) and API. Table 8.2 summarizes the comparison of the selected cloud service

Table 8.2 Comparison of popular cloud storage service providers

Cloud service provider	Pricing plan	Free storage	Maximum file size	Maximum storage capacity	Mobile device support	Platform compatibility	Security measure	SLA	API
Google Drive	$0.02 per GB per month	15GB	Upto 5TB	25TB	Android, iOS	Windows, Mac, Linux	SSL	Yes	Multiple platforms: Java, PHP, .NET, Python REST API
OneDrive	$4.70 per user per month	5GB	250GB	2TB	Android, Ios, Windows phone	Windows, Mac, Linux	SSL, not built-in encryption	Yes	No
Justcloud.com	$10.69 per month for home plan	1GB	10GB	4TB	Android, iOS, Blackberry	Windows, macOS, Linux	SSL, AES Encryption	No	No
Livedrive	$16 per month for 2TB	N/A	10GB	Unlimited Backup Storage & 5TB Briefcase Storage.	Android, iOS, Windows Phone	Windows, macOS	SSL, AES-256 Encryption	No	XML, SOAP Service
Dropbox	$12.50 per user per month for 5TB	2GB	3 TB		Android, iOS, BlackBerry and Kindle Fire	Windows, macOS, Linux	SSL, AES-256 Encryption	Yes	SDK for Major Platform (Java, PHP, Ruby, Android)
Box	15$ per month per user	10GB	150GB	Unlimited	Android, iOS, Windows Phone	Windows, macOS	AES –256 Encryption, SSL, SSAE	Yes	Yes

providers and provides an overview of the services offered by them. The analysis can help the users to have a better understanding of the service providers and will thus enable the users to select the provider that closely aligns with their specific needs and preferences.

It is evident from the discussion that while all distributed storage frameworks secure their data through secure sockets layer (SSL), the security of data stored on the server is not always 100 percent guaranteed. Organizations or individuals with higher security requirements have to adopt additional security measures like client-side encryption of information before moving the data to the cloud. The next section presents a novel and secure cloud storage framework that can be accessed by users using a web-based interface and provides AI-based data management and threat detection features.

8.4 PROPOSED CLOUD STORAGE ARCHITECTURE

Unlike public cloud storage, private cloud storage provides a greater level of performance by providing additional security and faster access time. This chapter presents CloudSync as a web-based private cloud storage service that can be integrated with various platforms such as web and mobile. A user can connect any application with this cloud service through the API. CloudSync provides a user-friendly web-based interface to the users to enable them to access the cloud storage. The user can register themselves on the website and then authenticate themselves by clicking the verification link sent to their registered email ids. Once a user is verified, the user can log in using their registered login credentials. After successful login, the user gains access to a personalized dashboard, which provides the option of uploading or downloading the data from the cloud. The dashboard also lets the user efficiently manage the stored data. The data management process is integrated with artificial intelligence (AI) based algorithms that assist in smart data management.

In order to provide security of data on CloudSync, AI-based threat detection algorithms are used, which identify the possible threats in real-time by analyzing the user activities and network traffic. Moreover, powerful encryption algorithms like Advanced Encryption Standard (AES) and SHA-256 are integrated with the proposed cloud storage service to provide an extra layer of security for the saved data. AES ensures secrecy of the stored data whereas SHA-256 is employed to ensure secure data transfer functions. Figure 8.3 provides a module-wise flow diagram of the proposed system.

The performance of the proposed cloud storage platform is evaluated using the uploading and downloading speeds on different PCs and different

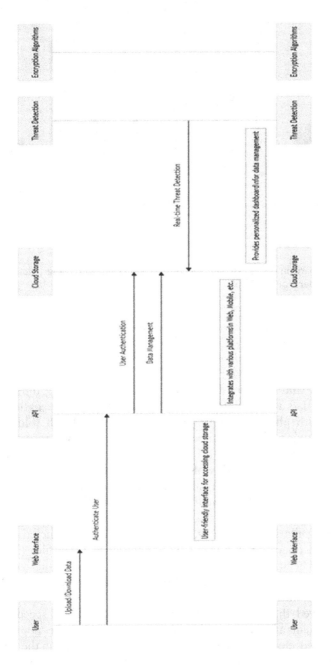

Figure 8.3 The proposed CloudSync data storage.

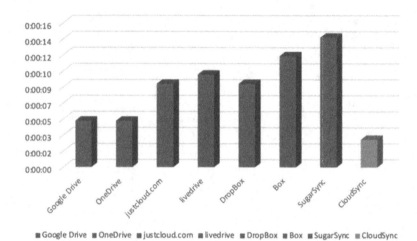

Figure 8.4 Comparison of download speed of CloudSync with other cloud service providers for a 3MB file.

routers. The performance evaluation is conducted to test the platform's operational efficiency across varied hardware configurations. The speed tests conducted also provide valuable insights into the performance of the proposed system in a real-world scenario.

The upload and download speeds are assessed by using different file sizes and formats to simulate the usual cloud storage user pattern. A 3 MB folder with photographs in JPG format and 300 MB folders with photos and movie files (.mov, .mp3 format) have been compressed and the upload and download speeds are analyzed. The test was conducted for three days, and the average download and upload completion time values were calculated each day. Figures 8.4 and 8.5 show the average download of the proposed system for small files (3 MB) and large files (300 MB) respectively and as expected, the average download time increases with the increasing file size. Similarly, Figure 8.6 and 8.7 depict the results of the upload operation for small files (3MB) and large files (300MB), respectively. The graphs are plotted against the popular cloud storage service providers like Google Drive, OneDrive, justcloud.com, live Drive, Dropbox, Box, and SugarSync.

It is observed that although the upload and download speeds of the proposed system are presently lower as compared to the popular and well-established cloud storage providers in the market, but the research provides valuable observations on the potential areas of improvement. The research can be extended to improve the presented system by using

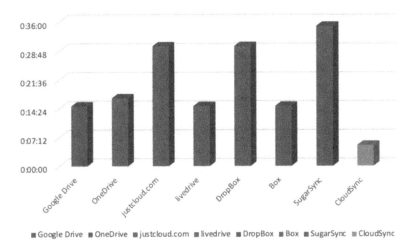

Figure 8.5 Comparison of download speed of CloudSync with other cloud service providers for 300MB file size.

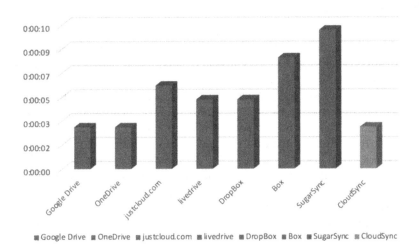

Figure 8.6 Comparison of upload speed of CloudSync with other cloud service providers for 3MB file size.

various optimization strategies like caching mechanisms, enabling parallel processing to maximize the available bandwidth and server load balancing. Moreover, the proposed system offers novelty by providing additional features like AI-driven data management and threat detection.

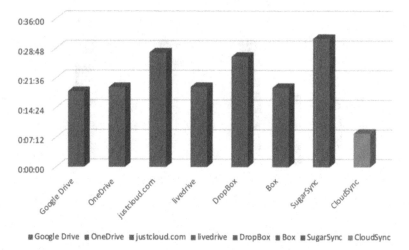

Figure 8.7 Comparison of upload speed of CloudSync with other cloud service providers for 3MB file size.

8.5 CONCLUSION AND FUTURE WORK

This study also provides a detailed understanding of various cloud-based deployment models along with their associated advantages and disadvantages. Moreover, a comparative analysis is performed to enable cloud users to efficiently choose from a variety of cloud storage service providers available in the market. The study did not aim to identify the best service provider but to facilitate a smart decision-making process for the users to select the most appropriate and well-suited cloud service provider by identifying and contrasting the key features and services provided by each service provider.

This chapter also presented an efficient web-based cloud storage solution, CloudSync for securely storing the data generated from smart IoT devices. CloudSync not only provides a secure data storage platform but also provides a user-friendly interface to efficiently manage the stored data. The novelty of the study lies in the integration of AI algorithms with the proposed cloud platform for efficient data management and threat prediction. The platform also provides an integration facility that makes it accessible through web browsers and mobile devices.

Although the study did not cover the scalability aspect of the proposed cloud system and the results of the system's performance tests were compared on the same network whereas in real-time the traffic loads can be dynamic, and location can have a significant impact on the results. The study can be further improved by performing tests on different network configurations under varying traffic loads and workloads. Moreover, various optimization techniques like caching mechanisms, parallel processing, and client and server-side encryption can be employed in the future to enhance the system by improving the uploading and downloading speeds.

REFERENCES

[1] T. Alam, "Cloud-based IoT applications and their roles in smart cities," *Smart Cities*, vol. 4, no. 3. 2021. doi: 10.3390/smartcities4030064.

[2] Q. Zhang, L. Cheng, and R. Boutaba, "Cloud computing: State-of-the-art and research challenges," *Journal of Internet Services and Applications*, vol. 1, no. 1, 2010, doi: 10.1007/s13174-010-0007-6.

[3] T. G. Peter Mell, "The NIST definition of cloud computing," *Observatorio Económico EEUU*, no. BBVA Research. 2016.

[4] S. P. T. Krishnan and J. L. U. Gonzalez, "Google compute engine," in *Building Your Next Big Thing with Google Cloud Platform*, 2015. doi: 10.1007/978-1-4842-1004-8_4.

[5] G. Juve et al., "Scientific workflow applications on amazon EC2," in *e-science 2009 – Proceedings of the 2009 5th IEEE International Conference on e-Science Workshops*, 2009. doi: 10.1109/ESCIW.2009.5408002.

[6] A. Shashi, "Google App Engine," in *Designing Applications for Google Cloud Platform*, 2023. doi: 10.1007/978-1-4842-9511-3_3.

[7] U. Akcil, H. Uzunboylu, and E. Kinik, "Integration of technology to learning-teaching processes and google workspace tools: A literature review," *Sustainability (Switzerland)*, vol. 13, no. 9. 2021. doi: 10.3390/su13095018.

[8] M. Amrit, J. Pherwani, M. Yadav, and K. Sorathia, "Dropbox," 2013. doi: 10.1145/2525194.2525285.

[9] T. Ahmad, R. Pandey, and M. Faisal, "Authorization model for securing cloud SaaS services (Netflix)," *International Journal of Distributed Systems and Technologies*, vol. 13, no. 8, 2022, doi: 10.4018/ijdst.307903.

[10] Z. Mahmood, "Cloud computing: Characteristics and deployment approaches," in *Proceedings – 11th IEEE International Conference on Computer and Information Technology, CIT 2011*, 2011. doi: 10.1109/CIT.2011.75.

[11] A. Alqahtani, "Usability testing of google cloud applications: Students' perspective," *J Technol Sci Educ*, vol. 9, no. 3, 2019, doi: 10.3926/JOTSE.585.

[12] AWS, "AWS Was ist Cloud Computing? – Amazon Cloud Services," Amazon Web Services. 2023.

[13] Microsoft, "What is Azure – Microsoft Cloud Services | Microsoft Azure," Azure. 2019.

[14] N. Subramanian and A. Jeyaraj, "Recent security challenges in cloud computing," *Computers and Electrical Engineering*, vol. 71, 2018, doi: 10.1016/j.compeleceng.2018.06.006.

[15] X. Zenuni, J. Ajdari, F. Ismaili, and B. Raufi, "Cloud storage providers: A comparison review and evaluation," in *ACM International Conference Proceeding Series*, 2014. doi: 10.1145/2659532.2659609.

[16] T. Sillmann, "iCloud," in *Das Swift-Handbuch*, 2019. doi: 10.3139/ 9783446457300.030.

[17] Microsoft, Communications, Microsoft, and E. B. Russell, "Get started with Microsoft OneDrive," *J. Cutan Pathol.*, vol. 30, no. 2, 2003.

[18] T. O. Gallaway and J. Starkey, "Google Drive," *The Charleston Advisor*, vol. 14, no. 3, 2013, doi: 10.5260/chara.14.3.16.

[19] M. Shariati, A. Dehghantanha, and K. K. R. Choo, "SugarSync forensic analysis," *Australian Journal of Forensic Sciences*, vol. 48, no. 1, 2016, doi: 10.1080/00450618.2015.1021379.

[20] Justcloud.com, www.justcloud.com/.

[21] Livedrive, www2.livedrive.com/.

[22] Box, www.box.com/.

[23] N. Aslanidis, A. F. Bariviera, and Ó. G. López, "The link between cryptocurrencies and Google Trends attention," *Financ Res Lett*, vol. 47, 2022, doi: 10.1016/j.frl.2021.102654.

Chapter 9

Blockchain technology-based biometric system

Mariya Ouaissa, Mariyam Ouaissa, and A. Prasanth

9.1 INTRODUCTION

In recent years, the world has experienced a revolution in the field of information security. This revolution is expected to gain even more attention in the coming years. Information systems security has become a highly interesting area of research. In a security context that has never been fully secured, passwords are known to be weak and easily hackable [1]. As a result, organizations are now taking the next step by seeking to use physiological and/or behavioral biometric data for identity management. This technique is increasingly becoming common in daily life, such as in the processing of banking transactions and access to certain military or industrial locations. However, like all aspects of our digital lives, biometric systems are also vulnerable to various attacks. These vulnerabilities can significantly degrade their functionality, making the security of these systems a critical necessity and a great challenge [2].

In the literature, there are biometric data security techniques that do not depend on specific domain requirements. Recently, a new technology, blockchain, has been proposed as a solution. Initially, blockchain technology was proposed and deployed to facilitate online payments directly from one party to another without the need for a financial institution, using the cryptocurrency Bitcoin. By integrating several techniques such as decentralization, distributed computing, asymmetric encryption, hashing, timestamping, and consensus algorithms, blockchain technology is now being used to secure other application domains [3].

However, research into how blockchain can be used in identity management is still in its early stages. In biometric systems, any alteration in the template base poses a significant risk, as an attack on this part of the system can prevent a legitimate user from gaining access or authorize an impostor. Additionally, channel interception can lead to unauthorized access by modifying information transmitted on the communication channel, destroying messages, inserting new messages, causing time shifts, or interrupting the dissemination of messages [4].

DOI: 10.1201/9781003497585-9

In this chapter, we provide a general overview of these two concepts, starting with their respective definitions, followed by an exploration of their operations and associated application areas. Finally, we highlight the synergy between blockchain and biometrics. The chapter is organized as follows: Section 9.2 presents biometric systems and their security, Section 9.3 introduces blockchain technology, and Section 9.4 explains how blockchain and biometrics can be combined for identity management.

9.2 OVERVIEW OF THE BIOMETRIC SYSTEM

Traditional passwords have long been a weak point in security systems. Biometrics aims to address this problem by linking proof of identity to our physical and behavioral characteristics. Biometrics is a technology that allows for the identification and verification of individuals based on unique physical or behavioral traits, making it extremely accurate and secure. These characteristics can include fingerprints, facial features, irises, voice, or even manner of movement. Among authentication technologies, biometrics has quickly stood out as the most relevant for identifying people reliably and quickly based on their unique biological traits. The goal of biometrics is to ensure accurate and reliable identification, providing a seamless and convenient user experience, and eliminating the need for passwords or personal identification numbers (PINs) that can be forgotten or stolen [5].

9.2.1 Definition

A biometric system is a set of technologies, software, and hardware that uses biometric data to identify or verify the identity of an individual. These systems are used in various contexts, including physical security, online authentication systems, government applications, and more. While biometrics is the scientific field that studies the unique biological characteristics of individuals, a biometric system is a collection of technologies that uses these characteristics to identify or verify a person's identity in different contexts. Biometrics involves the use of physiological and/or behavioral traits to determine or verify the identity of individuals. Despite the advantages of biometric systems over traditional authentication systems that use passwords and ID cards, they are still vulnerable to specific limitations that can significantly degrade their functionality [6].

Biometrics refers to an identification and authentication technique that involves transforming a biological, morphological, or behavioral characteristic into a unique identifier key. Its objective is to attest to the uniqueness of a person based on the measurement of an unchangeable or uncontrollable part of their body. In other words, it is the automated recognition of individuals based on their biological and behavioral characteristics. For recognition to be reliable and of high quality, the characteristics must meet the following conditions:

- *Universal*: Present in all individuals within the population.
- *Unique*: Distinguish one individual from another.
- *Permanent or persistent*: Remain consistent over time.
- *Recordable*: Allow the collection of characteristics from an individual.
- *Measurable*: Permit future comparison.
- *Non-reproducible*: Be difficult or impossible to falsify.

9.2.2 Applications of biometrics

9.2.2.1 Financial services

The banking and financial sector has rapidly adopted biometric technology for identity verification. Biometric authentication methods, such as fingerprint scanning or facial recognition, are used to secure access to online banking platforms and authorize transactions. This helps prevent unauthorized access and reduces the risk of fraudulent activity [7].

9.2.2.2 Healthcare

In healthcare, biometric identity verification plays a critical role in protecting patient privacy and preventing medical fraud. Biometrics can authenticate patients and healthcare providers when accessing electronic medical records or drug delivery systems, ensuring that only authorized individuals have access to sensitive information.

9.2.2.3 Mobile devices

The widespread adoption of smartphones has opened up new perspectives in biometric authentication. Many mobile devices now include fingerprint scanners or facial recognition technology to unlock the device or authorize digital payments. This increases the security of personal information stored on the device and protects against unauthorized access.

9.2.2.4 Travel and immigration

Many airports and border control agencies have implemented biometric identification systems, such as facial recognition, to improve the efficiency and accuracy of the immigration process. Biometrics can help streamline passenger processing, ensure the accuracy of travel documents, and detect potential security threats.

9.2.2.5 Biometric authentication

Biometrics allows the identification and authentication of a person based on recognizable and verifiable data that is specific and unique to them. Identification involves determining the identity of a person by capturing their biometric data, such as taking a photo of their face, recording their voice, or capturing the image of their fingerprint. This data is then compared to the biometric data of other individuals in a database. Authentication, also called verification, is the process of comparing a person's biometric data to their previously recorded biometric reference model to determine a match. The reference model is stored in a secure database, equipment, or personal object. This process verifies that the person presented is indeed who they claim to be.

9.2.3 Architecture of biometric systems and operating modes

Biometric systems rely on several distinct processes, namely registration, direct capture, pattern extraction, and pattern comparison. Pattern extraction involves signal processing of raw biometric samples to obtain a digital pattern. Models are typically generated and stored during registration to save time when processing subsequent comparisons. Comparing two biometric samples involves algorithmic calculations intended to evaluate their similarity. When comparing, a match score is assigned; if it exceeds a given threshold, the models are considered identical. As a general rule, biometric pattern extraction and comparison algorithms are proprietary, different, or secret, meaning they cannot be used interchangeably within the same system across different providers. For example, it is not possible to compare the models generated by different products or use one company's matching algorithm to compare models generated by another company's algorithms. A biometric system is essentially a pattern recognition system. It operates by acquiring biometric traits, building models, and then comparing these models with characteristics previously stored in a database. This comparison ultimately allows the system to execute an action or make a decision based on the result of the comparison [8].

9.2.3.1 Architecture of biometric systems

A biometric system is composed of the following five modules.

a. *Acquisition or capture module*: This module measures the original biometric characteristics using devices such as cameras, fingerprint readers, and security cameras. Preliminary treatments are performed at this level for reasons of efficiency and speed.

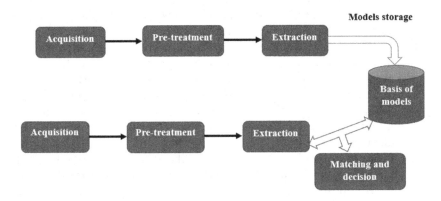

Figure 9.1 Architecture of a biometric system.

b. *Pre-processing module*: This module involves pre-processing and noise attenuation. It applies a series of continuous operations, such as filtering and normalization, to surface relevant and useful parameters.

c. *Feature extraction module*: This module represents the pre-processed biometric data with new representations, or models. These models are obtained by extracting the most relevant features. Ideally, these patterns should be unique to each individual and relatively constant despite intra-class changes.

d. *Storage module*: This module contains all the biometric models of registered users. Typically, the information stored is not the original images but rather a mathematical model of the elements that distinguish one biometric sample from another.

e. *Matching and decision module*: In this final step, appropriate decisions are made based on the application requirements after calculating the similarity between the sample and the baseline.

Figure 9.1 illustrates the architecture of biometric systems, detailing the flow from acquisition to decision-making.

9.2.3.2 Operating modes

Biometric systems can operate in two main modes: authentication and identification. There is also an initial stage before these modes called "enrollment."

a. *Enrollment*: Enrollment is the first phase of any biometric system. It is the stage where a user is registered in the system for the first time, and one or more biometric modalities are captured and recorded in a database. This registration may be accompanied by the addition of biographical information to the database.

b. *Authentication*: Authentication is used to prove the identity claimed by a user. The system must answer a question such as, "Am I the person I say I am?" Technically, the device checks against a code (identification) entered on a keyboard or read by passing a badge (smart card, magnetic, proximity, etc.) to ensure that the biometric sample provided corresponds to the template designated by the identifier.

c. *Identification*: Identification allows the system to verify whether the identity of an individual exists in the reference database. The system must determine the identity of the person, answering a question like, "Who am I?" From the biometric sample provided, the device searches for the corresponding template in its database. Identification and authentication are, therefore, two different problems. Identification can be a daunting task when the database contains millions of identities, especially when there are real-time constraints on the system. These difficulties are similar to those that multimedia document indexing systems aim to resolve.

9.2.4 Biometric modalities

There are a large number of biometric modalities, which can be grouped into three main categories: physiological (or morphological), behavioral, and biological [9].

a. *Physiological*: Physiological biometrics use parts of the human body for identification. This category includes the following.

b. *Fingerprint*: This is the most widespread and oldest biometric process. It is based on the patterns created by the ridges and valleys on the epidermis. A fingerprint is characterized by about a hundred unique points along the ridges, with 15 to 20 correctly located minutiae typically being sufficient for identification. Some fingerprint recognition modules also check the finger's temperature, conductivity, heartbeat, and other biological parameters.

c. *Ear*: Ears, like other parts of the body, present a unique imprint when pressed against a surface. This system identifies individuals based on the shape and dimensions of the external ear. However, even though ear shapes are unique, they grow from ages 0 to 20 and slightly deform after age 50.

d. *Iris*: The iris is the annular region located between the pupil and the white of the eye. This biometric trait is one of the most recent and effective methods. Iris patterns are formed during the first two years of life and remain stable throughout life.

e. *Retina*: Retina-based biometrics is seldom used and less well accepted by the public due to the need for close proximity to the sensor during measurement. This technique relies on the unique and stable pattern formed by the blood vessels in the retina.

f. *Hand Geometry*: Hand geometry is one of the most widespread biometric measurements, involving the measurement of several characteristics of the hand (up to 90) such as the shape, length, and width of the fingers. The technology primarily uses infrared imaging.

g. *Face*: Facial recognition is the most natural and popular biometric method. It involves measuring distinct features in the face, relying less on variable factors like hairstyle or cosmetics. However, the human face changes over time, posing challenges for face identification systems, especially due to factors like expression changes, illness, aging, and other normal variations. Environmental and human factors also play a significant role in the effectiveness of facial recognition systems.

h. *Voice Recognition*: Voice recognition can be easily falsified using a recording. Biometric voice measurement processes data influenced by physiological factors (age, gender, pitch, accent) and behavioral factors (speed, rhythm). These elements tend to be stable throughout an individual's life.

i. *Palm Recognition*: Palmprint recognition is one of the most effective new biometric modalities, based on the texture of the palm. The main lines and wrinkles in a palmprint image are unique, with most people having three main lines: the heart line, the head line, and the life line. Fine and irregular wrinkles around these lines also contribute to palmprint discrimination.

j. *Veins*: The vein patterns in the finger or palm serve as criteria for authenticating people. Using an infrared scanner and an integrated wide-angle camera, the system captures the unique venous structure within a few milliseconds, providing an unambiguous identity verification.

9.2.5 Behavioral

This category utilizes personal behavioral traits and is based on the analysis of certain behaviors of an individual. It involves studying the repetitive and habitual actions of people.

9.2.5.1 Recognition of keyboard typing dynamics

In this technique, statistical analysis is performed on factors such as the durations between keystrokes, the frequency of errors, and the duration of each keystroke. However, this technology is influenced by the physical and psychological state of the person using the keyboard. Factors like fatigue and stress can affect the quality of typing.

9.2.5.2 Recognition of signature dynamics

This identification system requires the user to sign with an electronic pen on a graphics tablet. The system analyzes variations in the pen's speed, accelerations, and pressures on the tablet. However, this technique may not be reliable if an individual does not consistently sign in the same manner, leading to potential access denial.

9.2.5.3 Recognition of gait

Each individual has a unique way of walking, which can be characterized by elements such as speed, acceleration, and body movements. Factors like shoe choice, walking surface, and clothing can also influence walking patterns. Gait recognition systems, which are still in development, use image processing to detect the human silhouette and associated spatiotemporal attributes.

9.2.6 Security of biometric systems

Over time and for enhanced security, biometric systems are increasingly utilized in numerous applications. Despite the advantages they offer compared to traditional authentication systems, biometric systems remain vulnerable to specific attacks, which can significantly impair their functionality.

9.2.6.1 Biometric model: Vulnerabilities and threats

Biometric systems possess several weaknesses, particularly when biometric templates are stored in the database without adequate protection. Among the threats and vulnerabilities affecting biometric models, the following are notable:

a. Risks of privacy violation

Privacy compliance analysis of biometrics-based automatic recognition systems is a crucial concern during both the system design phase and its deployment in real applications. The main concerns related to the use of biometrics include:

- Collection or sharing of biometric data without specific user authorization, adequate knowledge, or a specific purpose.

- Potential misuse of biometric data collected for specific purposes for unintended or unauthorized purposes.
- Violation of the "principle of proportionality," where biometric data is used excessively or inadequately in relation to the system's objective.
- Improper storage and/or transmission of biometric data, leading to exposure to external attacks.

b. Risks of identity theft

Identity theft risks arise when an individual collects another person's biometric information to create a "false identity." Counterfeiting biometric measurements is possible using various techniques. Other identity theft techniques include "replay attacks," bypassing biometric capture by accessing the system using a previously taken image, and "substitution attacks," inserting a hacker's biometric characteristics into another person's personal information database. Unlike passwords, biometric data is irrevocable and cannot be reused once stolen, complicating matters for legitimate users if their data is compromised.

9.2.6.2 Biometric model and security issues

Attacks on a generic biometric system can be classified into eight levels or classes. Figure 9.2 illustrates the possible locations of these attacks in a generic biometric system:

a. *Falsified biometric data*: Reproduced biometric data is presented to the biometric sensor, akin to presenting a copy of a signature.

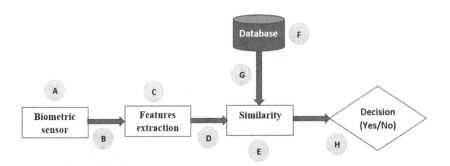

Figure 9.2 Locations of points of compromise of a biometric system.

b. *Transmission of intercepted biometric data*: Old recorded biometric data is replayed in the system without passing through the biometric sensor, similar to presenting an old copy of a fingerprint image.

c. *Attack on the feature extraction module*: This module could be replaced by a Trojan horse to produce information chosen by the attacker.

d. *Alteration of extracted characteristics*: After obtaining data from the characteristic extraction module, these are altered or replaced by other data defined by the attacker.

e. *Replacement of similarity calculation module with a malicious module*: This module could be substituted with a Trojan horse to artificially produce high or low scores.

f. *Alteration of the database*: The biometric model database may be available locally, remotely, or distributed across several servers. In this attack, the attacker modifies one or more models to authorize an imposter or prevent a legitimate user from accessing them.

g. *Attack on the channel between the database and the similarity calculation module*: In this attack, the models are altered on the transmission link connecting the model base and the similarity calculation module.

h. *Alteration of decisions (Accepted or Rejected)*: This attack alters the Boolean decision (yes or no) made by the similarity calculation module. This type of attack is highly dangerous, as even if the system performs robustly, it is rendered useless by this attack.

9.2.6.3 Securing the biometric model

Securing the biometric model is a crucial task in designing a secure biometric system. Before delving into the techniques used to secure biometric models, it's important to understand basic notions of cryptography, which are employed to achieve this goal.

a. *Symmetric cryptography*: Symmetric encryption relies on reversible mathematical functions. It operates on the principle of using a single key for both encryption and decryption.

b. *Asymmetric cryptography*: Asymmetric cryptography, a fundamental aspect of cybersecurity, uses two different keys—one for encryption and another for decryption. Unlike symmetric cryptography, it employs mathematically distinct keys for these operations.

c. *Cryptographic hash function*: A cryptographic hash function is a mathematical function that converts any input string (data) of any length into an alphanumeric string of fixed size, known as a hash value or fingerprint or checksum. Key properties of hash functions include the following:

- *Collision resistance*: This property makes it highly improbable for two random inputs to produce the same hash result. It's computationally infeasible to find a different dataset generating the same hash result given another dataset.
- *Preimage resistance*: Hash functions are unidirectional, meaning that given the output of a hash function, it's practically impossible to recover the original input.
- *Uniform distribution*: Hash results are uniformly distributed in the output space, ensuring that all possible outputs have an equal chance of occurrence.

d. *Digital signature*: Digital signatures are crucial for ensuring information security, providing authentication, data integrity, and non-repudiation of messages. It involves sending a digital signature with the message itself to prove its origin.

Blockchain technology, incorporating decentralization, distributed computing, asymmetric encryption, hashing, timestamping, and consensus algorithms, offers a secure, reliable, and transparent means of storing and transmitting information. Its adoption spans various sectors, including biometrics.

9.3 BLOCKCHAIN CONCEPT

9.3.1 Generalities

Blockchain is an information storage and transmission technology that maintains a decentralized, secure, and transparent ledger in the form of chained blocks with unique identifiers represented by cryptographic hashes. It serves as a shared and immutable ledger facilitating the recording of transactions and tracking of assets. By enabling a selected group of participants to share data without an intermediary, blockchain ensures data integrity through a single source of truth [10].

9.3.1.1 Basic concepts

To gain a deeper understanding of blockchain technology and its applications, the following key definitions are essential [11].

a. *Decentralized trust*: Businesses leverage blockchain technology to ensure data integrity without relying on a central authority. This concept, known as decentralized trust, provides assurance of reliable data.

b. *Blockchain blocks*: Data in blockchain is organized into blocks, with each block linked to the previous one, forming a chain structure. New blocks can only be added to the blockchain; once added, a block cannot be modified or deleted.

c. *Consensus algorithms*: Essential for securing and maintaining the reliability of a blockchain, consensus algorithms ensure agreement among network participants regarding the creation and sequence of blocks. Various consensus algorithms exist, each with its own advantages and drawbacks. Actors in the blockchain network participate in securing the network by verifying transactions and interactions, ensuring the accuracy and immutability of the transaction history.

d. *Blockchain nodes*: Blocks of blockchain data are stored on nodes, which are the units responsible for keeping the data synchronized. Nodes can quickly determine if a block has been altered since its addition to the chain. When a new full node joins the network, it downloads a copy of all current blocks. There are two main types of blockchain nodes:

   • *Full nodes*: These nodes store a complete copy of the blockchain.
   • *Lightweight nodes*: They store only the most recent blocks and can request older blocks when needed.

e. *Smart contracts*: These are self-executing contracts stored on a blockchain, ensuring their integrity and immutability. Smart contracts automate contract execution and eliminate the need for third-party intermediaries such as notaries or judges. They streamline processes, reduce costs and payment times, while enhancing transaction traceability and security.

9.3.1.2 *Types of blockchain*

• *Public blockchain*: A public, or permissionless, blockchain network is open to participation by anyone without restrictions. Most cryptocurrencies operate on public blockchains governed by consensus algorithms or rules. These networks are decentralized and do not rely on trusted third parties. Their defining characteristic is accessibility to all. Bitcoin's blockchain is the most well-known example, although numerous others exist. While public blockchains are secure, they lack the same level of flexibility as private blockchains.

• *Permissioned or private blockchain*: These blockchain technologies operate within a centralized system overseen by a network manager responsible for approving and admitting participants. The designated trusted third party retains sole authority to validate transactions within the network. Private, or permissioned, blockchains enable businesses to enforce access controls over blockchain data, allowing only authorized users to access specific datasets.

- *Federated or consortium blockchain*: Similar to a hybrid blockchain, a federated or consortium blockchain combines features of both private and public blockchains. However, it differs in that multiple members of an organization collaborate within a decentralized network. Essentially, a consortium blockchain is a private blockchain with restricted access limited to a specific group, mitigating the risks associated with a single entity controlling the network in a private blockchain setting. In a consortium blockchain, consensus mechanisms are managed by predetermined nodes. It typically includes a validator node responsible for initiating, receiving, and validating transactions, while member nodes have the capability to receive or initiate transactions [12].

9.3.1.3 How blockchain technology works

Blockchain technology functions as a ledger of transactions, with each block in the chain connected to the preceding one in a sequential manner, forming an immutable record on a peer-to-peer network. Each transaction is assigned a unique identifier or digital fingerprint known as a hash, ensuring trust and transparency. All participants maintain an encrypted record of every transaction within a decentralized, highly scalable, and resilient record-keeping mechanism, rendering the data tamper-proof and irrefutable. Having a single, decentralized source of truth reduces the operational costs associated with trusted business interactions between parties that may lack inherent trust. In a permissioned blockchain, commonly used by businesses, participants are granted access to the network, and each participant maintains an encrypted record of transactions. Any company or business consortium requiring secure, real-time, and shareable transaction recording can leverage this innovative technology. By dispersing data across multiple nodes, blockchain enhances security and availability, eliminating the risk associated with a central point of vulnerability.

9.3.2 Blockchain in different sectors

9.3.2.1 Health

Major pharmaceutical and medical device manufacturers are integrating blockchain technology to enhance access to patients' personal data, particularly in personalized therapies. Blockchain is recognized as a valuable tool for ensuring the traceability of medical products, reinforcing quality control, and combating counterfeiting. Collaborative efforts among hospitals, healthcare providers, and insurers are exploring blockchain solutions tailored to the healthcare sector to facilitate the development of secure and portable electronic health records (EHR). Furthermore, businesses are utilizing blockchain to address regulatory compliance requirements and to register clinical trials [13].

9.3.2.2 Energy

Blockchains are being employed to enhance the monitoring of decentralized energy production and to optimize network and meter management. Companies like Fortum are pioneering the use of blockchain in areas such as electric vehicle charging. Similarly, enterprises like Innogy are aiming to enable peer-to-peer energy trading through autonomous machine-to-machine (M2M) transactions.

9.3.2.3 Trade

In the retail sector, blockchain presents opportunities for process enhancement, particularly in tracking goods throughout the supply chain. Companies such as Walmart are leveraging blockchain to ensure product traceability and to take remedial action in case of supply chain issues.

9.3.2.4 Manufacturing industry

The manufacturing sector is mirroring the retail industry's adoption of blockchain to track products from raw materials to finished goods. There is an increasing demand for transparency in production chains, leading to initiatives utilizing blockchain to monitor every stage of production. Smart contracts are also utilized to automate certain aspects of the production chain, complementing traditional ERP systems. Numerous industry stakeholders are experimenting with and implementing such solutions, with companies offering comprehensive solutions to address these requirements, such as Block Verify [14].

9.4 THE SYNERGY OF BLOCKCHAIN AND BIOMETRICS

The integration of these two technologies offers several synergistic effects that are worth studying at each phase of the electoral process. Blockchain technology addresses some of the inherent difficulties of biometrics and introduces new advantages that neither technology could offer in isolation [15].

Combining biometric data with blockchain technology enhances security and privacy. Blockchain ensures immutability and transparency, making it an ideal platform for securely storing and managing biometric data. For instance, cryptocurrency wallet companies are incorporating biometric features like facial authentication and fingerprinting to bolster transaction security. Furthermore, the introduction of cold storage devices utilizing biometrics, is revolutionizing cryptocurrency security by merging blockchain technology with biometrics.

Numerous research efforts have gained significant importance in recent years, particularly those focusing on integrating the advantages and characteristics of public blockchains into biometric systems due to their high potential and benefits. The amalgamation of blockchain and biometrics can yield several advantages.

9.4.1 Blockchain for biometrics

The integration of blockchain and biometrics holds the potential to yield numerous benefits. Initially, blockchain technology could imbue biometric systems with several desirable attributes, including immutability, accountability, availability, and universal access. It could also serve to secure biometric templates and ensure privacy within biometric systems [16].

- By its very nature, a blockchain ensures the immutability of the records it houses, offering a secure foundation for storing biometric templates.
- Building upon this inherent property, a blockchain enhances the accountability and auditability of stored data, facilitating the demonstration to third parties, such as regulators, that biometric templates remain unaltered.
- Moreover, a public blockchain provides comprehensive availability and universal access to all users.

Furthermore, the incorporation of biometric technology could greatly enhance existing blockchain-based distributed digital identity schemes, among various other potential applications.

Another compelling application of biometrics in blockchain pertains to smart devices. These devices, whether digital or physical, can access a blockchain and execute actions or decisions based on the information stored therein.

Increasingly, blockchain is being viewed as a panacea for myriad issues. As discussed earlier, blockchain technology does offer solutions to challenges encountered in biometric systems, such as template security and privacy. However, it is important to acknowledge and address potential limitations inherent in blockchain technology before seamlessly integrating biometrics and blockchain.

9.4.1.1 Challenges and limitations of blockchains

Despite the new opportunities outlined, the fusion of blockchain and biometric technologies is not without its challenges, primarily due to the limitations inherent in current blockchain technology.

a. Limitations of current blockchains

- Low transaction processing capacity, currently limited to a few dozen transactions per second.
- The design of blockchain necessitates the storage of all transactions within the system, leading to rapid expansion in storage requirements.
- Insufficient exploration of its resilience against various types of attacks remains a concern.

b. Challenges of current blockchains

Among the challenges posed by public blockchain networks for the deployment and operation of biometric systems, several key issues stand out:

- *Economic cost of executing smart contracts*: Supporting smart contracts on blockchains requires payment of fees in cryptocurrency for each instruction executed. This poses a challenge in minimizing the cost of running biometric systems on the blockchain and coding efficient contracts involving biometrics.
- *Confidentiality*: Public blockchains inherently lack confidentiality, as all operations are visible to participating nodes. Preserving privacy involves ensuring anonymity for participants, keeping smart contract logic confidential, and encrypting data, including biometric templates, using cryptographic techniques such as zero-knowledge proofs and secure execution environments.
- *Processing capacity*: Limited transaction processing capacity, exemplified by Ethereum's capability of processing a few dozen transactions per second, poses a constraint for biometric systems. Additionally, varying confirmation times further affect the usability of blockchain for such systems.
- *Scalability*: The requirement for all nodes in a blockchain network to store all blocks poses scalability challenges, particularly evident in public blockchains like Bitcoin, where the blockchain size is growing rapidly. This scalability issue becomes critical for applications such as electronic health records and the Internet of Things (IoT).
- *Security*: As a nascent technology, blockchain's security characteristics are still under scrutiny. Concerns include vulnerabilities to attacks such as the 51% attack, highlighting the need for ongoing research and development in blockchain security.

9.4.1.2 Protection of blockchain-based biometric templates

Figure 9.3 illustrates the various compromise points of a biometric system from 1 to 8, highlighting how blockchain technology can secure points of compromise 6 (Alteration of the biometric model database) and 7 (Attack on the channel between the database and the similarity calculation module). A fundamental aspect contributing to the reliability of blockchain systems is immutability, whereby once a transaction is added to a blockchain, it cannot be deleted or modified. Consequently, the issue of altering the biometric template database can be effectively addressed. Attack 7 can similarly be mitigated by blockchain technology. Instead of transmitting the biometric models themselves, only a hash, utilized within the blockchain, would be sent. With each transaction recorded on the blockchain, any access to the chain would be detected. This approach ensures enhanced security for biometric systems by leveraging the inherent security features of blockchain technology.

9.4.1.3 Analysis of storage needs

One of the main limitations of the integration of the two technologies is the cost of operating (totally or partially) a biometric system based on blockchain. It is therefore crucial to estimate and minimize this cost [17].

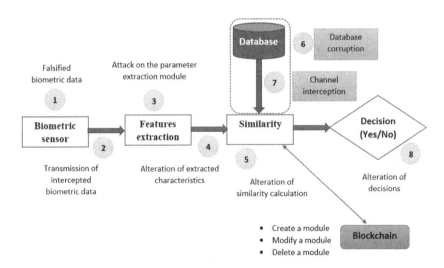

Figure 9.3 Points of compromise of a biometric system and protection of biometric templates based on blockchain.

a. *Complete on-chain storage*: This scheme, while the simplest, is the least efficient and costliest. It involves storing data directly in the blockchain without preprocessing. For instance, biometric templates could be stored as a data structure within a smart contract, forming part of a broader digital identity model. Storage space in public blockchains is notably expensive relative to computation to discourage misuse, rendering this approach generally prohibitively expensive for most biometric applications.

b. *Data hashing*: To address the challenges of the previous scheme, a more efficient approach involves storing data off-chain while maintaining intrinsic immutability. Here, only a hash value of the data is stored in the blockchain instead of the complete dataset. The complete model can then be stored in any traditional external storage system. This approach offers significant flexibility as the entire set of biometric models can be stored in interconnected server farms. However, a drawback is the necessity to ensure the availability of data stored outside the blockchain. Any loss or tampering with this data, though noticeable, could compromise the system's viability.

9.4.2 Biometric for blockchain

Within the blockchain ecosystem, participants exert control over their assets through the private key of an asymmetric key pair that pertains to them [18]. While this grants participants sovereignty over their assets, it also entails the responsibility of managing their keys. Presently, two major challenges exist in key management:

a. Users lack an efficient and secure method to store their keys.
b. In the event of key loss, no effective recovery mechanism exists.

9.4.2.1 Securing keys using biometric data

Asymmetric keys are pivotal in identifying network participants and controlling blockchain network assets. To execute a transaction in a blockchain network, each transaction is signed by the user's private key and verified by the public key, which can be shared with anyone. The corresponding private key must be stored securely, typically within the user's wallet folder. Consequently, the wallet's security primarily hinges on the security of the private key it contains. Access to the private key associated with an account is sufficient to manage and utilize that account. Among the solutions for safeguarding wallets containing sensitive information like financial and medical data is the utilization of biometric data.

9.4.2.2 Encryption and decryption of private keys using fingerprints

Employing traditional symmetric encryption methods like Data Encryption Standard (DES) involves using the same key for both encryption and decryption. However, fingerprints, being unique biometric traits, offer robust identification compared to conventionally chosen access codes. They can be utilized to generate the key for symmetric encryption. The process involves initially creating a symmetric key (hash) using the owner's fingerprint data and subsequently using this key to encrypt the private key. During decryption, if the generated key matches the one produced in the recording phase, the encrypted private key can be decrypted using the same symmetric algorithm and generated key used in encryption [19].

9.5 CONCLUSION

The convergence of biometrics and blockchain signifies a substantial progression in digital security and identity management. Biometrics provides robust authentication solutions by harnessing unique and difficult-to-falsify physical characteristics. However, it also raises concerns regarding privacy and the safeguarding of personal data. Blockchain, with its principles of decentralization, immutability, and transparency, introduces an additional layer of security and integrity to biometric systems. Integrating biometrics into blockchain networks not only fortifies authentication mechanisms but also ensures the preservation of biometric data from alteration or compromise. This synergy opens avenues for innovative applications across various sectors, including finance, healthcare, and utilities, where trust and security hold paramount importance.

REFERENCES

[1]   M. Ouaissa, and M. Ouaissa, "Cyber security issues for IoT based smart grid infrastructure," In IOP Conference Series: Materials Science and Engineering, IOP Publishing. vol. 937, no. 1, p. 012001. 2020.

[2]   S. Dargan, and M. Kumar, "A comprehensive survey on the biometric recognition systems based on physiological and behavioral modalities," *Expert Systems with Applications*, vol. 143, p. 113114, 2020.

[3]   B. K. Mohanta, D. Jena, S. S. Panda, and S. Sobhanayak, "Blockchain technology: A survey on applications and security privacy challenges," *Internet of Things*, vol. 8, p. 100107, 2019.

[4]   H. Guo, and X. Yu, "A survey on blockchain technology and its security." *Blockchain: Research and Applications*, vol. 3, no. 2, p. 100067, 2022.

[5]   M. Ouaissa, A. Rhattoy, and I. Chana, "New security level of authentication and key agreement protocol for the IoT on LTE mobile networks," In 2018 6th International Conference on Wireless Networks and Mobile Communications (WINCOM), p. 1–6, IEEE, 2018.

[6] M. Ouaissa, M. Ouaissa, and A. Rhattoy, "An efficient and secure authentication and key agreement protocol of LTE mobile network for an IoT system," *International Journal of Intelligent Engineering and Systems*, vol. 12, no.4, p. 212–222, 2019.

[7] S. A. Abdulrahman, and B. Alhayani, "A comprehensive survey on the biometric systems based on physiological and behavioural characteristics," *Materials Today: Proceedings*, vol. 80, p. 2642–2646, 2023.

[8] V. J. Rathod, N. C. Iyer, and S. M. Meena, "A survey on fingerprint biometric recognition system," In 2015 International Conference on Green Computing and Internet of Things (ICGCIoT), p. 323–326, IEEE, 2015.

[9] S. Sghaier, M. Krichen, A. O. Elfakki, M. Almutiq, M. Ouaissa, an M. Ouaissa, "Biometric Recognition Systems: A Short Survey," In International Conference on Advances in Communication Technology and Computer Engineering, pp. 557–568, Cham: Springer Nature Switzerland, 2023.

[10] M. Krichen, M. Ammi, A. Mihoub, and M. Almutiq, "Blockchain for modern applications: A survey," *Sensors*, vol. 22, no. 14, p. 5274, 2022.

[11] A. Ghosh, S. Gupta, A. Dua, and N. Kumar, "Security of cryptocurrencies in blockchain technology: State-of-art, challenges and future prospects," *Journal of Network and Computer Applications*, vol. 163, p. 102635, 2020.

[12] S. Sharma, and R. Dwivedi, "A survey on blockchain deployment for biometric systems," IET Blockchain, 2024, 4, no. 2, p. 124–151.

[13] P. Pawar, N. Parolia, S. Shinde, T. O. Edoh, and M. Singh, "eHealthChain— a blockchain-based personal health information management system," *Annals of Telecommunications*, vol. 77, no. 1, p. 33–45, 2022.

[14] F. A. Reegu, M. O. Al-Khateeb, W. A. Zogaan, M. R. Al-Mousa, S. Alam, and I. Al-Shourbaji, "Blockchain-based framework for interoperable electronic health record," *Annals of the Romanian Society for Cell Biology*, p. 6486–6495, 2021.

[15] A. Singh, R. K. Dhanaraj, M. A. Ali, B. Balusamy, and V. Sharma, "Blockchain technology in biometric database system," In 2022 3rd International Conference on Computation, Automation and Knowledge Management (ICCAKM), p. 1–6, IEEE, 2022.

[16] S. H. G. Salem, A. Y. Hassan, M. S. Moustafa, and M. N. Hassan, "Blockchain-based biometric identity management," *Cluster Computing*, p. 1–12, 2023.

[17] Lee, Y. K., and Jeong, J. (2021). Securing biometric authentication system using blockchain. *ICT Express*, 7(3), 322–326.

[18] E. Barka, M. Al Baqari, C. A. Kerrache, and J. Herrera-Tapia, "Implementation of a biometric-based blockchain system for preserving privacy, security, and access control in healthcare records," *Journal of Sensor and Actuator Networks*, vol. 11, no. 4, p. 85, 2022.

[19] M. Al Baqari, and E. Barka, "Biometric-based blockchain EHR system (BBEHR)," In 2020 International Wireless Communications and Mobile Computing (IWCMC), p. 2228–2234, IEEE, 2020.

Chapter 10

Exploring the integration of artificial intelligence and blockchain for enhanced face detection and human tracking in IoT

Oussama Lachihab, My Ahmed El Kiram, and Latifa Er-rajy

10.1 INTRODUCTION

Recent advancements in artificial intelligence (AI) have spurred revolutionary strides in face detection and human tracking technologies. These AI-based systems have become fundamental tools in a variety of applications, from security and surveillance to personalized user experiences in smart environments. The capacity of AI-driven algorithms to analyze and comprehend complex visual data is rapidly transforming Internet of Things ecosystems, enabling them to become more responsive and intelligent. We begin by examining the foundational role of AI in modern detection and tracking applications, highlighting its ability to revolutionize object detection and tracking algorithms. We then discuss the evolution of traditional methods in face detection and the significant advancements brought about by AI-driven techniques, such as deep learning approaches with convolutional neural networks (CNNs). Furthermore, we delve into the concept of hybrid architectures, which combine algorithms with deep learning to achieve superior performance and efficiency. We also explore the role of Edge AI in bringing real-time analytics and decision-making to the edge of the network, a crucial capability for IoT applications requiring immediate responses to detected events. We discuss how blockchain technology enhances the security and trustworthiness of IoT-based detection and tracking systems. By ensuring data integrity and providing a decentralized and tamper-proof ledger for transaction verification, blockchain addresses key security challenges in IoT environments. Overall, this chapter aims to provide a comprehensive overview of the integration of AI and blockchain technologies for enhanced face detection and human tracking in IoT environments. By examining the latest research and experimental findings, this work aims to demonstrate how AI can push the envelope in visual object recognition, offering more reliable and efficient solutions.

DOI: 10.1201/9781003497585-10

10.2 ARTIFICIAL INTELLIGENCE IN FACE DETECTION AND HUMAN TRACKING

10.2.1 Object detection

Object detection is a fundamental task in computer vision that involves identifying instances of a predefined set of object classes (e.g., people, bikes, animals) and indicating the location of each detected object in the image with a bounding box. It's crucial for various applications such as intelligent surveillance, autonomous driving, and medical imaging. Traditional methods, relying on handcrafted features like HOG [12] and SIFT [28] have limitations in adaptability and generalization. The advent of deep learning has revolutionized object detection, with models categorized into regression/classification-based and region-proposal-based methods. Object detection models can be categorized into three main types based on their underlying methodologies.

1. Conventional image processing techniques are traditional approaches to object detection that often rely on handcrafted features and classical machine learning algorithms. Techniques such as edge detection and histogram of oriented gradients (HOG) have been employed to detect facial features and human figures in images or video streams.
2. Two-stage deep learning algorithms: The adoption of deep learning in object detection has led to the development of two-stage algorithms. Various models, such as R-CNN, fast R-CNN, faster R-CNN, mask R-CNN, and mesh R-CNN, are among the most popular and commonly used two-stage object detection algorithms [30]. These models typically involve a regional proposal mechanism followed by object classification, achieving higher accuracy but at the expense of increased computational complexity.
3. Stage deep learning algorithms, including models like YOLO, RetinaNet, and SSDs, have gained prominence for their speed and competitive accuracy in object detection tasks. These models adopt a single-stage approach, prioritizing real-time processing while maintaining satisfactory precision levels [40]. Object detection primarily relies on two approaches: CNN-based and transformer-based methods [41].

Object detection: Transformer-based architecture. Carion et al. [8] introduce a framework called DEtection TRansformer (DETR), which simplifies the object detection pipeline by treating the task as a direct set prediction problem, eliminating the need for hand-designed components like non-maximum suppression or anchor generation. Object Detection with Transformers [33] provides a comprehensive review of 21 recently proposed advancements in the original DETR model, including modifications to the backbone structure, query design strategies, and refinements to attention mechanisms.

"Toward transformer-based object detection" [5]: This work investigates the application of vision transformers as a backbone for common detection task heads, proposing the ViT-FRCNN model and demonstrating its properties and performance.

A novel transformer-based adaptive object detection method [36] addresses the limitations of traditional CNN models in capturing global information by introducing transformer-based architectures like DaViT. By combining spatial window attention and channel group attention, the method successfully captures both local and global features, enhancing object detection accuracy.

Vision Mamba (Vim), a recent vision backbone model that leverages the bidirectional state–space model for efficient visual representation learning. This means that Vim can effectively process and understand visual information, making it suitable for tasks like object detection, image classification, and more. Efficient modeling power and hardware-aware design position it as a next-generation vision backbone with great potential for object detection and various computer vision applications [43].

In summary, one- and two-stage models offer distinct benefits. The two-stage algorithm offers high accuracy, but it is slower due to the time required for the selective search algorithm during detection. On the other hand, one-stage algorithms prioritize speed over accuracy [40]. Transformers aim to balance these aspects by providing a more unified and streamlined approach to object detection but often require longer training times to converge compared to one and two-stage models [3].

Vim's hardware-aware design enables faster inference speeds and lower memory usage compared to vision transformers (ViTs) when processing high-resolution images.

10.2.2 Traditional methods in face detection

10.2.2.1 Active shape models

Active shape models (ASMs) are statistical models designed to interpret the shape of objects within images. They were first introduced by Cootes et al. in the early 1990s as a method to locate and recognize objects whose shapes can vary in a predictable manner. ASMs are a prime example of the feature-based approach. There are generally three main types of ASMs such as Snakes, point distribution model (PDM), and deformable templates.

Snakes, also known as active contour models, are energy-minimizing splines guided by external forces. They are particularly designed to adapt to the approximate shape of the boundary, allowing for a degree of flexibility in detecting features within an image. Snakes were first proposed by Kass et al. in 1987 [23]. They are commonly used to localize the boundaries of the head [32].

Point distribution model (PDM) is a statistical model developed by Erikand Lows [44]. It relies on landmark points to represent the shape of an object, which are then analyzed using statistical methods to understand the correlation of movement among these points.

PDMs play a crucial role in building ASMs and find extensive application in face detection. Deformable part models were introduced by Felzenszwalb et al. [45] as an effective approach for object detection, including face detection. DPM leverages several key characteristics to improve detection accuracy. Parts representation corresponds to facial features like eyes, nose, and mouth, with each part represented using low-level features such as histogram of oriented gradients (HOG) to capture local information. DPM also captures spatial relationships between these parts, understanding how they are arranged relative to each other. This is crucial for handling variations in pose, lighting conditions, and occlusion, which are common challenges in face detection. DPM constructs a structure model that combines the root model (representing the overall object, e.g., the face) and part models (representing individual parts). This combination allows DPM to handle complex object structures and deformations.

Deformable template matching (DTM) is categorized as an active shape model due to its ability to actively deform the predefined boundaries to conform to a given face. Template matching is a method used to compare images with a template image in order to find highly similar (matching) patterns. In addition to delineating the face boundary, the extraction of other facial features such as the eyes, mouth, eyebrows, nose, and ears is a critical task in the face detection process. The concept of "snakes" was advanced by Blake and Yuille in 1992 [46], where they integrated information from the eyes as a global feature to enhance the extraction process. While the conventional template-based approach is suitable for detecting faces with rigid shapes, it encounters challenges when faced with faces of varying shapes. DTM addresses this limitation by adapting to the diverse shapes of faces, making it particularly effective for non-rigid face shapes [17].

10.2.2.2 Low-level analysis

Low-level analysis in face detection refers to the preliminary phase of the detection process, where algorithms sift through basic image elements—pixels, edges, and color gradients—to discern patterns or features indicative of a human face. Unlike high-level analysis that involves a more abstract recognition of facial features (eyes, nose, mouth), low-level analysis is concerned with extracting basic or fundamental visual information from an image. In the context of detecting faces, low-level analysis involves identifying simple visual cues or features that are characteristic of faces, such as edges, skin colors, textures, and shapes.

Skin color-based analysis is a crucial feature of human faces, offering several advantages for tracking and detection. The uniform color of human skin distinguishes it from many objects, making it resistant to variations in facial patterns. Algorithms for skin detection based on color histograms and thresholds in YCbCr and HSV color spaces are discussed [27].

1. RGB color model is the basic color model used for detecting skin color, but it has limitations in distinguishing skin-colored regions accurately.
2. HSV color model provides a better representation for skin color discrimination, particularly in low saturation situations.
3. YCbCr color model is used for skin color clustering as it is less sensitive to luminosity changes.
4. CIELAB color model is a perceptually uniform color scale that can be used for comparing color values across different devices and environments.

Motion-based analysis can be used to locate moving objects, including faces, in video sequences. Gray scale-based analysis, dark facial features like eyebrows and lips can be detected using local gray minima within segmented facial regions. Edge-based analysis, face detection based on edges involves detecting facial features by analyzing line drawings or edge images of faces.

10.2.2.3 Feature analysis

Feature-based analysis stands out for its precision in detecting facial features, allowing for the accurate localization of faces within images. Its ability to decompose the face into features makes it robust against partial occlusions and variations in facial expression, pose, and orientation.

Feature searching involves some techniques where distinctive and identifiable characteristics or key points of a face such as edges, contours, textures, or specific facial features like the eyes, nose, and mouth are extracted from images. These unique attributes serve as critical markers to locate, identify, and differentiate faces within an image or across multiple images. The process involves analyzing these facial features in detail to perform tasks such as face detection, recognizing a person, tracking facial movements, or identifying facial expressions. Viola–Jones algorithm is a boosted cascade of classifiers, a powerful technique used in object detection popularized by Viola and Jones for face detection [38]. It combines the efficiency of simple features with the effectiveness of boosting to create a robust and computationally efficient method for detecting objects in images or video streams. The technique works by breaking down the detection process into a series of stages, starting with Haar features that are utilized to capture characteristic properties common to human faces, such as variations in intensity between the eye and nose regions. These features are computed using Haar basis functions, providing a digital representation of image features.

Integral images are then generated, consolidating the information from neighboring rectangles into a single image representation. This integration process significantly accelerates subsequent computations. After that, the Adaboost algorithm is used to train a classifier. Adaboost helps choose important visual features from many possible ones, making the classifier more accurate.

The final step involves cascading classifiers, where a series of classifiers are combined. This cascading process efficiently filters out background windows, enabling more focused computation on regions resembling the object of interest, such as a human face.

10.2.3 Tracking algorithms

10.2.3.1 Kalman filters

Tracking algorithms are fundamental in numerous fields, such as robotics, autonomous vehicles, aerospace, and surveillance. Among these, the Kalman filter stands out as one of the most and widely used estimation methods.

The Kalman filter, introduced by Rudolf Emil Kalman to address the linear filtering problem in aircraft and aviation (Rudolph, Citation1960), is a recursive algorithm used for estimating the state of a linear dynamic system from a series of noisy measurements. It is often described using the framework of state–space equations. These equations represent the evolution of the system's state over time, taking into account both the system dynamics and the influence of noise.

The system dynamics are modeled as a linear time-invariant dynamic system represented by the state–space equations:

$$x_{k+1} = Ax_k + Bu_k + wk$$

$$y_k = Cx_k + v_k$$

where x_k is the state of the system at time k, y_k is the observation at time k, u_k is the control input at time k, and w_k and v_k are zero-mean white Gaussian noise processes representing process and measurement noise, respectively. The matrices A, B, and C define the system dynamics.

In the context of tracking individuals across frames, the Kalman filter predicts the position and size of objects (e.g., people) in upcoming frames recursively. This implies that to compute the current state estimate, only the estimated state from the previous time step and the current measurement are required. Here is an overview of how a recursive algorithm such as the Kalman filter supports people tracking across frames:

Initialization: The Kalman filter is initialized with a state vector containing some parameters that can vary depending on the specific implementation and tracking requirements, These parameters include the x and y coordinates for position, providing information about the object's current location within the frame, as well as velocity parameters for the object's speed in the x and y directions, aiding in predicting its future position based on its current velocity. Acceleration parameters, if included, account for changes in velocity over time, providing a more dynamic representation of the object's motion. Size parameters, such as the width and height of the object or bounding box, can be included to track changes in size, which can help distinguish between different objects in the scene. Additionally, other parameters like angular orientation, angular velocity, or higher-order motion models can be added based on specific tracking requirements, offering more detailed information about the object's motion and improving tracking accuracy.

The Kalman filter operates through several key steps to track a person in a video sequence. First, it performs state prediction, where the next state of the person is predicted using a state transition matrix based on the current state. This prediction provides the anticipated coordinates and dimensions of the person in the next frame. Upon identifying persons in the next frame, a measurement update is conducted using a measurement equation, which incorporates the measured coordinates, the person's width, and white Gaussian noise with diagonal variance. To handle noisy measurements, the Kalman filter prioritizes the prediction if the measurements deviate significantly from the predicted position by a predefined threshold, discarding the unreliable measurement. The state correction step follows, where the position, velocity, and acceleration of the person are updated based on the current frame's values and previous frame data, thereby improving tracking accuracy. This process is iterative, with the Kalman filter continuously cycling through prediction and correction steps for each frame, updating the estimated state of the person with new measurements and predictions.

To enhance the Kalman filter's performance in dealing with nonlinearities, extensive research has been conducted, resulting in the development of methods such as the extended Kalman filter (EKF), unscented Kalman filter (UKF), and cubature Kalman filter (CKF) [14]. These advanced filtering techniques offer improved capabilities for handling nonlinear systems and non-Gaussian noise, thereby enhancing the accuracy of state estimation in complex real-world scenarios.

ConfTrack is a Kalman filter-based multi-person tracking system that tackles noisy detection results in crowded environments. It introduces novel algorithms to handle low-confidence detection boxes and has shown robust performance in various datasets, achieving high scores in metrics like HOTA and IDF1 [22].

MambaTrack, a learning-based motion model that surpasses traditional Kalman filter-based tracking algorithms in challenging scenarios like sports and dance [20]. MambaTrack improves tracking accuracy and adaptability, with MambaTrack+ enhancing performance through state–space model trajectory feature extraction.

10.2.3.2 Mean shift tracking

Mean shift is a nonparametric clustering algorithm widely used for the purpose of tracking objects. The mean shift algorithm is founded on kernel density estimation, a method of estimating the probability density function of random variables. For tracking, the algorithm considers the color distribution (or another feature distribution) of the target to create a probability density function. It then iterates to locate the maximum density, which corresponds to the target's new position in the subsequent frame.

In people tracking, the mean shift algorithm starts by identifying the initial location and size of a person within the frame, often represented as a bounding box. It analyzes the color histogram within this box to model the target's appearance. As the video progresses, the algorithm computes the mean shift vector to the target's predicted location in the new frame.

The mean shift algorithm begins with initialization, where a search window W is established around the target object (person) in the first frame of the video sequence. This search window defines the region where the algorithm will search for the target in subsequent frames. The target object is then represented in a feature space, typically based on attributes such as color or intensity, and the algorithm calculates the centroid of the target object in this feature space. The iteration process of mean shift involves kernel density estimation, which estimates the probability density function of the target object in the feature space using a kernel function. The probability density function is given by

$$p(x) = \frac{1}{n} \sum_{i=1}^{n} k(x - xi)$$

where k is the kernel function and xi are the points in the search window. The algorithm calculates a mean shift vector m that points toward the mode (peak) of the probability density function. This vector indicates the direction in which the centroid of the target should be shifted to converge toward the target object. The mean shift vector is calculated as

$$\frac{\sum_i K\left(x - x_i\right)x_i}{\sum_i K\left(x - x_i\right)} - x$$

The centroid of the target object is then updated by shifting it in the direction of the mean shift vector:

$$C_{\text{new}} = C_{\text{old}} + m$$

where C_{old} is the old centroid and C_{new} is the updated centroid. The mean shift algorithm iterates this process of kernel density estimation, mean shift vector calculation, and centroid update until convergence is achieved. Convergence occurs when the centroid stabilizes within a certain threshold, indicating that it has reached the target object's location. In subsequent frames of the video sequence, mean shift uses the updated centroid from the previous frame as the initial estimate for the target object's location. The algorithm repeats the mean shift iteration process in each frame to track the movement of the target object over time.

By employing a grid-based density estimation approach, MeanShift++ significantly reduces computational complexity, achieving linear runtime and maintaining theoretical consistency. It is up to 10,000 times faster than the traditional MeanShift, delivering competitive clustering quality and efficient image segmentation [21].

10.2.4 Deep learning approaches

10.2.4.1 Convolutional neural networks (CNNs) for detection

CNNs achieve remarkable accuracy in detecting and classifying objects within images, surpassing traditional machine learning techniques. It has critical applications across various fields such as autonomous driving, security surveillance, and medical imaging. Convolutional neural networks (CNNs), with their ability to learn hierarchical representations of visual data, have become the backbone of advanced object detection systems, enabling more accurate and real-time processing.

While there are various CNN model variations, they generally follow a predefined paradigm as shown in Figure 10.1, maintaining a consistent overall architecture. which includes an input layer, followed by a series of convolutional and pooling layers, one or more fully connected layers, activation functions, and an output layer at the end [42]:

The input layer receives raw data, such as images, which are often preprocessed for better performance. Convolutional layers apply filters to extract features like edges and textures, defined by parameters such as filter

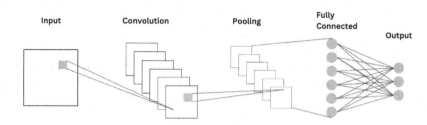

Figure 10.1 A general structure of the CNN architecture for object detection.

size and number of filters. Pooling layers, like max pooling, reduce spatial dimensions and computational complexity by summarizing the regions of the feature map.

Fully connected layers combine features from previous layers to make predictions for classification or regression tasks, adjusting weights through backpropagation. Activation functions (ReLU, sigmoid, softmax) introduce non-linearity, enabling the network to learn complex patterns. Batch normalization normalizes activations to improve training speed and stability, allowing higher learning rates and acting as regularization.

The output layer handles the final predictions, such as bounding boxes for object locations and class probability scores. It uses specialized loss functions to guide training and post-processing techniques like non-maximum suppression to refine detection results, providing accurate and structured output for further analysis.

CNNs have revolutionized the field of computer vision, enabling automatic feature learning from large training datasets. Li et al. [26] propose the use of CNNs for face detection, highlighting their ability to capture complex visual variations and their suitability for parallelization on graphic processing unit (GPU) cores for accelerated processing. The paper emphasizes the automatic feature learning capabilities of CNNs from large training datasets, making them well-suited for robust face detection in uncontrolled environments.

10.2.4.2 Recurrent neural networks (RNNs) for tracking

Recurrent neural networks (RNNs) are distinguished by their ability to process inputs sequentially and maintain a memory of previous inputs via their internal state, making them ideal for tasks where historical data influence current decisions. Over the years, RNN architectures have evolved significantly with developments such as long short-term memory (LSTM) [19] units and gated recurrent units (GRUs) [10] as shown in Figure 10.2, which mitigate challenges like the vanishing gradient problem. These advancements have bolstered the ability of RNNs to capture long-term dependencies

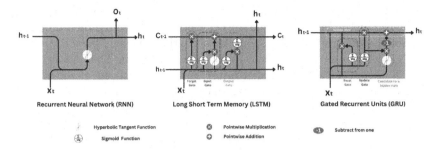

Figure 10.2 RNN, LSTM, and GRU architectures.

within data, a critical feature for modeling human movements that exhibit complex temporal dynamics.

RNNs is an extension of a conventional feedforward neural network that can process variable-length sequences of inputs. Unlike feedforward networks, which process inputs in a single pass, RNNs have a hidden state that persists over time and is updated at each step based on the current input and the previous hidden state. This allows RNNs to model sequential data and capture dependencies between elements in the sequence.

Given a sequence of input vectors $x_1, x_2, ..., x_T$, where T is the length of the sequence, and a sequence of hidden states $h_1, h_2, ..., h_T$, the hidden state C_t at time step t is computed as:

$$h_t = f\left(W_h.h_{t-1} + W_x.x_t + b_h\right)$$

where

- W_h is the weight matrix for the recurrent connections,
- W_x is the weight matrix for the input connections,
- b_h is the bias term,
- f is the activation function (commonly the tanh or ReLU function).

The output of the network at each time step can be computed as:

$$y_t = g\left(W_y.h_t + b_y\right)$$

where W_y is the weight matrix for the output connections, b_h is the bias term, and g is the activation function for the output layer.

The use of RNNs for tracking involves leveraging the sequential nature of data to predict and track human movements in various scenarios. RNNs have emerged as a powerful tool for tracking people in video sequences. We will be examining the application of RNNs in single-person tracking, multi-person tracking, and handling occlusions, highlighting their predictive capabilities and robustness in complex scenarios. In single-person tracking, RNNs excel in environments with minimal occlusion. They leverage historical movement data to predict future positions, adapting to the person's dynamic behavior. Studies have shown that RNNs can effectively learn individual movement patterns and anticipate their trajectories [24].

The predictive nature of RNNs is attributed to their internal memory, which captures temporal dependencies. This allows for continuous tracking even when the subject's movements are erratic or nonlinear [18].

Multi-person tracking using RNNs are employed in scenarios with multiple individuals, where they must distinguish and track several targets. The challenge lies in maintaining the identity of each individual without confusion. RNNs address this by learning distinctive features and movement patterns of each person [24].

The literature indicates that RNNs can handle simultaneous tracking by employing mechanisms like attention models, which focus on specific targets while filtering out irrelevant data. This enables RNNs to track multiple people in crowded scenes [18].

Handling occlusions is a significant challenge in people tracking. RNNs demonstrate an ability to manage temporary occlusions by inferring obscured trajectories. They achieve this by drawing on learned movement patterns to fill in gaps when visual data is incomplete [24].

The effectiveness of RNNs in occlusion scenarios is further enhanced by their capacity to learn and predict complex movement patterns. This allows them to maintain tracking continuity even when subjects are partially or fully obscured for short periods [18].

RNNs are inherently suited for time-series data, making them a natural choice for tracking applications where temporal consistency is key. Their ability to remember past information allows for more accurate predictions of an individual's trajectory in a dynamic environment. The performance of RNN architectures is typically evaluated using metrics such as intersection over union (IoU) and tracking accuracy. These metrics provide a quantitative measure of the model's ability to maintain consistent tracking of individuals over time [6]. Comparing LSTM and GRU models reveals trade-offs between computational efficiency and tracking accuracy. LSTMs tend to be more accurate but computationally intensive, while GRUs offer a more balanced approach suitable for real-time applications [31].

10.2.4.3 Hybrid architectures

Hybrid architectures that combine different neural network models have emerged as a promising approach to address the challenges posed by dynamic environments, occlusions, and real-time processing requirements.

Recent literature emphasizes the use of deep convolutional neural networks for their powerful feature extraction capabilities in human detection tasks. These networks have been adapted to work under constraints such as noise and occluded scenes, improving the reliability of human detection systems [16].

For tracking, the integration of recurrent neural network architectures, including LSTM and GRUs, with CNNs has shown promise. These hybrid systems capitalize on the sequential data processing strength of RNNs and the spatial feature recognition of CNNs to track human movement accurately over time [9].

Babaee et al. [4] present an approach that combines CNN and RNNs for accurate and efficient tracking of multiple individuals in complex scenarios. The proposed method follows a tracking-by-detection paradigm, where a CNN is trained to measure the similarity of two detection boxes, and a graph is constructed for data association using the output of the CNN as edge costs. Additionally, an RNN is utilized to predict the nonlinear motion of people, addressing occlusion and ID-switch problems in tracking. The study demonstrates the effectiveness of the dual CNN–RNN approach through experiments on the MOT2016 dataset, showcasing improved tracking performance and motion prediction capabilities.

The field is moving toward more sophisticated hybrid models that may include transformer-based architectures for their ability to handle long-range dependencies and provide context-aware tracking. These models aim to further improve the accuracy and efficiency of human detection and tracking systems, particularly in complex and crowded environments [9].

10.3 CURRENT STATE OF EDGE AI-BASED DETECTION AND TRACKING SYSTEMS

The advent of Edge AI has revolutionized detection and tracking systems, providing critical capabilities for a variety of applications. By processing data locally, Edge AI enhances system responsiveness and reliability, making it an indispensable component in modern surveillance and monitoring. The integration of AI with blockchain further augments these systems, offering improved performance through enhanced security and data integrity. Edge devices, such as sensors, cameras, and AI chips, are the frontline components in Edge AI systems. These devices vary in complexity from simple sensors to sophisticated AI-enabled cameras capable of performing on-device analytics.

Local processing in Edge AI involves performing AI computations near the users at the network's edge, rather than at a centralized location such as a cloud service provider's data center [39].

The communication infrastructure of Edge AI systems facilitates the interaction between edge devices and cloud servers, establishing a data flow hierarchy that prioritizes local processing while allowing for cloud-based oversight when necessary [25].

Edge AI-based detection and tracking systems offer several significant benefits. A hallmark feature is real-time processing, enabling immediate analysis and response to detected events, which is crucial for applications requiring prompt action [37] such as surveillance and monitoring. Additionally, these systems exhibit reduced latency compared to cloud-based systems. Singh and Gill [35] identify important open challenges and potential research directions in the field of edge computing and Edge AI. These aspects underscore the transformative potential of Edge AI across diverse sectors while acknowledging the need for continued innovation and research to address existing challenges. This report "State of Edge AI Report, Exploring the Dynamic World of Edge AI Applications across Industries" is a comprehensive analysis of Edge AI's current state and its transformative potential in different sectors. It discusses the impact of Edge AI across various industries, highlighting real-time data processing and AI model deployment at the source of data generation. At the end, it covers insights into the challenges and future developments of Edge AI, emphasizing its potential to transform industries with efficient and sustainable solutions. alternatives, significantly improving system responsiveness and user experience [13]. By processing data locally, Edge AI optimizes bandwidth usage, reducing transmission costs and alleviating network congestion. Moreover, local data processing offers enhanced privacy, as sensitive information can be analyzed without leaving the device, ensuring compliance with stringent privacy regulations [7]. Lastly, Edge AI systems improve reliability by maintaining operational continuity even during connectivity issues, with fail-safe mechanisms ensuring uninterrupted service. These advantages make Edge AI a robust and efficient solution for modern detection and tracking applications.

10.4 BLOCKCHAIN TECHNOLOGY FOR SECURING IOT-BASED DETECTION AND TRACKING SYSTEMS

Blockchain operates on the principles of decentralization, immutability, and consensus, ensuring that data stored on the network is resistant to unauthorized alterations and cyber-attacks. The technology's inherent features, such as cryptographic hashing and smart contracts, provide a secure framework for IoT operations, from data collection to device maintenance. Advancements in blockchain technology have focused on addressing the unique security requirements of IoT systems. Lightweight cryptographic schemes have been proposed to accommodate the resource-constrained nature of IoT devices, ensuring secure data handling without compromising performance [2]. Furthermore, hybrid models combining blockchain with other security frameworks, such as recurrent neural elliptical curve blockchain (RNECB), have shown promising results in securing agricultural IoT monitoring systems [29].

Applications in IoT Security using blockchain has found applications in various domains of IoT security, including intrusion detection systems (IDSs) for monitoring and preventing malicious activities, and providing tamper-proof storage for IoT devices and networks [1]. In the context of face detection and human tracking, blockchain can secure the transmission and storage of sensitive biometric data, ensuring privacy and preventing identity theft.

Blockchain technology holds the key to addressing the security vulnerabilities inherent in IoT-based detection and tracking systems. By leveraging its decentralized architecture and cryptographic security measures, it can provide a resilient framework for protecting IoT networks. As the technology continues to evolve, it is expected to play a pivotal role in the advancement of secure and efficient IoT systems.

10.5 CHALLENGES AND FUTURE DIRECTIONS

The integration of artificial intelligence and blockchain technology in IoT environments has opened up new frontiers in face detection and human tracking. While this convergence offers numerous benefits, it also presents a unique set of challenges that must be addressed to realize its full potential. Scalability is a critical concern as IoT networks expand, with AI models requiring substantial computational resources, particularly deep learning algorithms, which may be limited on edge devices [11]. Additionally, blockchain networks must manage increasing transaction volumes without compromising performance. Interoperability is another challenge, given the heterogeneity of IoT devices and blockchain platforms, necessitating seamless communication and data exchange between different systems and standards.

Privacy and security concerns arise from the integration of blockchain, which enhances data security, with AI models processing sensitive biometric data, necessitating a balance between robust security and individual privacy rights [15]. Furthermore, the energy consumption of blockchain operations, particularly energy-intensive consensus mechanisms like Proof of Work, poses a challenge, requiring the development of more energy-efficient solutions suitable for IoT environments. Regulatory compliance, in the context of evolving regulations such as General Data Protection Regulation (GDPR) presents additional challenges for developers and implementers of these technologies. To address these challenges, future directions include research into lightweight AI models that maintain high accuracy while being computationally efficient, enabling broader deployment on resource-constrained edge devices [34]. Innovations in blockchain technology, such as more energy-efficient consensus algorithms and exploration of sharding techniques, will also be crucial. Enhanced privacy mechanisms, such as the implementation of advanced cryptographic techniques within blockchain networks, can provide additional layers of privacy for sensitive data processed by AI systems. Cross-disciplinary collaboration and standardization efforts in protocols and interfaces for AI and blockchain integration in IoT will also be essential for facilitating interoperability and accelerating adoption. Through these efforts, the integration of AI and blockchain in IoT-based face detection and human tracking systems can be significantly advanced, leading to more robust, secure, and efficient solutions.

10.6 CONCLUSION

This chapter has examined the face detection and human tracking using AI, beginning with object detection, which enables precise identification and categorization within images. While traditional methods laid the groundwork, AI-driven techniques now offer superior accuracy and adaptability. The evolution of tracking algorithms, enhanced by AI, has greatly improved human tracking capabilities. Deep learning, particularly with CNN, has significantly enhanced the accuracy and reliability of face detection.

Edge AI has introduced real-time analytics and decision-making to the edge of the network, which is crucial for IoT applications. Blockchain ensures data integrity and trust, addressing security challenges in IoT environments. This integration not only enhances the capabilities of face detection and human tracking systems but also addresses critical challenges such as data security, privacy, and system scalability moving forward. Further research and development are crucial to overcome existing limitations and fully realize the potential of AI and blockchain in IoT environments. The convergence of these technologies promises to drive innovation, improve security, and usher in a new era of intelligent monitoring systems.

Future research in this area should concentrate on developing more efficient AI models that can operate effectively on resource-constrained edge devices. Additionally, there is a need for further exploration of advanced cryptographic techniques to enhance privacy in blockchain-based systems. Collaboration between researchers, industry experts, and policymakers will be crucial in addressing these challenges and ensuring the responsible deployment of AI and blockchain technologies in IoT environments.

In conclusion, the integration of AI and blockchain in IoT-based face detection and human tracking systems represents a significant technological advancement with far-reaching implications. By addressing key challenges and pursuing innovative solutions, we can unlock the full potential of these technologies, leading to safer, more efficient, and more secure IoT environments.

REFERENCES

[1] Love Allen Chijioke Ahakonye, Cosmas Ifeanyi Nwakanma, and Dong-Seong Kim. Tides of blockchain in IoT cybersecurity. *Sensors*, 24(10):3111, 2024.

[2] Abraham Ayegba Alfa, John Kolo Alhassan, Olayemi Mikail Olaniyi, and Morufu Olalere. Blockchain technology in IoT systems: current trends, methodology, problems, applications, and future directions. *Journal of Reliable Intelligent Environments*, 7(2):115–143, 2021.

[3] Ershat Arkin, Nurbiya Yadikar, Xuebin Xu, Alimjan Aysa, and Kurban Ubul. A survey: object detection methods from CNN to transformer. *Multimedia Tools and Applications*, 82:21353–21383, 6 2023.

[4] Maryam Babaee, Zimu Li, and Gerhard Rigoll. A dual CNN–RNN for multiple people tracking. *Neurocomputing*, 368:69–83, 2019.

[5] Josh Beal, Eric Kim, Eric Tzeng, Dong Huk Park, Andrew Zhai, and Dmitry Kislyuk. Toward transformer-based object detection. arXiv, 2012: 09958, 2020.

[6] Niccol´o Bisagno, Bo Zhang, and Nicola Conci. Group LSTM: Group trajectory prediction in crowded scenarios. In *Proceedings of the European conference on Computer Vision (ECCV) Workshops*, pages 123–225, 2018.

[7] Stevan Cakic, Tomo Popovic, Srdjan Krco, Daliborka Nedic, Dejan Babic, and Ivan Jovovic. Developing edge AI computer vision for smart poultry farms using deep learning and HPC. *Sensors*, 23(6):3002, 2023.

[8] Nicolas Carion, Francisco Massa, Gabriel Synnaeve, Nicolas Usunier, Alexander Kirillov, and Sergey Zagoruyko. End-to-end object detection with transformers In European Conference on Computer Vision (pp. 213–229). Cham: Springer International Publishing, 2020.

[9] Shiyao Chen and Dale Chen-Song. Detection, recognition, and tracking: A survey. *arXiv preprint arXiv*:2203.11900, 2022.

[10] Junyoung Chung, Caglar Gulcehre, KyungHyun Cho, and Yoshua Bengio. Empirical evaluation of gated recurrent neural networks on sequence modeling. *arXiv preprint arXiv*:1412.3555, 2014.

[11] Pinchen Cui, Ujjwal Guin, Anthony Skjellum, and David Umphress. Blockchain in IoT: Current trends, challenges, and future roadmap. *Journal of Hardware and Systems Security*, 3:338–364, 2019.

[12] Navneet Dalal and Bill Triggs. Histograms of oriented gradients for human detection, In *2005 IEEE Computer Society Conference on Computer Vision and Pattern Recognition (CVPR'05)* (vol. 1, pp. 886–893). IEEE, 2005.

[13] Duc-Liem Dinh, Hong-Nam Nguyen, Huy-Tan Thai, and Kim-Hung Le. Toward AI-based traffic counting system with edge computing. *Journal of Advanced Transportation*, 2021:1–15, 2021.

[14] Shuo Feng, Xuegui Li, Shuai Zhang, Zhen Jian, Hanxu Duan, and Zepeng Wang. A review: state estimation based on hybrid models of Kalman filter and neural network. *Systems Science & Control Engineering*, 11(1):2173682, 2023.

[15] Prerna Gulati, Aditi Sharma, Kartikey Bhasin, and Chandrashekhar Azad. Approaches of blockchain with ai: Challenges & future direction. In

Proceedings of the International Conference on Innovative Computing &
Communications (ICICC), 2020.

[16] Ejaz Ul Haq, Huang Jianjun, Kang Li, and Hafeez Ul Haq. Human
detection and tracking with deep convolutional neural networks under
the constrained of noise and occluded scenes. *Multimedia Tools and
Applications,* 79(41):30685–30708, 2020.

[17] Md Khaled Hasan, Md Shamim Ahsan, Abdullah-Al-Mamun, S. H. Shah
Newaz, and Gyu Myoung Lee. Human face detection techniques: A comprehensive review and future research directions. *Electronics (Switzerland),*
10:10, 2021.

[18] Saif Hassan, Ghulam Mujtaba, Asif Rajput, and Noureen Fatima. Multi-
object tracking: a systematic literature review. *Multimedia Tools and
Applications,* 83(14), 43439–43492, 2023.

[19] Sepp Hochreiter and J¨urgen Schmidhuber. Long short-term memory.
Neural Computation, 9(8):1735–1780, 1997.

[20] Hsiang-Wei Huang, Cheng-Yen Yang, Wenhao Chai, Zhongyu Jiang, and
Jenq-Neng Hwang. Exploring learning-based motion models in multi-
object tracking. *arXiv preprint arXiv:*2403.10826, 2024.

[21] Jennifer Jang and Heinrich Jiang. MeanShift++: Extremely fast mode-
seeking with applications to segmentation and object tracking. In
*Proceedings of the IEEE/CVF Conference on Computer Vision and Pattern
Recognition,* pages 4102–4113, 2021.

[22] Hyeonchul Jung, Seokjun Kang, Takgen Kim, and HyeongKi Kim.
Conftrack: Kalman filter-based multi-person tracking by utilizing con-
fidence score of detection box. In *Proceedings of the IEEE/CVF Winter
Conference on Applications of Computer Vision,* pages 6583–6592, 2024.

[23] Michael Kass, Andrew Witkin, and Demetri Terzopoulos. Snakes: Active
contour models. International Journal of Computer Vision, 1(4):321–331,
January 1988.

[24] Chanho Kim, Fuxin Li, and James M Rehg. Multi-object tracking with
neural gating using bilinear LSTM. In *Proceedings of the European conference on computer vision (ECCV),* pp. 200–215, 2018.

[25] Seongjin Lee, Seungeon Baek, Wang-Hee Woo, Chiwon Ahn, Jinwon Yoon,
et al. Edge ai-based smart intersection and its application for traffic signal
coordination: A case study in Pyeongtaek city, South Korea. *Journal of
Advanced Transportation,* , 2024(8): 8999086, 2024.

[26] Haoxiang Li, Zhe Lin, Xiaohui Shen, Jonathan Brandt, and Gang Hua. A
convolutional neural network cascade for face detection. In *Proceedings
of the IEEE Conference on Computer Vision and Pattern Recognition,*
pp. 5325–5334, 2015.

[27] Qiong Liu and Guang-zheng Peng. A robust skin color based face detection algorithm. In *2010 2nd International Asia Conference on Informatics
in Control, Automation and Robotics (CAR 2010),* 2, pp. 525–528.
IEEE, 2010.

[28] David G. Lowe. Object recognition from local scale-invariant features.

[29] Nagarajan Mahalingam and Priyanka Sharma. An intelligent blockchain technology for securing an IoT-based agriculture monitoring system. *Multimedia Tools and Applications*, 83(4):10297–10320, 2024.

[30] Widad K. Mohammed, Mohammed A. Taha, Haider D. A. Jabar, and Saif Ali Abd Alradha Alsaidi. Object detection techniques: A review. *Wasit Journal of Computer and Mathematics Science*, 2:59–68, 9 2023.

[31] Jianjun Ni, Yongchun Wang, Guangyi Tang, Weidong Cao, and Simon X Yang. A lightweight GRU-based gesture recognition model for skeleton dynamic graphs. *Multimedia Tools and Applications*, pp. 1–26, 2024.

[32] Athanasios Nikolaidis and Ioannis Pitas. Facial feature extraction and pose determination. *Pattern Recognition*, 33(11):1783–1791, 2000.

[33] Tahira Shehzadi, Khurram Azeem Hashmi, Didier Stricker, and Muhammad Zeshan Afzal. Object detection with transformers: A review. arXiv:2306.04670, 2023.

[34] Ashish Singh, Suresh Chandra Satapathy, Arnab Roy, and Adnan Gutub. Ai-based mobile edge computing for IoT: Applications, challenges, and future scope. *Arabian Journal for Science and Engineering*, 47(8):9801–9831, 2022.

[35] Raghubir Singh and Sukhpal Singh Gill. Edge AI: a survey. *Internet of Things and Cyber-Physical Systems*, 3:71–92, 2023.

[36] Shuzhi Su, Runbin Chen, Xianjin Fang, and Tian Zhang. A novel transformer-based adaptive object detection method. *Electronics (Switzerland)*, 12:2, 2023.

[37] Doan Viet Tu, Pham Minh Quang, Huynh Phuc Nghi, and Tran Ngoc Thinh. An edge AI-based vehicle tracking solution for smart parking systems. In *International Conference on Intelligence of Things*, pp. 234–243. Springer, 2023.

[38] Paul Viola and Michael Jones. Rapid object detection using a boosted cascade of simple features. In *Proceedings of the 2001 IEEE Computer Society Conference on Computer Vision and Pattern Recognition. CVPR 2001*, volume 1, pp. 511–518. IEEE, 2001.

[39] Jie Yang, Thar Baker, Sukhpal Singh Gill, Xiaochuan Yang, Weifeng Han, and Yuanzhang Li. A federated learning attack method based on edge collaboration via cloud. *Software: Practice and Experience*, 54(7), 1257–1274, 2022.

[40] Hang Zhang and Rayan S Cloutier. Review on one-stage object detection based on deep learning. *EAI Endorsed Transactions on e-Learning*, 7:174181, 6 2022.

[41] Minying Zhang, Tianpeng Bu, and Lulu Hu. A dynamic dual-processing object detection framework inspired by the brain's recognition mechanism. In Proceedings of the IEEE/CVF International Conference on Computer Vision. 2023. p. 6264–6274.

[42] Xia Zhao, Limin Wang, Yufei Zhang, Xuming Han, Muhammet Deveci, and Milan Parmar. A review of convolutional neural networks in computer vision. *Artificial Intelligence Review*, 57(4):1–43, 2024.

[43] Liao B. Zhang Q. Wang X. Liu W. Wang X. Zhu, L. Vision mamba: Efficient visual representation learning with bidirectional state space model. *arXiv preprint arXiv:2401.09417*, 2024.

[44] Hjelmås Erik and Lows Boon Kee. Face detection: A survey. *Computer Vision and Image Understanding*, 2001, 83(3): 236–274.

[45] Pedro Felzenszwalb, David McAllester, and Deva Ramanan, A discriminatively trained, multiscale, deformable part model. In *2008 IEEE Conference on Computer Vision and Pattern Recognition* (pp. 1–8), 2018, IEEE.

[46] Andrew Blake and Alan Yuille, Active Vision, MIT Press, p.368, 1992.

Chapter 11

Education and training revolution

AR, VR, and IoT integration

Sahiti Mummadi, C. Kishor Kumar Reddy,
D. Manoj Kumar Reddy, and Srinath Doss

11.1 INTRODUCTION TO AR, VR, AND IOT

Augmented reality is a digital interactive interface that uses computer-generated perceptual information to improve the physical world. It refers to the ability of technology to superimpose virtual or digital material onto physical reality, which can be viewed through "AR-enabled" glasses, smartphones, or tablets. In augmented reality model where the user's real-world environment is overlaid or blends digital information and objects, the sense of reality is enhanced as the computer-generated matter simply overlies the physical environment. Several industries, including gaming, retail, healthcare, and education, may benefit from this technological advancement, which integrates computerized information into the environment to generate live information, interactive experiences, and dormant visualization.

Augmented reality (AR) is one of the advanced technologies in modern society that has possibilities for use in education. Despite the vast amount of investment and research that has been done in the development of AR, limited literature exists in the area of education. The research has extended to AR research as the results of this technology have proved fruitful in the recent past. AR has been utilized in various domains of learning. Specifically, AR is useful when using a development model that requires the ability to visually depict certain data. AR also cooperates with the manipulation of the integration of the real and the virtual world as well as enables a tangible interface metaphor for the printable object [1].

Virtual reality (VR) refers to an environment that can be interactively encountered in actual and physically presented three-dimensional space managed by a computer. Virtual reality is created through the use of technologies applied to enable visualization and provide interaction of a virtual environment.

The Internet of Things (IoT) is a system of interconnected device objects designed to combine these devices via software, actuators, and sensors that create freedom and information exchange by connecting to other

DOI: 10.1201/9781003497585-11

devices systems and each other through the internet. "Smart" devices may appear from things in everyday life, such as wearable technology and home appliances, to complex machinery and metropolitan infrastructure. The IoT makes it possible to monitor, govern, and automate physical processes long distance by reaching better output, accuracy, and monitoring across various companies such as manufacturing, transportation, healthcare, and smart cities.

The concept of augmented reality first appeared in the 1960s thanks to Morton Heilig—he created Sensorama, a machine that provided multimodal vibrant experiences; it became fully developed only in the 1990s with such projects as Boeing's Virtual Fixtures and Tom Caudell's AR term at Boeing. The progress of global positioning system (GPS)-enabled smartphones in the 2000s allowed the rise of consumer AR applications. Pokémon GO in 2016 became an international hit and presented AR to ordinary people with its gaming and entertainment potential. Since then, the development of AR technology has become fast-paced, providing hardware, software, and promotion to numerous spheres like manufacturing, retail, healthcare, and education.

The word "virtual reality" (VR) was first developed in the 1980s by Jaron Lanier, although some of the earliest known VR ideas came from the 1960s and 1970s, including Ivan Sutherland's "Sword of Damocles" and Myron Krueger's "Video Place." Although VR initially infiltrated the gaming arena, other industries were piqued by curiosity. Over the 2010s, VR made it to the healthcare, education, architecture, and virtual tourism industry. IoT consist of various information-sensing units like radiofrequency identification (RFID), infrared sensing unit, laser shinning, GPS, which collect and provide real-time information, which demand monitoring, connecting, interacting, and many more [19].

Tables 11.1, 11.2, and 11.3 respectively outline the evolution of VR, AR, and IoT. Table 11.1 details key milestones in VR, from Charles Wheatstone's invention of 3D imaging in 1838 to the release of the Apple Vision Pro in 2024. Table 11.2 highlights AR advancements, from Ivan Sutherland's early AR head-mounted display in 1968 to the widespread adoption of AR in enterprise solutions by 2024. Table 11.3 tracks IoT progress, from the initial concept discussions in the 1980s to the advancements in edge computing and IoT cybersecurity in 2024, while Figure 11.1 shows the increase in VR/AR users.

11.2 ROLE OF TECHNOLOGY IN EDUCATION

The advances in technology in education marked a breakthrough that offered new methods of education, substituting old and traditional ones with more accessible and effective ones. First introduced in the early twentieth century, educational radio broadcasts became the first step in the development of

Table 11.1 Evolution of virtual reality

Year	Evolution in VR
1838	The invention of 3D imaging by Charles Wheatstone
1957	Martin Heilig invented the Sensorama
1960	Heiling invented the Telesphere Mask
1975	Computer artist Myron Krueger created artificial reality
1985	The VPL Research company sold VR goggles and gloves
1990s	A system by NASA for driving the Mars *Rover*, video games by SEGA and Virtuality Group, and post-traumatic stress disorder (PTSD) therapies for Vietnam veterans by university researchers
2007	Launch of Google Street View, which used 360-degree cameras and later 3D imagery
2010	Palmer Luckey created a prototype headset
2014	Facebook bought Luckey's Oculus VR company, Google released Cardboard
2015	Snapchat launched Lenses, Samsung released Gear VR
2016	Google released Daydream, Microsoft released its Windows Mixed Reality, Sony released the PlayStation VR headset and associated VR games for the PS4, and HTC and Valve partnered up to create their virtual headset, Vive
2018	Facebook released the Oculus Go and later the Oculus Quest
2020	Facebook introduced controller-free hand tracking to the Quest and released the updated Oculus Quest 2
2021	Facebook officially rebranded to Meta to create a virtual world called Metaverse
2023	Reality Labs by Meta released Quest 3, Sony Interactive Entertainment released The PlayStation VR2 (PS VR2)
2024	Release of the Apple Vision Pro

Table 11.2 Evolution of augmented reality

Year	Evolution in AR
1968	Ivan Sutherland's "The Sword of Damocles"—first AR head-mounted display (HMD)
1992	Louis Rosenberg's Virtual Fixtures at U.S. Air Force Research Laboratory
1997	Ronald Azuma publishes a survey of AR, defining its key characteristics
2000	Hirokazu Kato develops AR Toolkit, enabling AR development using webcams and markers
2009	Launch of Layar, the first AR browser for mobile devices
2014	Microsoft announces HoloLens, a mixed reality (MR) headset combining AR and VR
2016	Pokémon GO by Niantic becomes a global phenomenon, popularizing mobile AR gaming
2017	Apple releases ARKit, a development platform for creating AR applications on iOS
2018	Google releases ARCore, an AR development platform for Android devices

(continued)

Table 11.2 (Cont.)

Year	Evolution in AR
2019	Microsoft releases HoloLens 2, improving on its predecessor with better comfort and functionality
2020	AR applications expand into various industries such as retail, healthcare, education, and industrial maintenance
2021	Snapchat and Facebook (Meta) push AR filters and effects in social media applications
2022	Continued advancements in AR glasses, with new models from companies like Nreal and Vuzix
2023	Apple introduces its own AR glasses, further integrating AR into daily consumer technology
2024	Ongoing improvements in AR technology, with more widespread adoption in enterprise solutions, AR navigation, and entertainment

Table 11.3 Evolution of the Internet of Things

Year	Evolution of IoT
1980	The concept of connected devices discussed by university researchers.
1999	Kevin Ashton coins the term "Internet of Things" during a presentation at Procter & Gamble
2000	Early IoT implementations in industrial and business settings begin
2003	RFID technology adoption increases, fueling early IoT applications
2005	UN's International Telecommunication Union (ITU) publishes its first report on IoT
2008	IPSO Alliance was formed to promote the use of IP in smart object communications
2010	Google's self-driving car project highlights the potential of IoT in transportation
2011	IPv6 adoption begins, allowing for an exponentially larger number of IP addresses for IoT devices
2013	Industry standards such as AllJoyn by the AllSeen Alliance and Thread Group established
2016	Launch of commercial IoT platforms like Amazon AWS IoT, Microsoft Azure IoT Suite, and Google Cloud IoT Core
2018	The introduction of 5G networks begins, promising faster and more reliable IoT communications
2019	IoT device management becomes a key focus, with advancements in analytics and data management
2020	Integration of artificial intelligence (AI) and machine learning (ML) with IoT devices for smarter data processing
2021	Smart city initiatives grow globally, with IoT applications in traffic management, energy efficiency, and public safety
2022	IoT adoption in healthcare is accelerating, with remote patient monitoring and telemedicine becoming more prevalent
2023	Expansion of industrial IoT in manufacturing, logistics, and supply chain management
2024	Ongoing advancements in edge computing and IoT cybersecurity, with more robust and secure IoT ecosystems

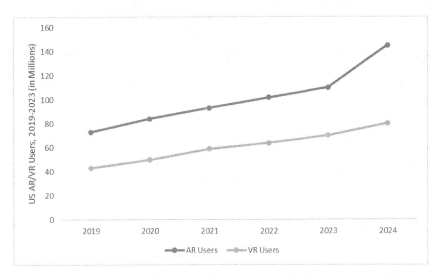

Figure 11.1 Increase in VR/AR users.

educational technologies, followed by television programming at the end of the same century. Computer-based learning was introduced at the end of the twentieth century when schools began to use personal computers with preinstalled software. As a result, interactive lessons and educational games became accessible to thousands of students.

Education in the nineteenth century saw the prospect of new technology such as the rise of the internet in the 1990s helped initiate distance learning and the start of online courses and e-learning. These made it possible for students all over the world to pursue courses offered by prestigious institutions, which means that geographical factors posed no impediment with regard to access to education. Since then, the advancement in technology continued to develop with new concepts such as digital classrooms, online learning platforms, gamification, adaptive learning technologies, and blended learning models being introduced as tools that introduced dynamism and mechanics specific to individual learners. AR and VR technologies have revolutionized learning approaches through immersive digital experiences, interactive environments, simulation, and engagement [8].

11.3 CURRENT APPLICATIONS OF AR, VR, AND IOT

11.3.1 Augmented reality (AR)

The implementation of AR systems has been researched in numerous fields since the beginning of the 1990s: medicine and health sciences, engineering and manufacturing, aeronautics and space, robotics, cinema and video games, tourism and travel, and consequently, social network and multimedia communication, and at the time being learning environments [3].

Retail: The use of AR in retail has changed the way people shop, allowing them to see how products will look like before purchasing. AR-enabled applications by IKEA and Sephora help customers preview furnishings and makeup at home.

Healthcare: Some areas of application for AR are medical education, surgical aids, and patient consultation. Digital images can be superimposed on a patient's body during surgery so that surgeons can have exact guidance while medical trainees can execute some medical routines in a virtual environment.

Education: In other words, AR is meant to improve learning encounters through interaction with material as well as creating an immersive experience. Educational AR apps like Wonderscope bring stories alive via animated characters, which assists pupils to remain attentive to class content.

Manufacturing: Companies also use AR technology to make manufacturing processes faster and more accurate; they digitally overlay instructions and schematics onto physical objects. Workers are provided with direct online guides, hence reducing the number of mistakes made as well as downtime from their machines.

Tourism: In tourism activities, one can enhance experiences by augmenting them with location-based information or immersive storytelling. Guides like Google Lens or Citymapper provide interactive pointers and even give you a chance to see what different landmarks would ideally appear like in case you were there.

11.3.2 Virtual reality (VR)

Gaming: VR gaming is a kind of game that has got the ability to make the players feel as if they are in the virtual world. Some popular platforms for VR gaming include Oculus Rift, PlayStation, and HTC Vive, which provide real visuals and interactive gameplay.

Training and simulation: Numerous industries such as aviation, military, healthcare, and manufacturing use VR for training simulations. Through this method, trainees can practice complicated procedures in a secure environment without putting themselves at risk thus facilitating an effective learning process.

Therapy and rehabilitation: Among other uses of VR therapy and rehabilitation are phobia treatment, post-traumatic stress disorder (PTSD) management, chronic pain relief, and motor disabilities support system. In this case, patients are exposed to computer-generated environments aimed at confronting their fears or difficulties.

Architecture and design: The use of VR is helpful to architects as well as designers as it offers a more interactive method to view 3D models of building plus spaces. When applied in addition to geographic information system (GIS) technologies, the user can navigate through real or model information with a great amount of freedom, yet with great caution because the world presented in VR is represented with a high level of spatial reference. This breaks the inside-click static man–machine interface mode with just buttons, turning it to a dynamic outdoor mode helpful in fields of geoscience research and education among others [7].

Entertainment and media: Beyond gaming, VR experiences involve immersive storytelling, virtual concerts, and virtual tours interactive narratives, among others. For example, Oculus Quest and Samsung Gear VR are some of the headsets used by many people while watching movies or attending concerts in the VR world.

11.3.3 Internet of Things (IoT)

Smart Home: Smart thermostats, lights, and security cameras are IoT devices that enable homeowners to control and manage their homes while they are away. Amazon Alexa, among others, is a smart home ecosystem that comes with voice-activated control for connected devices.

Healthcare: Remote patient monitoring, medication adherence, and preventive care are some of the services provided by IoT gadgets. These include wearable health trackers and smart medical devices, which combine to provide real-time health monitoring, personalized data insights, and improved patient care management. Thus, over the recent past, there has been an escalation in the adoption of healthcare applications that have integrated wearable technologies. They claimed that the medical devices they use to monitor the human body are not comfortable to wear [9]. This is beneficial for developing new medical clothes and comfortable-to-wear devices that include electrocardiogram (ECG), accelerometer, and SpO2 sensors in one product [11].

Transportation: Connected infrastructure, intelligent traffic management, and smart cars are some examples of how IoT technology is transforming transportation systems. Road safety as well as efficiency is improved through vehicle-to-vehicle communication and autonomous driving technologies.

Smart cities: The use of IoT enables development of sustainable urban environments that are effective through use of smart infrastructure, especially producing energy or public service delivery. In this context, we can say that deploying IoT sensors plus data analytics assist in optimizing usage of resources, cutting down pollution levels while increasing the quality levels within cities.

11.4 THE NEED FOR INNOVATION IN EDUCATION AND TRAINING

11.4.1 Strategies for integration

Assess needs and objectives: Decide on the specific educational object-ives for which you want to use AR, VR, and IoT. Additionally, determine which subjects or topics are best suited to these technologies.

Professional development: Educators should be educated in how to effectively use AR, VR, and IoT learning tools. Workshops on their professional growth and ongoing support are required.

Start small: Implement the technologies in a few pilot projects to evaluate their success and address any issues you encounter. The feedback you receive from these pilots will assist you in shortening your learning curve.

Curriculum integration: Develop classroom lesson plans that include AR, VR, and IoT activities. Finally, ensure these plans comply with the curriculum.

Collaborate and share: Encourage collaboration among teachers to share resources and best practices. Create a community of practice to support continuous improvement and innovation (Figure 11.2).

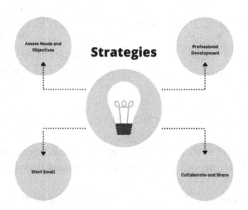

Figure 11.2 Strategies for integration.

11.4.2 Challenges facing traditional education and training methods

Conventional learning practice has encountered a myriad of unique challenges that hamper learning. The are failure of student involvement due to extended use of direct instruction, lecture methods, and rote learning that reduce the enthusiasm of the learners. These features also fail to allow for separate coherent approaches to learning, thus discouraging individuality. Other challenges include accessibility since teachers are physically present in classrooms, thus excluding students who are unable to attend classes or those who have disabilities and need the assistance of the tech company's remote learning solutions. The decline in education quality is due to a critical issue in schools' ability to provide standard teaching materials and technology. In many cases, the improved curricula do not align with industrial growth.

Furthermore, the teacher-centered approach also prevents active participation and critical thinking by the participants. The traditional methods of assessment, like paper–pencil tests and memorized behaviors, do not assess a deep understanding of concepts. Thus the students come out of the classrooms ill-prepared for real-life problems. The traditional system also involves little fieldwork and actual practice, which forms vital components in the training and preparation of employees. *Time tables and classroom schedules*: Fixed time tables and class locations are rigid, and problems arise for students with jobs and other commitments. Lastly, the high cost associated with the establishment of some form of physical infrastructure and material requirements, which are fundamentally required in traditional educational forms, are quite prohibitive. Hence the call to embrace more innovative and socially sensitive approaches to education.

11.5 OPPORTUNITIES PRESENTED BY AR, VR, AND IOT

Despite all the opportunities that information technologies provide when it comes to education and training with the help of AR, VR, and IoT, there are a lot of challenges that are quite similar to the one faced by traditional education system. Endowing learning with these technologies can revolutionize it, making it more captivating and enjoyable for everyone involved, thus leading to better learning results. Bringing learning materials to life through augmented reality could greatly enhance students' engagement and motivation. Through augmented reality, for example, interactive and immersive experiences like virtual field trips or 3D representations for complex scientific concepts found within some AR apps have been developed, in this way making it easier to remember what has been learned as well as making it enjoyable.

IoT technologies will be useful in ensuring that there are no more students who just shift from place to place without everyone getting what they actually need as regards academic knowledge. Instructors can change their teaching approaches to suit individual needs by collecting information about student learning levels and progress through the use of IoT devices. For instance, smart classrooms have Internet of Things sensors installed within them, which enable monitoring of students' interest levels while they attend classes. As such, this information can be used to make immediate changes to the teacher's approach during lessons. By utilizing these data, adaptive learning platforms can incorporate their efforts to provide unique learning paths for each individual student to receive the exact experience that he or she requires in terms of challenge or support.

Online VR classrooms and AR-based learning apps can provide students with flexible access to educational content, anytime and anywhere. This is particularly beneficial for adult learners, professionals seeking further training, and students in remote or underserved areas. These technologies aid in the advancement of a more student-centered approach to learning. Through AR and VR, students can engage in interactive, experiential learning in which they are active participants. The use of IoT devices helps in connecting students for real-time communication, data sharing, as well as increased interaction during collaborative projects that involve peer instruction. These technologies enhance assessment and feedback processes by collecting real-time data and analytics by using the IoT, and teachers can continuously monitor how students' progress and give immediate feedback that is applicable. VR can mimic assessment environments that assess practical skills along with decision-making capacity in an all-inclusive manner better than conventional examination approaches.

11.6 INTEGRATION OF AR, VR, AND IOT IN EDUCATION AND TRAINING

AR-enabled textbooks turn still images into 3D models, animations, and videos that are interactive. They promote creativity and understanding among students. For example, in a biology textbook, AR brings the human heart into reality for students who can study different parts of it up close. Details and illustrations help to explain complex subjects easily and attractively. One way in which students can better understand complex topics such as mathematics, physics, and the sciences, is through the use of AR, which allows for both seeing and interacting with those subjects. One such app for demonstration purposes could show students how atoms are arranged within space in three dimensions, based on distance between atoms, type of atoms, and structural arrangement; alternatively, an AR program might assist pupils in performing real-world tests, like those from chemistry laboratories, to prove existing theories or discover new ones, or provide tools for working with geometric shapes in 3D environments so that it becomes possible to touch them directly on the screen.

The blend of AR, VR, and IoT in education is a significant step forward in the way teaching is done. Students are presented with immersive experiences through which learning becomes exciting and enjoyable, especially for those who do not like books. For example, traditional methods cannot allow people to gain experience in astronomy because it requires traveling through space that never ends. AR involves superimposing digital information to the physical environment enabling students to interact with dynamic contents like 3D models and simulations without leaving their rooms. VR takes this a step further by creating entirely immersive virtual environments where students can explore and engage with complex concepts in a controlled, risk-free setting, making subjects like history, science, and engineering more tangible and understandable.

IoT, on the other hand, connects various devices and sensors to the internet, enabling real-time data collection and interaction. In educational settings, IoT can facilitate smart classrooms where environmental conditions, such as lighting and temperature, are automatically adjusted for optimal learning conditions. A study analyzed that the IoT and cloud platform VR service system for college physical education provides new scientific outlook to the modern construction of college physical education. The IoT is, therefore, a new type of internet that takes place from cyberspace into the physical world [2].

11.6.1 Technologies for AR systems

AR and VR differ in major elements though they employ similar technologies and bonding as well as touching on other points such as computer-generated scenes or objects, interaction, and three dimensions. Outside of the head-mounted display, other components relevant to AR include the computer, input device, and tracking system. Among the many categories of displays used to support and provide for AR, there are see-through and monitor-based categories [4].

Microsoft HoloLens: This device is applied in the learning process to produce realistic and engaging content, for instance, demonstrating simulations or 3D diagrams of human organs.

ARKit (Apple): This device allows for the creation of AR educational applications that could be deployed on iPhone and iPad to allow kids to engage in augmented learning activities such as virtual learning trips and augmented texts.

Vuforia: This enables teachers create mobile AR apps where learning content can be placed over real textbooks, which often come as physical texts.

Merge Cube: It is gadget that, connected with AR applications, enables students to study tangible objects and use their own hands to deal with various digital objects, which can help visualize various ideas that are difficult to illustrate in any other way.

Google Expeditions AR: It enables students to focus on learning concepts in a 3D context, with cases and virtual objects that can be viewed and manipulated through AR.

11.6.2 Technologies for VR systems

Oculus Rift: The development of VR has been adopted in education to help the creation of such facilities as virtual field trips, simulation, as well as interactive storytelling.

Google Expeditions VR: A VR that can be used to transport students from their classrooms and take them for around-the-world education session that can augment the geography and history lessons.

ClassVR: A VR system for schools to teach and learn more in an online environment with the help of a variety of educational materials.

zSpace: It merges VR and AR technologies so that the students can interact with the 3D model and simulation learners get an opportunity to learn science, technology, engineering, and mathematics (STEM) and medical programs.

Labster VR: It offers tutorials in laboratory techniques and concepts and allows students to perform experiments in a safe and real-life environment within cyberspace.

Apple Vision Pro: Apple's vision of a higher end VR, Vision Pro, boasts of the highest pixel density for a VR headset alongside incorporation of AR overlays (Figure 11.3).

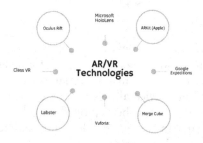

Figure 11.3 List of technologies.

11.7 ENHANCING EDUCATION AND TRAINING THROUGH AR, VR, AND IOT: APPLICATIONS AND BENEFITS ACROSS VARIOUS FIELDS

- *Medical education and training*

  AR *Anatomy*: Learning enthusiasts can incorporate AR applications in learning, where students can place virtual models that are anatomically correct on the samples for hands-on exploration.

  VR *Surgical Simulations*: Students can rehearse authentic surgeries through high-technology simulators that mimic real operating theatres equipped with medical mannequins and equipment.

  IoT *Patient Monitoring*: Some of the elements that can be found in manikins are IoT devices that can actually share physiological data with students; they can work as medical professionals to monitor patient vital signs and respond to hypothetical patient situations.

- *STEM Education*

  AR *Science Labs*: To address the issue of students' lack of access to materials and equipment, learners can use AR applications to perform safe virtual experiments that help them understand reactions and similar processes.

  VR *Physics Simulations*: Educational applications of VR may include enhancing academic content through discovery, for instance, physics students can have force assignments and exercise gravitational body experience in electromagnetic field through VR simulation.

  IoT *Environmental Monitoring*: Technological devices placed in outdoor environment, that is, electronic sensors can be used in the gathering of information like temperatures, humidities, and pollution levels, making it easier for students to use real environmental information when studying science.

- *Language Learning*

  AR *Language Translation*: Another way through which AR can assist language learners is through the use of translation apps using augmented reality to display translated strings over real physical objects, thus associating the object with real-life translated strings.

11.7.1 Cospaces in education

The use of web-based VR authoring tools like InstaVR, WondaVR, and CoSpaces help users design own VR artifacts without any programming skills. This study focused on CoSpaces as a VR environment to create simulations because of its sustained ease of use and compatibility with education purposes. It is important to note that in CoSpaces, the background can range from being chosen from available scenes by the user or create a new one by using 360/panoramic images to use in VR artifacts. They add to the scene in ways that include sprites, objects, gestures, and interactions. When students are done with the design, development, and coding of virtual worlds through the use of the CoSpaces web app, they can access their world through the use of mobile devices with the CoSpaces mobile creating VR in a business and technology, which are both compatible with Android and iOS devices. For visitor experiences to be fully immersive, easy to navigate using a Google Cardboard, or similar VR viewers, the app allows users to visit the virtual worlds. Virtual worlds are the main built-in feature that allows users to create content in Aurora, and it can be shared with others via link or a QR code or integrated into a blog or website [5].

11.7.2 IoT-enabled smart education environments

11.7.2.1 Smart learning

Smart learning environments allow for the use of the IoT to specially design and connect learning environments to provide students relevant and adaptive because information and feedback. These environments use IoT devices, sensors, and other smart technologies that enhance learning through personalization and effective use of the available resources.

11.7.2.2 Smart classroom

Smart classes include the use of gadgets like internet-enabled whiteboards and IoT devices that assist in making teaching and learning a more excellent experience. Such a classroom enables students to collaborate with their counterparts on the same task in real time and access a broad range of online resources.

11.7.2.3 Smart teaching

Smart teaching is done through utilizing technology in teaching, learning, and assessment, as well as the effective use of information and communication technology, learning technologies, and educational data mining. It enables educators to make recommendations or change how they facilitate lessons in response to the requirements of the learners.

11.7.2.4 Smart assessment

Intelligent testing applies technology and statistical approach in the assessment of an individual's performance, flexibly and efficiently. Such

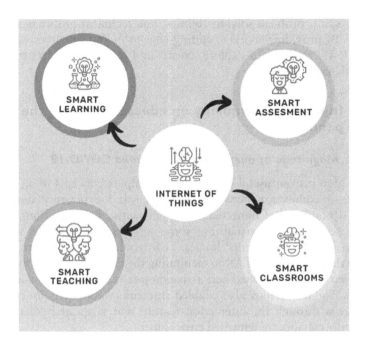

Figure 11.4 Integration of IoT in smart education systems.

techniques involve online quizzes and the use of analytical tools that enable one to receive feedback or be assessed constantly in their approach.

11.7.2.5 Smart university

A smart university is therefore defined as an educational institution where IoT, AI, and digital platforms are employed in the management of facilities services and academic processes. These institutions enrich examination, increase productivity, and engender unique access to knowledge with integrated facilities (Figure 11.4).

11.8 IMPACT ASSESSMENT AND OUTCOMES

These initiatives have demonstrated positive impacts on student engagement, learning outcomes, and career readiness. Educators report increased student motivation, curiosity, and retention of knowledge when using AR, VR, and IoT technologies in the classroom. Students benefit from immersive, hands-on learning experiences that prepare them for future careers in STEM, healthcare, and other fields. Furthermore, institutions and organizations implementing these technologies have observed improvements in critical thinking skills, problem-solving abilities, and technical proficiency among students. By providing access to cutting-edge tools and resources, educators can empower students to explore, create, and innovate in ways that were previously not possible.

11.8.1 Impact of technology on education during the pandemic

11.8.1.2 Magnitude of augmented reality amid COVID-19

AR has been proven useful in explaining complex concepts in an attempt to create a connection between knowledge and experience during the COVID-19 outbreak. Connected classrooms with AR applications allowed learning scenarios and visualizing some subjects, for example, anatomy or engineering from students' homes. Learners had reported that teachers adopted the application of AR in facilitating the design of lessons that could easily keep learners engaged and active despite the absence of face-to-face tutorials. The technology also enabled students to complete project-based assignments through the interaction feature that facilitated collaborative work in the enhanced augmented environment.

11.8.1.3 Magnitude of virtual reality amid COVID-19

VR was revealed as a crucial medium for education during the COVID-19 pandemic as the technology that can provide as engaging learning experiences as possible to replace physical ones. Students can carry out visual experiments, visit historical places, and engage in activities that where strenuously off bound due to the COVID-19 pandemic and its repercussions of social distancing. It also helped in creating virtual classes in which it allows students as well as their tutors to interact in the same 3D mode as the actual classroom setting [7]. Users appreciated that VR eliminated the distant feeling during distance learning or other restrictive online activities.

11.8.1.4 Magnitude of the Internet of Things in the midst of COVID-19

The advent of COVID-19 changed the ways of delivering knowledge in university education, making the adoption of new learning approaches and models indispensable for offering high-quality courses [1]. The IoT also makes it easier to identify and invite various experts to the smart classrooms in real time using such instruments as video recordings and solutions for remote conferencing, which in turn enhances the quality of educational processes. Out of all IoT possibilities in the COVID-19 context, one of the most influential was the use of IoT in distance education, where a large number of devices needed to be interconnected in order to obtain collective data, to be followed by instant correction. The situation that has developed due to the COVID-19 pandemic makes education institutions switch to e-learning tools with the aim of continuing the educational process [20]. Otherwise, in smart learning environments, the IoT sensors also contribute by adjusting light and temperature to make the home learning environment more comfortable for the learners.

11.8.2 Challenges and considerations in AR, VR, and IoT

It is crucial to note that even though concepts like AR, VR, and the IoT have the ability to reform education and training in general, they have some limitations and concerns that one needs to think through to bring them into practice.

Cost and accessibility: The initial investment in hardware, software, and infrastructure can be significant, making it difficult for some schools and institutions to afford. Additionally, ensuring equitable access to these technologies for all students, regardless of socioeconomic background, is essential to avoid widening existing disparities in education.

Technical complexity: Another challenge is the technical complexity involved in deploying and managing AR, VR, and IoT systems. Educational institutions may lack the expertise and resources needed to set up and maintain these technologies effectively. Training educators and IT staff on how to use and troubleshoot AR, VR, and IoT systems is crucial to ensure smooth operation and maximize their educational impact.

Content development: Developing high-quality educational content for AR, VR, and IoT platforms can be challenging and time-consuming. Educators need access to tools, resources, and training to create engaging and pedagogically sound experiences that align with curriculum standards and learning objectives. Collaboration between educators, instructional designers, and content developers is essential to ensure the development of effective educational materials.

Integration with curriculum: Integrating AR, VR, and IoT technologies into existing curricula and educational practices can be challenging. Educators need guidance on how to effectively incorporate these technologies into lesson plans, learning activities, and assessments. Professional development opportunities and ongoing support are essential to help teachers adapt their teaching practices to leverage the potential of AR, VR, and IoT for enhanced learning outcomes.

Privacy and security: Privacy and security concerns are significant considerations when implementing AR, VR, and IoT technologies in educational settings. Collecting and storing data from sensors, devices, and user interactions raises privacy issues related to student information and data protection. Educational institutions must implement robust security measures and adhere to relevant regulations and policies to safeguard sensitive data and ensure user privacy.

Ethical and social implications: AR, VR, and IoT technologies raise ethical and social considerations that educators and policymakers need to address. These include issues related to digital citizenship, online safety, information literacy, and the ethical use of technology. Educators must integrate discussions about responsible technology use and digital ethics into their curriculum to prepare students to navigate the ethical challenges of living in an increasingly digital world.

Evaluation and assessment: Assessing the effectiveness of AR, VR, and IoT implementations in education presents challenges due to the lack of established evaluation frameworks and metrics. Educators need tools and methodologies to measure learning outcomes, engagement levels, and the impact of these technologies on student achievement. Developing standardized assessment tools and conducting empirical research are essential steps in evaluating the efficacy of AR, VR, and IoT in education.

Cognitive overload: The use of AR in learning could pose challenges such as information overload, whereby students are exposed to a wealth of information; multiple device engagement, where a learner is expected to engage several technologies; and multitasking since the task expected of a student could be complex. In other words, it is becoming aware that students have to be busy in AR environments, that is, multitasking. Sharing the above concerns, it has been documented that student's experiences in a multi-user AR simulation left them anxious or confused because they directly involved with unfamiliar technologies as well as complex tasks [10].

11.9 CONCLUSION

The potential of integrating AR together with VR and IoT to advance learning and teaching practices vis-a-vis traditional training methodologies is evident. These technologies provide engaging, interactive, and personalized learning solutions that are very effective in making lesson points clearer to the students and improve their ability to remember them. The history and modern uses of AR, VR, and IoT in education prove the efficiency of these technologies across some learning disciplines. However, it is also crucial to consider some of the problems where the use of these technologies is becoming a problem, for instance, cognitive overload, accessibility barriers, and the need for teachers' professional development.

Although these technologies hold incredible potential, they also pose some fairly unique problems like cognitive overload, accessibility concerns, and the fact that a teacher will need a very long time to learn to use them. These tasks can only be accomplished through the development of an effective strategic plan and allocation of proper resources to build educational infrastructure with a focus placed on the enhancement of educators' professional development. However, there are some factors that should be noted, and they include ethical features like data privacy and equity in the implementation of advanced technologies.

Employing AR, VR, and IoT was not just possible, but necessary during the COVID-19 crisis and its disruption to education systems around the world. Hence, with these innovations, education applications are expected to advance in the future, more improvements in learning processes will be made to allow interaction, inclusiveness, and efficiency. In conclusion, embracing AR, VR, and IoT in education and training offers a path to a more engaging and efficient educational landscape.

REFERENCES

1. Nor Farhah Saidin, Noor Dayana Abd Halim, Noraffandy Yahaya, "A Review of Research on Augmented Reality in Education: Advantages and Applications", *International Education Studies, 8*(13), 1–8, 2015.
2. Yu Ding, Yuhang Li, Lei Cheing, "Application of Internet of Things and Virtual Reality Technology in College Physical Education", *IEEE Access, 8*, p. 96065–96074, 2020.
3. Matt Bower, Cathie Howe, Nerida McCredie, Austin Robinson, David Grover, Augmented Reality in Education"—*Cases*, Places and Potential. Taylor & Francis, 2014.
4. Mehmet Kesima, Yasin Ozarslan, *Augmented Reality in Education: current Technologies and the Potential for Education*, Elsevier, 2012.
5. M Claudia Tom Dieck, Timothy H. Jung, Sandra M.C. Loureiro, Augmented Reality and Virtual Reality: New Trends in Immersive Technology, Springer, 2021
6. Juan Jose Fuertes, Miguel Angel Prada, Jose Ramon Rodriguez-Ossorio, Raul Gonzalez-Herbon, Daniel Perez, Manuel Dominiguez. "Environment for Education on Industry 4.0", IEEE *Access, 9*, 144395–144405, 2021.
7. P.R. Anisha, C.K.K. Reddy, N.G. Nguyen, "Blockchain Technology: a Boon at the Pandemic Times—A Solution for Global Economy Upliftment with AI and IoT", *Springer, Blockchain Security in Cloud Computing*, 2022.
8. M. Al-Ansi, Mohammed Jaboob, Askar Garad, Ahmed Al-Ansi, *Analyzing Augmented Reality (AR) and Virtual Reality (VR) Recent Development in Education*, Elsevier, 2023.
9. Steve Chi-Yin Yuen, Gallayanee Yaoyuneyong Erik Johnson, "Augmented Reality: An Overview and Five Directions for AR in Education", *Journal of Educational Technology Development and Exchange (JETDE), 4*(1), 11, 2011.
10. Hsin-Kai Wu a, Silvia Wen-Yu Lee b, Hsin-Yi Chang, Jyh-Chong Liang, *Current Status, Opportunities and Challenges of Augmented Reality in Education*, Elsevier, 2013.
11. Ravi Kishore Kodali, Govinda Swamy and Boppana Lakshmi, "An Implementation of IoT for Healthcare", *IEEE Access*, RAICS, 2015.

12. C. Kishor Kumar Reddy, P. R Anisha, Marlia Mohd Hanafiah, Srinath Doss, Kari Lippert, *Intelligent Systems and Industrial Internet of Things for Sustainable Development*, Routledge Taylor and Francis, 2024.

13. P.R. Anisha, C. Kishor Kumar Reddy, Nguyen Gia Nhu, *Big Data: Trends, Challenges, Opportunities, Tools, Success Factors, and the Way Toward Pandemic Analytics*, Apple Academic Press, 2022.

14. M Akcayir, G Akcayir, "Advantages and Challenges Associated with Augmented Reality for Education: A Systematic Review of the Literature," *Educational Research Review*, 20, 1–11, 2017.

15. Iulian Radu, *Augmented Reality in Education: a Meta-review and Cross-media Analysis*, Springer, Personal and Ubiquitous Computing, 2013.

16. Dosheela Devi Ramlowat, Binod Kumar Pattanayak, "Exploring the Internet of Things (IoT) in Education: A Review", *Advances in Intelligent Systems and Computing Information Systems Design and Intelligent Applications*, 245–255, 2019.

17. Shahbaz Pervez, Shafiq ur Rehman, and Gasim Alandjani, "Role of Internet of Things in Higher Education", *International Conference on Advances in Education*, 2018.

18. Katie Ellis, Mike Kent, Leanne McRae, *The Internet of Things: Education and Technology*, 2018.

19. Jinhua Liu, Caipang Wang, Xianchun Xiao, "IoT Technology for the Development of Intelligent Decision Support Education Platform", Hindawi, Scientific Programming, 2021.

20. Marinela Mircea, Marian Stocia, and Bogdan Ghilic-micu. "Investigating the Impact of Internet of Things in Higher Education Environment", IEEE Access, 9, p. 33396-33409, 2021.

21. Hannes Kaufmann, "Collaborative Augmented Reality in Education", Institute of Software Technology and Interactive Systems, 2013.

Chapter 12

IoMT-blockchain-based secured remote patient monitoring framework for neuro-stimulation devices

Md Sakib Ullah Sourav, Mohammad Sultan Mahmud,
Md Simul Hasan Talukder, and Rejwan Bin Sulaiman

12.1 INTRODUCTION

The Internet of Things (IoT), artificial intelligence (AI), machine learning (ML), robotics, blockchain, and other smart technologies have revolutionized engineering and manufacturing. The healthcare industry is no exception. The healthcare system has been boosted by new technology, making it more viable and accessible to the general public. Since the 1970s, there has been a substantial change in the way technology is used in this field. Because of the rapid expansion and use of the IoT and Cloud computing, today's generation, known as Industry 4.0, is entirely reliant on intelligent gadgets and their use. IoT is used in a variety of fields, including smart cities, smart homes, smart grids, security and emergency situations, smart agriculture, smart monitoring, and so on [1]. Many sensors are employed for use in the creation of various intelligent wearable devices that aid in the monitoring of human activities as well as the recording of health data. In the field of biomedical engineering, the Internet of Medical Things (IoMT) allows doctors to treat patients remotely. Models must be in place, however, to guarantee that the treatments are carried out properly, considering the security issues connected with the IoMT [2]. COVID-19's recent events demonstrate the need for a remote patient monitoring (RPM) system to be developed because of the benefits of protecting vulnerable patients by reducing the need for visits to hospitals and other clinical settings, as well as reducing risk to physicians by reducing physical patient contact [3].

For many years, neurorehabilitation has employed transcranial direct current stimulation (tDCS) to effectively boost or reduce mental function and learning [4] and it is considered to be safe and widely accepted [5]. Several studies have looked at using tDCS to treat neurological illnesses including Parkinson's disease and other movement-related disorders [6,7]. Such therapies have been shown to be successful in a wide spectrum of individuals with neuro diseases, with tDCS therapy improving quality of life (QoL) in people who would otherwise suffer greatly [8]. tDCS systems require researchers to collaborate with patients in order to achieve the desired outcomes. This is due to the fact that these systems must be able to accurately target and focus on certain parts of the brain in order to stimulate them [9]. Furthermore, tDCS devices can be quite costly, limiting their application to specialized units with available resources [10]. As a result, new methods for conducting tDCS have been developed in order to improve patient outreach. For instance, the approaches described by Sourav et al. [11] and Herring et al. [12] are based on an open source framework and deliver the same medicines to a larger number of patients. However, such systems are still in the early stages of research and are subject to restrictions such as the accuracy of real output currents and the system's effectiveness. Treatment monitoring and delivery are crucial components of any new tDCS system, as tDCS therapies require specialized clinical supervision. More patients might be served by providing remote and cloud-based services for such therapy. This research will look into how clinicians can use tDCS remotely using cloud-based tools. Legal and ethical considerations, as well as the requirement for safe testing and development prior to clinical trials, must all be considered in such a system. As a consequence, these automated remote solutions must be safe and secure, with no risk of patient privacy or tDCS treatment abuse or misuse. This project will look into using off-the-shelf components in the hardware design to keep costs down and make the device more accessible to patients.

Doctors rely on sensitive healthcare data to monitor and diagnose their patients' health. Data acquired from devices or diagnoses of patients is frequently kept in a centralized system called electronic health records (EHR) for later study. Storing all of a patient's data in one location increases the danger of data loss, manipulation, and hacking. Furthermore, storing all data in a central repository makes it impossible to establish transparency. Furthermore, these records should be individualized and accessible to both patients and physicians from any location, which may be accomplished with the use of a decentralized storage system. However, data decentralization must ensure that data is not tampered with and is accessible to everyone in a secure manner. To address all the issues, blockchain, a secured and consistent decentralized storage technology can be introduced.

Nonetheless, integrating blockchain with IoT in healthcare is difficult, and there are just a few researches on the topic. This chapter has a twofold contribution from us.

- We created a hardware prototype of a tDCS device with unique characteristics that may be used at home with real-time guidance and instructions from a doctor.
- To incorporate in our suggested model, we evaluated the current literature that blends IoMT with blockchain.

This chapter is structured as follows. Brain simulation and devices are described in Section 12.2. Section 12.3 discusses the optimal conditions reported in the literature for tDCS treatments. Section 12.4 highlights the specifications of our proposed framework. Finally, Section 12.5 concludes the work with future directives.

12.2 BRAIN SIMULATION AND DEVICES

Brain stimulation is emerging as a highly promising treatment option for various disorders, particularly epilepsy. This advanced method involves the precise application of scheduled stimulation to specific cortical or subcortical targets, using commercial devices designed to deliver electrical pulses at set intervals. The main objective of this technique is to modify the intrinsic neurophysiologic properties of epileptic networks effectively, potentially leading to transformative therapeutic outcomes.

Among the extensively researched targets for scheduled stimulation, the anterior nucleus of the thalamus and the hippocampus have attracted significant attention. Studies have shown that stimulating the anterior nucleus of the thalamus can substantially reduce seizures, with effects lasting for months after the implantation of the stimulator [13]. Furthermore, significant progress has been made in treating cluster headaches (CH) using temporary stimulating electrodes at the sphenopalatine ganglion (SPG), with patients experiencing rapid pain relief within minutes of stimulation [14].

The advancement of brain stimulation techniques has also extended beyond invasive methods involving implanted electrodes. Innovative researchers have developed a transparent zirconia "window" implanted in mice skulls, allowing optical waves to penetrate more deeply, similar to the principles of optogenetics. This non-invasive technique enables precise stimulation or inhibition of individual neurons, expanding the possibilities for brain research and potential therapeutic breakthroughs.

12.2.1 Invasive of brain stimulation

Invasive techniques involve surgical procedures to implant electrodes or other devices directly into the brain to deliver electrical impulses or stimulation. The invasive stimulation devices are listed in Table 12.1.

12.2.1.1 Deep brain stimulation (DBS)

Deep brain stimulation (DBS) is a surgical procedure and neuromodulation technique used to treat certain neurological conditions by delivering electrical impulses to specific brain regions [15]. This process involves implanting a small, battery-operated medical device, commonly known as a "brain pacemaker," into the brain. The device includes electrodes that are

Table 12.1 Invasive neurostimulation devices

S. No.	Name of the non-invasive stimulation
1	Deep brain stimulation (DBS)
2	Epidural cortical stimulation

precisely placed in targeted brain areas and connected to a pulse generator, usually implanted under the skin in the chest or abdomen [16].

The principle behind DBS is to modulate abnormal neural activity within the brain circuits linked to various movement and neuropsychiatric disorders [17]. The electrical stimulation from the electrodes helps regulate the firing patterns of neurons, effectively suppressing or facilitating specific brain pathways, thereby alleviating symptoms and enhancing overall brain function.

12.2.1.2 Epidural cortical stimulation

Epidural cortical stimulation (ECS) is a relatively new brain stimulation technique that involves placing electrodes on the brain's surface, specifically the cerebral cortex, to deliver electrical impulses and modulate brain activity [18]. ECS, a form of neuromodulation, is used to explore brain function, investigate neural circuits, and potentially treat certain neurological and psychiatric disorders [19].

The ECS procedure typically involves surgically implanting a thin sheet or grid of electrodes directly on the brain's surface, just beneath the dura mater (the outermost protective membrane surrounding the brain). These electrodes are used to apply electrical currents to the cortical surface, allowing researchers or clinicians to stimulate or inhibit specific brain regions or neural circuits.

ECS is believed to work by directly influencing the electrical activity of targeted brain areas [20]. By modulating neural firing patterns and synaptic transmission, ECS can potentially alter brain network dynamics and influence various cognitive and motor functions.

As a research tool, ECS allows scientists to study brain function with high spatial and temporal resolution, providing valuable insights into brain organization and connectivity. Clinically, ECS is being investigated as a potential treatment for conditions such as epilepsy, chronic pain, movement disorders, and certain cases of traumatic brain injury or stroke rehabilitation [21]. The therapeutic potential of ECS is still being explored, with its use in clinical settings limited to specialized centers and research studies.

It's important to note that ECS is an invasive procedure and carries potential risks, including infection, bleeding, and damage to brain tissue. As with other brain stimulation techniques, careful patient selection, thorough evaluation, and appropriate post-operative care are crucial to ensure safety and optimize outcomes. Additionally, given the continuous evolution in the fields of neuroscience and neuromodulation, there may have been further advancements or updates in ECS research beyond my knowledge cutoff date.

12.2.2 Non-invasive brain stimulation

Non-invasive techniques do not require surgery and involve the application of external stimuli to the scalp or other peripheral areas to influence brain activity. The non-invasive neurostimulation devices are enlisted in Table 12.2.

12.2.2.1 Transcranial magnetic stimulation (TMS)

Transcranial magnetic stimulation (TMS) is a non-invasive medical procedure used to treat certain neurological and psychiatric conditions [22]. It involves the use of electromagnetic induction to create small electrical currents in specific areas of the brain.

During a TMS session, a magnetic coil is placed against the scalp of the patient. When an electrical current pass through the coil, it generates a magnetic field that can penetrate the skull and stimulate the underlying brain regions [23]. The stimulation can either increase or decrease the activity of the targeted brain area, depending on the frequency and intensity of the magnetic pulses. The structure of it is depicted in Figure 12.1.

There are two main types of TMS:

• Repetitive transcranial magnetic stimulation (rTMS): In this method, multiple magnetic pulses are delivered in rapid succession to the targeted brain region. rTMS can either increase or decrease neuronal activity and is often used as a therapeutic tool for various neurological and psychiatric disorders.

Table 12.2 Non-invasive neurostimulation devices

S. No.	Name of the non-invasive stimulation
1	Transcranial magnetic stimulation (TMS)
2	Transcranial direct current Stimulation (tDCS)
3	Transcranial alternating current stimulation (tACS)
4	Transcranial random noise stimulation (tRNS)

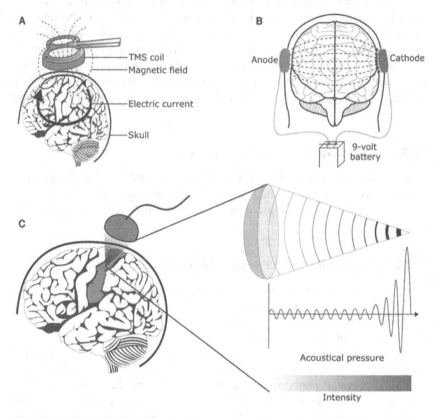

Figure 12.1 TMS of the brain.

- Deep transcranial magnetic stimulation (dTMS): dTMS is a variation of TMS that uses H-coils to target deeper brain structures. It is commonly used to treat conditions like depression and obsessive-compulsive disorder.

TMS has shown promise as a treatment option for various conditions, including depression, anxiety disorders, migraines, and certain types of chronic pain. However, its exact mechanisms of action are still not fully understood, and research in this field is ongoing.

12.2.2.2 Transcranial direct current stimulation (tDCS)

Transcranial direct current stimulation (tDCS) is a non-invasive brain stimulation technology used to modulate the excitability of the central nervous system in individuals [24]. The objective of this stimulation is to alter neuronal firing in the brain, which can have beneficial or harmful effects on the patient. Numerous studies have investigated the optimal testing parameters for tDCS therapy, including session lengths (minutes), current dosages (mA), and session timelines, with the goal of enhancing long-term cognitive plasticity [25].

Bikson et al. [26] established safety limits for tDCS treatments, recommending an average treatment length of 20 min, with a range of 5–30 min. Thair et al. [27] confirmed that the duration of therapy should be determined by the neurophysician's prescription for each session. Consequently, any tDCS system must be capable of operating optimally for up to 30 min [26, 27]. Additionally, studies have assessed whether current tDCS levels are both safe for patients and effective in achieving beneficial effects. Parazzini et al. [28] found that 1 mA does not interfere with the brainstem, making it a suitable dosage for sustained tDCS therapy up to 30 min. Furthermore, Parazzini et al. [29] demonstrated that a current dosage of less than 2 mA had no effect on the heart, indicating a safe current range of 1 to 2 mA, with specific doses prescribed by a doctor [28, 29].

The number of sessions required for optimal neurological and cognitive outcomes is also a critical aspect of treatment. Castillo-Saavedra et al. [30] identified five sessions per week as ideal, while Loo et al. [31] found similar results with treatments lasting between two and eight weeks. However, no additional benefits were observed after six weeks, and exceeding the recommended number of sessions posed a risk of minor adverse effects [31]. Therefore, the platform must include a scheduling or control mechanism to ensure patient safety according to the doctor's orders.

Randomized sham tDCS trials have been conducted to verify the effectiveness of tDCS systems. In these trials, the device indicates to the patient that it is delivering current, while in reality, no current is applied—this is known as a sham or placebo tDCS study [32, 33]. While these studies demonstrate how to conduct sham tDCS trials, they do not detail a device-specific method to automate the process, providing both false and genuine treatments. Previous research has only suggested a random crossover mechanism during a study, randomly assigning patients to sham or genuine tDCS treatments [32]. Therefore, further research is needed to automate the integration of placebo and genuine therapies into the hardware platform.

12.2.2.3 Transcranial alternating current stimulation (tACS)

Transcranial alternating current stimulation (tACS) is a cutting-edge, non-invasive brain stimulation technique that shows great promise for understanding and modulating brain activity [34]. tACS works by applying weak alternating electrical currents to the scalp, aiming to influence brain oscillations and neural synchronization at specific frequencies [35]. This alternating current alters the excitability of neurons, leading to the entrainment of brainwave patterns linked to various cognitive functions. Unlike transcranial direct current stimulation (tDCS), which uses a constant electrical current, tACS targets the frequency of the brain's natural electrical rhythms, enabling researchers to fine-tune the effects and achieve more precise, frequency-specific brain modulation. This specificity makes tACS a valuable tool for investigating the causal relationship between brain oscillations and cognitive processes, as well as exploring its potential in enhancing cognition or treating neurological and psychiatric disorders.

12.2.2.4 Transcranial random noise stimulation (tRNS)

Transcranial random noise stimulation (tRNS) is another non-invasive brain stimulation technique that involves applying random electrical noise to the scalp to modulate brain activity [36]. Similar to transcranial alternating current stimulation (tACS), tRNS aims to influence neural excitability and brain oscillations. However, unlike tACS, which uses a specific alternating current frequency, tRNS delivers random electrical noise across a broad frequency range [37]. This random noise is thought to increase overall neural excitability in the targeted brain regions, making neurons more responsive to incoming stimuli and potentially enhancing cortical plasticity. Although the exact mechanism is not fully understood, it is believed that tRNS may induce a random firing of neurons, leading to a "stochastic resonance" effect, where noise enhances the detection and transmission of weak signals in the brain.

One advantage of tRNS is that it does not require fine-tuning the stimulation frequency, making it a simpler and potentially more broadly applicable technique compared to tACS [38]. Additionally, tRNS may be beneficial in situations where the optimal frequency for brain modulation is unknown or where multiple frequencies are involved in a particular cognitive process. Research and clinical studies are exploring tRNS to understand its effects on various cognitive functions, learning, memory, motor skills, and its potential as a treatment for neurological and psychiatric disorders. Like other brain stimulation techniques, tRNS requires careful investigation and supervision to ensure its safety and efficacy for specific applications.

12.3 PROPOSED IOMT-BLOCKCHAIN-BASED TDCS FRAMEWORK

Our suggested tDCS platform includes cloud communication as a crucial component to ensure both patient and physician privacy and confidentiality. Patients are treated remotely after getting the specialty gadget, and doctors deal with patients remotely via video conference, according to studies [39]. Despite the fact that this framework provided a way to provide

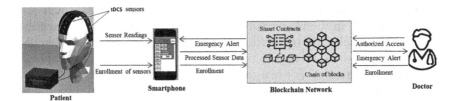

Figure 12.2 Proposed framework for IoMT-blockchain-based neuro-stimulation system.

a patient's needed dosage in accordance with existing tDCS safety rules and recommendations, [5,26] it did not deliver a guideline for grasping real-time data about individual treatment parameters or details regarding patient's conditions. It also doesn't go over further safety features like the device's ability to administer the right amount to the patient or the doctor's ability to operate it remotely. This research presents a unique IoMT-blockchain-based architecture for bi-directional communication between a patient's tDCS device held remotely (such as at home) and a physician's software interface. Figure 12.2 demonstrates the treatment process in the proposed tDCS framework.

Patients and doctors are the two sorts of users who connect to the system via their cell phones. The system contains all of the components of a distributed network, with the exception of a blockchain network at the network layer, which offers all of the distributed ledger technology's capabilities.

12.3.1 Components of the proposed tDCS framework

The components of this proposed framework are briefly explained in this section.

Patients: Each patient will become a node in the network. To read health data, various IoT gadgets will be implanted on their bodies. The data from the sensors will be collected and processed by a mobile app on the patient's smartphone before being sent to the network. As a result, in our system, the mobile app may be thought of as a virtual patient.

Doctors: Doctors are registered individuals who are in charge of monitoring and treating the patients in the system.

Blockchain network: The system will have a blockchain network that will connect all of the system's components. To be included in this network, all of the nodes in it must be confirmed. Because the data must be accessible to everybody, the network will be peer-to-peer, and the blockchain will be permissioned. The network is devoid of rogue nodes thanks to permissioned blockchain. Because there is no rogue node in the system, the Practical

Byzantine Fault Tolerance consensus process should be used to ensure the legitimacy of each transaction in the network. Healthcare data will not be directly kept in the blockchain; rather, data storage and access will be recorded as blockchain transactions. The patients' processed data should be saved on a cloud server. To provide safe data access, all users should have digital signatures. For real-time monitoring, each transaction must be coupled with many smart contracts. They will be activated in response to data values and peer behavior.

Cloud storage: Because monitoring data is acquired on a continual basis and must be retained in the system, the amount of healthcare data will grow with time. If the data is stored on a blockchain ledger, the devices at the user's end will require a large amount of storage. Furthermore, if we wish to store data in the blockchain, a node's disconnection may result in data loss. As a result, cloud storage may be used to store actual data, with the blockchain network storing the link to the data in the cloud server as part of the transaction.

12.3.2 Operations in the framework

The tDCS architecture we propose focuses on continuously reading health data, storing it, and notifying authorized people in the event of an emergency. As a result, we can highlight three key processes that must be completed within the constraints.

i. *Doctors' registration and assignment:* Patients and doctors will request registration providing all the information to the hospital. Then, the hospital authority will validate them using a defined smart contract in the system. Because of smart contracts, the system is responsive and act in real time [40]. After being validated by the smart contracts, information of the patients and doctors will be added to the ledger of the blockchain. Lastly, hospital authorities will assign a doctor to a patient.

ii. *Data collection and storage on a continuous basis:* All health data is constantly gathered and kept in the system, and any odd occurrence must be reported to the appropriate parties. Raw sensor and device values will be delivered to the patient's smartphone or tablet through a mobile application. The raw data is then formatted and processed by the mobile application. The data is processed and then passed through a smart contract for additional analysis. Because the system requires real-time monitoring, smart contracts should be developed to detect any abnormalities in the patient's condition based on the monitoring data. The data from the smart contract should be kept in the cloud storage after it has been analyzed. Each information upload and data access event must be recorded in the ledger as a transaction.

Patient name: Haydar Mahmud

Treatment length: 5 mins

```
Date:2021/9/21, Time:13-1-7, Current:1,
Date:2021/9/21, Time:13-1-23, Current:1,
Date:2021/9/21, Time:13-1-26, Current:1,
Date:2021/9/21, Time:13-1-29, Current:1,
Date:2021/9/21, Time:13-1-31, Current:1,
Date:2021/9/21, Time:13-1-33, Current:1,
Date:2021/9/21, Time:13-1-36, Current:1,
Date:2021/9/21, Time:13-6-57, Current:1,
Date:2021/9/21, Time:13-7-30, Current:0,
Date:2021/9/21, Time:13-8-5, Current:25,
Date:2021/9/21, Time:13-8-19, Current:25,
Date:2021/9/21, Time:13-8-58, Current:18,
```

Figure 12.3 tDCS session data stored in cloud.

All monitoring data should be kept in the cloud (Figure 12.3) and adhere to the Health Insurance Portability and Accountability Act (HIPAA) procedure to prevent data mapping.

iii. *Data requests and access*: Doctors may also view a patient's monitoring data, which is an important feature of the system. A request is issued to the system when a doctor wants to view a patient's data. If the patient wants the doctor to have access to his or her monitor data, he or she will provide the doctor his or her key in exchange for the request. When a doctor submits a request to the system, a smart contract is launched to verify the doctor's identity before granting access to the patient's data. After being authenticated in the system, the doctor may access the patient's data from the ledger.

12.4 HARDWARE PROTOTYPE OF PROPOSED TDCS FRAMEWORK

The system framework is depicted in Figure 12.4 as a block diagram. The essential component of a tDCS device is the circuit board. A processor ATMEGA328P handles this circuit board. Some current-regulating ICs make up the IC panel (LM334). The amount of current supplied by each IC is varied. On the basis of current requirements, the CPU adjusts the supply power to power up the ICs. The CPU is linked with a real-time clock and an SD card module. The stimulation period is counted in real time. The real-time data is stored in the cloud module. ATMEGA328P is also linked to a Bluetooth device. Bluetooth establishes a link between the mobile app and the circuit board. Anode refers to the positive side of an electrode. It connects to the IC panel and delivers the output to the brain's scalp. The cathode is the electrode that is linked to the ground and is the negative component of the electrodes. A power source is included with the board to provide the system with the necessary electricity.

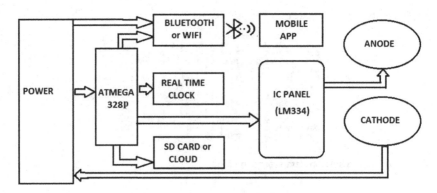

Figure 12.4 Block diagram of the system.

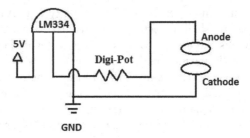

Figure 12.5 Current regulating circuit.

We utilized LM334 with a digital potentiometer to control a little amount of current (digi-pot). For different values of digi-pot, we receive varied amounts of current from this circuit (Figure 12.5). The main idea for obtaining the desired amount of current at the electrodes of this device is as follows.

One of the most crucial components of this tDCS gadget is the headband (Figure 12.6). The headband has a numerical basis that goes from (–V) to (+V). The base is made up of two hands that are numbered from (I) to (V) (III). These two hands are able to move in tandem with the base. Each hand has two square compartments in which electrodes are put. These square boxes may also be moved around freely, allowing electrodes to be put wherever on the user's head. Different disorders necessitate various electrode locations.

The circuit board can be viewed in Figure 12.7 to show all of the system's components. The board now has a real-time clock and cloud module,

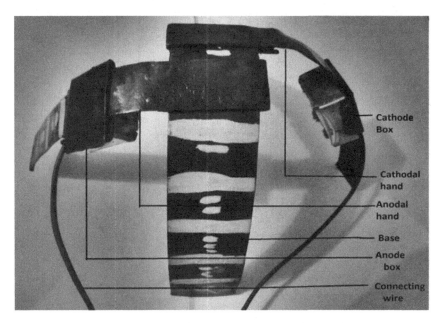

Cathode Box

Cathodal hand

Anodal hand

Base

Anode box

Connecting wire

Figure 12.6 tDCS headband.

Figure 12.7 The circuit board of the device.

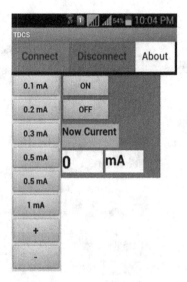

Figure 12.8 Mobile app interface.

allowing the system to retain current passing data in real time and date. This information will be useful to both the user and the clinician for future treatment.

To control this advanced tDCS gadget, we created an Android app (Figure 12.8). This software must use Bluetooth to communicate with the circuit board. From this app, we can provide commands for the needed current.

12.5 CONCLUSION AND FUTURE DIRECTION

We intended to address a pressing issue that requires more attention in the field of biomedical engineering research. This research focuses on using blockchain and Internet of Medical Things (IoMT) technologies to provide efficient and secure remote patient monitoring (RPM) in tDCS devices. In the future, the prototype should be enhanced more so that it may be utilized in clinical trials and provide a more seamless experience for physicians. The IoMT-blockchain-based neurostimulation solutions may be used with machine learning technologies to automatically customize smart contracts for each patient. Such integration is something we'll work on in the future.

REFERENCES

[1]   V. Hassija, V. Chamola, V. Saxena, D. Jain, P. Goyal, and B. Sikdar, "A survey on IoT security: application areas, security threats, and solution architectures," *IEEE Access,* vol. 7, pp. 82721–82743, 2019.

[2] J. L. Hall and D. McGraw, "For telehealth to succeed, privacy and security risks must be identified and addressed," *Health Affairs,* vol. 33, pp. 216–221, 2014.

[3] A. C. Smith, E. Thomas, C. L. Snoswell, H. Haydon, A. Mehrotra, J. Clemensen, *et al.,* "Telehealth for global emergencies: Implications for coronavirus disease 2019 (COVID-19)," *Journal of Telemedicine and Telecare,* vol. 26, pp. 309–313, 2020.

[4] M. Bucur and C. Papagno, "A systematic review of noninvasive brain stimulation for post-stroke depression," *Journal of Affective Disorders,* vol. 238, pp. 69–78, 2018.

[5] M. Bikson, P. Grossman, C. Thomas, A. L. Zannou, J. Jiang, T. Adnan, *et al.,* "Safety of transcranial direct current stimulation: evidence based update 2016," *Brain Stimulation,* vol. 9, pp. 641–661, 2016.

[6] P. S. Boggio, R. Ferrucci, S. P. Rigonatti, P. Covre, M. Nitsche, A. Pascual-Leone, et al., "Effects of transcranial direct current stimulation on working memory in patients with Parkinson's disease," *Journal of the Neurological Sciences,* vol. 249, pp. 31–38, 2006.

[7] J.-P. Lefaucheur, A. Antal, S. S. Ayache, D. H. Benninger, J. Brunelin, F. Cogiamanian, et al., "Evidence-based guidelines on the therapeutic use of transcranial direct current stimulation (tDCS)," *Clinical Neurophysiology,* vol. 128, pp. 56–92, 2017.

[8] J. Leite, O. F. Gonçalves, and S. Carvalho, "Facilitative effects of bi-hemispheric tDCS in cognitive deficits of Parkinson disease patients," *Medical Hypotheses,* vol. 82, pp. 138–140, 2014.

[9] J.-H. Park, S. B. Hong, D.-W. Kim, M. Suh, and C.-H. Im, "A novel array-type transcranial direct current stimulation (tDCS) system for accurate focusing on targeted brain areas," *IEEE Transactions on Magnetics,* vol. 47, pp. 882–885, 2011.

[10] S. Zaghi, N. Heine, and F. Fregni, "Brain stimulation for the treatment of pain: a review of costs, clinical effects, and mechanisms of treatment for three different central neuromodulatory approaches," *Journal of Pain Management,* vol. 2, p. 339, 2009.

[11] M. S. U. Sourav, A. Rahman, A. Al Mamun, and F. M. Alamgir, "Standard Transcranial Direct Current Stimulation (tDCS) Model," *International Journal of Computer Networks and Communications Security,* vol. 5, pp. 264–270, 2017.

[12] S. S. Herring, M. H. B. Azhar, and M. Sakel, "Tele-tDCS: A Novel Tele-neuromodulation Framework using Internet of Medical Things," in *Biodevices,* 2022, pp. 84–93.

[13] Fisher, R., Salanova, V., Witt, T., Worth, R., Henry, T., Gross, R., ... & SANTE Study Group. (2010). Electrical stimulation of the anterior nucleus of thalamus for treatment of refractory epilepsy. *Epilepsia,* 51(5), 899–908.

[14] Schoenen, J., Jensen, R. H., Lanteri-Minet, M., Láinez, M. J., Gaul, C., Goodman, A. M., ... & May, A. (2013). Stimulation of the sphenopalatine ganglion (SPG) for cluster headache treatment. Pathway CH-1: a randomized, sham-controlled study. *Cephalalgia,* 33(10), 816–830.

[15] Mayo Clinic: www.mayoclinic.org/tests-procedures/deep-brain-stimulation/about/pac-20384562

[16] Montgomery Jr, Erwin B., and John T. Gale. (2008). "Mechanisms of action of deep brain stimulation (DBS)." *Neuroscience & Biobehavioral Reviews* 32(3), 388–407.

[17] Montgomery Jr, E. B., and Baker, K. B. (2000). Mechanisms of deep brain stimulation and future technical developments. *Neurological Research*, 22(3), 259–266.

[18] Lefaucheur, J. P. (2008). Principles of therapeutic use of transcranial and epidural cortical stimulation. *Clinical Neurophysiology*, 119(10), 2179–2184.

[19] Priori, A., and Lefaucheur, J. P. (2007). Chronic epidural motor cortical stimulation for movement disorders. *The Lancet Neurology*, 6(3), 279–286.

[20] Cherney, L. R., Erickson, R. K., and Small, S. L. (2010). Epidural cortical stimulation as adjunctive treatment for non-fluent aphasia: preliminary findings. *Journal of Neurology, Neurosurgery Psychiatry*, 81(9), 1014–1021.

[21] Seo, H., and Jun, S. C. (2021). Computational exploration of epidural cortical stimulation using a realistic head model. *Computers in Biology and Medicine*, 135, 104290.

[22] Klomjai, W., Katz, R., and Lackmy-Vallée, A. (2015). Basic principles of transcranial magnetic stimulation (TMS) and repetitive TMS (rTMS). *Annals of Physical and Rehabilitation Medicine*, 58(4), 208–213.

[23] Transcranial Magnetic Stimulation (TMS): https://my.clevelandclinic.org/health/treatments/17827-transcranial-magnetic-stimulation-tms

[24] Woods, A. J., Antal, A., Bikson, M., Boggio, P. S., Brunoni, A. R., Celnik, P. et al. (2016). "A technical guide to tDCS, and related non-invasive brain stimulation tools," *Clinical Neurophysiology*, 127, 1031–1048.

[25] Fertonani, A., Brambilla, M., Cotelli, M., and Miniussi, C. (2014). "The timing of cognitive plasticity in physiological aging: a tDCS study of naming," *Frontiers in Aging Neuroscience*, 6, 131.

[26] Bikson, M., Datta, A., and Elwassif, M. (2009). "Establishing safety limits for transcranial direct current stimulation," *Clinical Neurophysiology*, 120, 1033.

[27] Thair, H., Holloway, A. L., Newport, R., and Smith, A. D. (2017). "Transcranial direct current stimulation (tDCS): a beginner's guide for design and implementation," *Frontiers in Neuroscience*, 11, 641.

[28] Parazzini, M., Rossi, E., Ferrucci, R., Liorni, I., Priori, A., and Ravazzani, P. (2014). "Modelling the electric field and the current density generated by cerebellar transcranial DC stimulation in humans," *Clinical Neurophysiology*, 125, 577–584.

[29] Parazzini, M., Rossi, E., Rossi, L., Priori, A., and Ravazzani, P. (2013). "Numerical estimation of the current density in the heart during transcranial direct current stimulation," *Brain Stimulation: Basic, Translational, and Clinical Research in Neuromodulation*, 6, 457–459.

[30] Castillo-Saavedra, L., Gebodh, N., Bikson, M., Diaz-Cruz, C., Brandao, R., Coutinho, L., et al. (2016). "Clinically effective treatment of fibromyalgia pain with high-definition transcranial direct current stimulation: phase II open-label dose optimization," *The Journal of Pain*, 17, 14–26.

[31] Loo, C. K., Sachdev, P., Martin, D., Pigot, M., Alonzo, A., Malhi, G. S. et al. (2010). "A double-blind, sham-controlled trial of transcranial direct current stimulation for the treatment of depression," *The International Journal of Neuropsychopharmacology*, 13, 61–69.

[32] Palm, U., Schiller, C., Fintescu, Z., Obermeier, M., Keeser, D., Reisinger, E., et al. (2012). "Transcranial direct current stimulation in treatment resistant depression: a randomized double-blind, placebo-controlled study," *Brain Stimulation*, 5, 242–251.

[33] Palm, U., Reisinger, E., Keeser, D., Kuo, M.-F., Pogarell, O., Leicht, G., et al. (2013). "Evaluation of sham transcranial direct current stimulation for randomized, placebo-controlled clinical trials," *Brain Stimulation*, 6, 690–695.

[34] Antal, A., and Paulus, W. (2013). "Transcranial alternating current stimulation (tACS)." *Frontiers in Human Neuroscience*, 7, 317.

[35] Elyamany, O., Leicht, G., Herrmann, C. S., and Mulert, C. (2021). "Transcranial alternating current stimulation (tACS): from basic mechanisms towards first applications in psychiatry". *European Archives of Psychiatry and Clinical Neuroscience*, 271(1), 135–156.

[36] Van der Groen, O., Potok, W., Wenderoth, N., Edwards, G., Mattingley, J. B., & Edwards, D. (2022). Using noise for the better: The effects of transcranial random noise stimulation on the brain and behavior. *Neuroscience & Biobehavioral Reviews*, 138, 104702.

[37] Mulquiney, P. G., Hoy, K. E., Daskalakis, Z. J., & Fitzgerald, P. B. (2011). "Improving working memory: exploring the effect of transcranial random noise stimulation and transcranial direct current stimulation on the dorsolateral prefrontal cortex". *Clinical Neurophysiology*, 122(12), 2384–2389.

[38] Palm, U., Chalah, M. A., Padberg, F., Al-Ani, T., Abdellaoui, M., Sorel, M., ... and Ayache, S. S. (2016). "Effects of transcranial random noise stimulation (tRNS) on affect, pain and attention in multiple sclerosis". *Restorative Neurology and Neuroscience*, 34(2), 189–199.

[39] Cucca, A., Sharma, K., Agarwal, S., Feigin, A. S., and Biagioni, M. C. (2019). "Tele-monitored tDCS rehabilitation: Feasibility, challenges and future perspectives in Parkinson's disease," *Journal of Neuroengineering and Rehabilitation*, 16, 1–10.

[40] Ashraf, F. B. and Reaz, R. (2021). "IoT-Blockchain in remote patient monitoring," in The 5th International Conference on Future Networks & Distributed Systems, pp. 186–194.

Chapter 13

Exploring generative intelligence systems for sustainability in transformative healthcare 6.0

Thota Akshitha, C. Kishor Kumar Reddy,
D. Manoj Kumar Reddy, and Srinath Doss

13.1 INTRODUCTION TO AI-DRIVEN HEALTHCARE INTELLIGENCE

Artificial intelligence technology integrated with healthcare helps create a new space for everyone where various medical services can be provided to different people remotely [1]. It creates an active digital environment in which associates can work together and analyze how these virtual healthcare services are delivered to different people. This concept of artificial intelligence helps overcome many limitations, like physical boundaries, and allows medical professionals, and even researchers to interact and access different types of medical services and information. Artificial intelligence creates a medical environment that is like realistic scenarios [2]. It helps the consumers feel real and truly involved. This technology helps both the medical professionals and the patients to communicate effectively, analyze the problems of the patient, and provide a feasible solution. Patients can schedule virtual sessions, learn more about their health conditions and the necessary precautions, and contact doctors for support. Doctors can use this virtual technology for recommendations and training [21].

As depicted in Figure 13.1, the projected growth of artificial intelligence in healthcare helps in customizing the preferences of an individual to suit their needs. Preferences such as their culture, language, and other aspects are considered to make each person using the platform feel included. This virtual world is all about making healthcare easier to access, improving how doctors and patients work together, and ultimately making sure everyone gets better care.

13.1.1 Evolution of healthcare information systems

The traditional handwritten paper records that were used earlier have now transitioned to high-level digital ecosystems that support the need of the modern age. The complexities that arose due to the usage of manual record on paper charts that were stored and organized in the enormous cabinets have

DOI: 10.1201/9781003497585-13

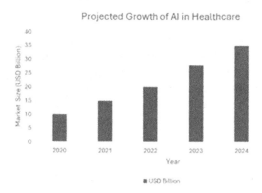

Figure 13.1 Projected growth of AI in healthcare.

promoted the adoption of electronic health records (EHRs) and healthcare information technology to smooth the data management and improve efficiency in healthcare [4]. The transitional shift to EHRs in medical data management enables effortlessly accessing the information, securely storing the data, and smooth exchange of information across healthcare facilities by digitalizing the patient record.

The EHR system initially focused mainly on capturing and storing patient data, thereby creating a strong framework that allows different medical institutions to effectively and smoothly communicate and exchange important data, which in turn promotes the collaboration and improvement of overall quality of medical services. With the new technologies and changes in regulations, more developed health information systems (HIS) have come into existence [1]. This new technology offers a wide range of functions and supports different medical workflows, administrative tasks, and decision-making processes. Beginning in the 1960s and 1970s, many hospitals and medical institutions introduced basic computer systems for assistance in tasks like billing and maintaining databases.

By the 1980s, healthcare professionals started digitalizing patient data using EHRs. In the 1990s, the development of health information exchange (HIE) systems started allowing data sharing between the providers. The early 2000s introduced clinical decision support systems (CDSS) to improve diagnostics and treatment. The late 2000s saw policy changes that promoted widespread EHR adoption. The 2010s witnessed telemedicine and remote monitoring, while advances in data analytics and AI in the late 2010s further enhanced HIS capabilities. By the 2020s, HIS had evolved into a comprehensive system supporting diverse medical and administrative functions, significantly improving healthcare efficiency and quality.

13.2 FOUNDATIONS AND TECHNIQUES OF GENERATIVE INTELLIGENCE SYSTEMS

Generative artificial intelligence describes a course of artificial intelligence versions made to create brand-new artificial information that resembles a provided collection of training information [19]. Unlike discriminative versions, which concentrate on identifying or anticipating based upon input information, generative designs intend to comprehend the underlying circulation of the input information and develop brand-new instances that are depictive of this circulation.

13.2.1 Key techniques in generative artificial systems

Generative intelligence uses several innovative strategies, each with distinct approaches as well as applications. One of the most noticeable strategies consist of the following.

Generative adversarial networks (GANs)

- *Structure*: Generative intelligence contains two neural networks: one is the generator and the other is a discriminator. The generator produces artificial information and then the discriminator checks the correctness of the produced information with that of the actual information here in the GANs [1].
- *Educating Process*: GANs are directed with a process called adversarial training. The generator tries to create information that is identical to genuine information while the discriminator intends to boost its capacity to compare actual along phony information [10]. With time, these competitors drive both the networks to boost, leading to very reasonable artificial information.
- *Applications*: GANs are highly used in photo generation, boosting clinical pictures, information enhancement, and creating reasonable personal information for research study [2].

Variational auto encoders (VAEs)

- *Structure*: VAEs will encode input information into a lower-dimensional room and after that decrypt it back into the initial information layout. This procedure includes a probabilistic technique where the encoder creates a circulation over the distinct area as opposed to an existing factor.
- *Educating Process*: During training, VAEs maximize both the restoration precision as well as the routine of the distinct area to guarantee

smoothness along with connection. This allows the designer to create brand-new information by sampling from the distinct area plus decoding it.

- *Applications*: VAEs are specifically reliable in producing complicated information such as clinical pictures, messages, as well as sound. They are likewise made use of in anomaly discovery plus information compression [10].

Transformers

- *Structure*: Transformers utilize self-attention devices to version reliance in between various components of the input information, making them extremely efficient for consecutive information. They were at first established for natural language handling jobs; however, they have been extended to numerous generative applications.
- *Educating Process*: Transformers are educated on huge datasets to discover contextual partnerships within the information. The self-attention device permits them to produce natural plus contextually appropriate series such as message, songs, as well as pictures.
- *Applications*: Transformers are made use of in message generation picture synthesis, as well as also creating artificial digital wellness documents for research study objectives [11].

In the developing area of medicine, several AI structures have gotten importance because of their one-of-a-kind abilities as well as applications. Recognizing the toughness and constraints of these structures is important for choosing the ideal design for medical jobs [21].

As shown in Table 13.1, the relative summary of three commonly used AI structures, namely, generative adversarial networks (GANs), variational autoencoders (VAEs), and transformers are compared against each other stating the description and the corresponding advantages and disadvantages involved with structural model. Each of these structures has distinct features that make them appropriate for various sorts of health care applications, from information enhancement to consecutive information modeling [19].

13.2.2 Comparison of generative and discriminative models

Generative AI stands for an effective strategy within the more comprehensive area of expert system using ingenious services as well as making it possible to produce beneficial brand-new information throughout numerous applications, especially in medical care. By recognizing and leveraging these methods, scientists as well as professionals can provide extra efficient, tailored, plus reliable medical treatment [5].

Table 13.1 Comparison of AI frameworks commonly used in healthcare applications

Framework	Description	Advantages	Disadvantages
Generative adversarial networks (GANs)	GANs consist of two neural networks, a generator and a discriminator; trained adversarial [10].	It can generate realistic synthetic data for training.	Mode collapse may occur, leading to limited diversity in generated samples.
Variational autoencoders (VAEs)	VAEs encode input data into a latent space and decode it back into the original format.	It provides a probabilistic approach to data generation.	Challenges to optimize the reconstruction accuracy and latent space smoothness.
Transformers	Transformers use self-attention mechanisms to model dependencies in sequential data.	It is highly effective for generating coherent and contextually relevant sequences, such as text and images.	Require large amounts of data and computational resources [3].

Table 13.2 Comparison of generative vs. discriminative models

Aspect	Generative Models	Discriminative Models
Goal	Model data distribution	Classify input data
Example techniques	GANs, VAEs, Transformers	SVM, logistic regression, neural networks
Data requirements	High	Variable
Computational cost	High	Moderate
Applications	Image generation, medical image enhancement	Disease diagnosis, image classification

- *Generative Models*: The aim to make the joint chance circulation of the input information to develop brand-new information circumstances. Instances of generative designs consist of GANs, VAEs, and transformers [2]. These designs generally need huge quantities of information to precisely record the underlying circulation. This information need makes certain that the version can produce reasonable and varied information examples. Nonetheless generative designs are typically a lot more computationally extensive because of the demand to create as well as review artificial information.
- *Discriminative Models*: Determining the limits from the provided information helps to identify or make forecasts. Instances of discriminative designs consist of support vector machines (SVMs), logistic regression, coupled with semantic networks utilized for category jobs. These versions commonly accomplish outstanding efficiency with reasonably much less information relying on the intricacy of the job available. On top of that, discriminative versions are typically much less computationally requiring as they focus only on category or regression jobs, instead of producing brand-new information.

As depicted in Table 13.2, the two models are compared on a range of factors which include the vital properties such as the goals associated with the models, example methodologies, along with the computational costs involved, states the applications associated with both and applications generative and discriminative models in the patient diagnosis.

13.3 BENEFITS AND CHALLENGES OF GENERATIVE AI IN HEALTHCARE

- *Information enhancement*: Generative variations can boost limited datasets especially in professional imaging, where determined info may be arranged. This enhancement improves the toughness along with abstraction of expert system variations, resulting in much more exact evaluation plus visualized results [4].

- *Synthetic data generation*: Generative AI can create synthetic professional pictures together with individual details, which are useful for training and screening formulas without endangering a person's personal privacy [21].
- *Personalized medicine*: Generative designs make it possible for the generation of individualized therapy intends based upon private individual information consisting of hereditary details, case history, and therapy actions. This tailored method to medical care boosts individual end results by boosting therapy efficiency and getting rid of negative impacts [19].
- *Drug discovery*: Generative AI accelerates medication exploration by producing unique molecular frameworks with preferred homes. This simplifies the medication growth procedure causing the exploration of brand-new restorative substances for numerous conditions [13].
- *Optimization of healthcare operations*: Generative AI can boost health care procedures by projecting person need boosting source allocation plus boosting process performance. This improves client circulation, minimizes delay times, and enhances total health care distribution [5].

Despite its capacity, generative AI in healthcare additionally deals with numerous difficulties:

- *Reliability and safety*: Ensuring the reliability plus safety of the produced information together with formulas is vital in healthcare setups. Mistakes or predispositions in generative versions can cause wrong medical diagnoses, therapy referrals, or negative impacts for individuals [8].
- *Data privacy and security*: Generative AI frequently calls for accessibility to delicate person information, increasing problems concerning personal privacy and protection [9]. Shielding own personal privacy as well as sticking to regulations such as Health Insurance Portability and Accountability Act (HIPAA) are important yet challenging facets of using generative AI in healthcare.
- *Interpretability and explainability*: Generative AI designs are typically intricate along with tough to analyze, making it screening for medical professionals to comprehend their options plus count on their end results. Making sure openness plus explainability in generative AI formulas is important for acquiring individual consent along with governing permission.
- *Integration with the existing systems*: Integrating generative AI right into existing medical care systems combined with operations can be

intricate plus taxing. Compatibility problems and interoperability obstacles, in addition to resistance to alter from the doctors, pose obstacles to fostering [20].

The fostering of generative AI in health care adheres to a typical innovation fostering contour, mirroring the progressive boost in approval as well as usage with time. Originally, generative AI was accepted by trendsetters together with very early adopters, consisting of leading proving ground as well as highly sophisticated health care service providers that agree to explore brand-new devices. As these very early individuals show the advantages as well as resolve preliminary difficulties, the innovation acquires reputation as well as starts to bring in the very early bulk [24]. This team is extra sensible and searches for tested worth prior to devoting it to brand-new innovations. At some point, bulk of the people that are a lot more doubtful as well as risk-averse start to embrace generative AI.

AI has come to be a common technique in the sector. Ultimately laggards, one of the most immune to change, take on the innovation just when it ends up being inescapable. Comprehending this contour aids stakeholders prepare for the steady combination of generative AI in medical care systems [14]. The generative expert system (AI) holds assurance for changing medical care through supplying a variety of advantages, yet it additionally provides several obstacles.

Table 13.3 supplies a review of the advantages as well as difficulties associated with the execution of generative AI in healthcare. The advantages consist of tailored therapy strategies customized to specific person requires, improved clinical imaging for boosted analysis precision, and anticipating

Table 13.3 Benefits and challenges of generative AI in healthcare

Aspect	Benefits	Challenges
Personalized Treatment	Tailor interventions to individual patient needs	Requires accurate, diverse patient data
Enhanced Medical Imaging	Improves image quality and diagnostic accuracy	High computational demands
Predictive Analytics	Forecasts disease progression and patient outcomes	Must validate AI predictions thoroughly
Cost Reduction	Automates tasks, optimizes resources, reduces errors	Initial implementation costs
Data Privacy	Protects sensitive patient information	Risk of data breaches and misuse
Ethical Concerns	Promotes fairness and transparency	Ensures algorithmic bias is minimized
Regulatory Issues	Complies with rigorous standards	Navigates complex approval processes

analytics for projecting condition development as well as person end results. Nonetheless, there are numerous obstacles to take into consideration such as the demand for precise and varied client information, high computational needs for clinical imaging improvement as well as the requirement to extensively confirm AI forecasts [20].

13.4 ETHICAL AND REGULATORY CONSIDERATIONS

13.4.1 Moral effects of AI decisions

The mix of AI in healthcare enhances significant moral factors to consider, especially concerning the choices provided by AI solutions. These choices can have extensive repercussions for people, healthcare service providers as well as culture all at once. Some vital moral effects consist of the following:

- *Fairness and bias*: AI formulas might inadvertently continue or intensify predispositions existing in the information made use of for training. Influenced formulas can result in unreasonable therapy or disparities in treatment influencing patients with a weak heart or at-risk populaces unjustifiably [22]. It's essential to understand and relieve predispositions in AI formulas to ensure reasonable results for all individuals.
- *Transparency in AI systems*: AI formulas are commonly intricate and opaque, making it testing to recognize just how they get to their choices. The absence of openness along with explainability can weaken the trust on AI systems as well as threaten their approval by medical care specialists and clients [12].
- *Privacy and data security*: AI formulas frequently need accessibility to substantial quantities of delicate individual information to educate together with run properly. Shielding individual personal privacy and making certain information protection are very important to keeping person count on and sticking to regulative needs such as HIPAA. Medical care suppliers must execute durable information safety steps along with stringent personal privacy criteria when setting up AI systems [23].
- *Autonomy and informed consent*: AI formulas might affect professional decision-making and also therapy suggestions, possibly influencing people's self-reliance as well as right to self-determination. It's essential to involve people in the decision-making procedure as well as guarantee that they recognize the function of AI in their treatment. Valuing a person's freedom and getting educated approval are basic concepts of moral medical care technique [9].

- *Accountability and liability*: Determining obligation for choices made by AI formulas can be testing. In case of negative results or mistakes, it might be uncertain who is responsible—the designer, the doctor, or the formula itself. Developing clear lines of duty and obligation is essential for guaranteeing responsibility in addition to dealing with damage brought on by AI systems.

Resolving these moral issues needs a multidisciplinary team including medical care specialists, information researchers, ethicists, policymakers as well as personal supporters [22]. Collective initiatives to develop moral standards, finest methods as well as governing structures can aid guarantee that AI is released suitably and truthfully in medical care setups, eventually profiting people as well as culture.

13.4.2 Study: Regulatory approvals of AI applications in healthcare

In this study, we look at the governing authorization procedure for AI applications in medical care concentrating on a theoretical AI-powered analysis device for identifying diabetic person retinopathy as a leading reason for loss of sight.

- *Development plus recognition*: A team of researchers develops an AI formula informed on a massive dataset of retinal images to find indicators of diabetic person retinopathy [18]. The formula goes through extensive recognition research to evaluate its performance, precision paired with safety and security in professional setups.
- *Submission to regulatory authorities*: The designers send a premarket notice additionally called access to the Food and Drug Administration (FDA) summing up the AI formula's desired usage technical specs, recognition information plus professional proof sustaining its security in addition to efficiency.
- *Review plus evaluation*: The FDA assesses the entry reviewing the AI formula's efficiency, scientific proof plus adherence to regulative needs. They might ask for added info or clarification from the designers to make sure a comprehensive assessment.
- *Approval plus market authorization*: If the AI formula fulfills the FDA's regulative requirements for security along with efficiency, it gets governing authorization or clearance for business circulation combined with usage in a professional environment [25]. The programmers can then market and supply the AI-powered analysis device to doctor for patient treatment.

- *Post-market surveillance*: After market authorization, the designers proceed to check the AI formula's efficiency coupled with security with postmarked security tasks such as real-life information collection, inaccurate occasion coverage, and recurring quality control actions.

This study highlights the relevance of regulative authorizations in making certain the security, efficiency plus moral use AI applications in medical care. By sticking to regulative structures coupled with conformity demands, designers can bring ingenious modern AI technologies to market while preserving individual security along with personal privacy [20].

13.5 CURRENT FRAMEWORKS FOR HEALTHCARE APPLICATIONS

13.5.1 Overview of popular frameworks

- *TensorFlow*: Established by Google Brain, TensorFlow is just one of the most made use of open-source expert system structures. It makes use of comprehensive assistance for deep discovery consisting of neural network style, training as well as release throughout numerous systems [23].
- *Py Torch*: Developed by Facebook's AI Research laboratory (FAIR) Py Torch is recognized for its high-level computational chart that makes it very user-friendly and versatile for scientists.
- *OpenAI*: OpenAI establishes artificial intelligence innovations together with research study. In addition, they have launched countless devices and structures to sustain AI growth consisting of OpenAI Gym for support knowing jobs together with OpenAI API for all-natural language handling.
- *DeepMind*: DeepMind, developed by Google, focuses on artificial basic knowledge (AGI). They have not released a certain structure. Tuition fees influence the development of artificial intelligence frameworks and algorithm.

As depicted in Figure 13.2, a relative evaluation of the efficiency metrics of numerous structures in healthcare applications. The metrics assessed consist of precision, accuracy, recall, coupled with F1-score, which are generally utilized to analyze the efficiency of artificial intelligence versions in category jobs [8]. Each structure, consisting of TensorFlow, Py Torch, OpenAI coupled with DeepMind, is examined based upon these metrics to establish their category efficiency. These efficiency metrics offer a beneficial understanding right into the toughness and weak points of each structure, helping in the choice of one of the most appropriate structures for detailed healthcare jobs [16].

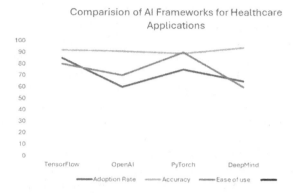

Figure 13.2 Performance comparison of machine learning frameworks in healthcare applications.

13.5.2 Real-world examples: Deployment in hospitals and clinics

Real-world applications of AI use in healthcare facilities and centers together with advantages of AI advancements in healthcare setups are given below:

- *Medical imaging*: AI formulas can instantly find irregularities, section body organs or sores coupled with a focus on instances for analysis, aiding radiologists enhance the precision of medical diagnosis and performance [18].
- *Clinical decision support*: AI-based assistance systems are released in hospitals and to help doctors. These systems analyze client information and their medical histories with evidence-based standards to give personalized therapy with drug application assistance with threat analysis [18]. The Medical Decision Support Advisor is utilized by clinical specialists to access evidence-based therapy suggestions and scientific standards at the factor of treatment, boosting medical decision-making and individual safety and security.
- *Remote patient monitoring*: With the increase of telemedicine plus remote medical care distribution designs, AI-enabled remote person tracking options are becoming significantly common in medical facilities and also centers. These services make use of wearable tools, sensing units, and also AI formulas to continually keep track of clients' important indications task degrees as well as wellness from another location [7]. By evaluating real-time information streams,

AI formulas can find very early indications of wearing down and anticipate negative occasions prompting sharp medical professionals to interfere immediately. Instances consist of BioForm's' Bio vitals system, which makes use of AI to keep track of people with persistent problems and find adjustments in wellness condition from another location, making it possible for aggressive treatments and minimizing hospital stays [12].

- *Optimization of healthcare operations*: Modern AI technologies are released in medical facilities and centers to enhance health care procedures and processes as well as boost source appropriation. AI formulas examine functional information such as person circulation, team organizing to determine traffic jams, and ineffectiveness coupled with chances for enhancement [15]. Real-world applications of AI release in expert facilities and centers give the beneficial applications and advantages of AI advancements in medical care setups by maximizing source use plus process performance. AI aids health centers as well as centers enhance client treatment distribution, minimize delay times, and take full advantage of staffing degrees [17]. As an example, GE Healthcare's Command Center makes use of AI formulas to assess real-time information from healthcare facility systems combined with anticipating a person's need, allowing aggressive administration of sources as well as enhancing functional performance.

These real-world situations show the different applications of modern AI technologies in healthcare facilities and centers varying from clinical imaging evaluation to professional choice assistance to remote person surveillance plus medical care procedures optimization [14]. By making use of the power of AI, medical professionals can enhance results, identify the correct medical procedures, and provide a more reliable and individualized treatment.

13.6 APPLICATIONS OF GENERATIVE AI IN HEALTHCARE

13.6.1 Tailored treatment recommendations

- *Customized therapy referrals*: Generative AI can examine client information consisting of hereditary details, case history, and therapy results to produce tailored therapy suggestions [3]. By thinking about specific individual attributes, generative AI assists doctors to enhance therapy for much better effectiveness and minimize negative effects.
- *Medical imaging analysis*: Generative AI methods such as generative hostile networks (GANs) with variational autoencoders (VAEs) are used for clinical picture generation, renovation, and evaluation.

These designs can improve the quality of clinical photos and identify problems, section body organs or sores and help radiologists in medical diagnosis along with treatment preparation [17].

- *Predictive analytics*: Generative AI allows expert analytics by finding the patterns and connections from healthcare information to show future results [20]. The expected versions by generative artificial intelligence can give illness development, recognize high-risk individuals for therapy, and enhance source appropriation for boosted healthcare shipment.

- *Carpet exploration with growth*: Generative AI can speed up medication administration by producing unique molecular frameworks with the required residential properties. By mimicking just how various molecular mixes connect with organic targets, AI can determine appealing prospects for brand-new medicines quicker better than conventional techniques. This strategy not just fastens the medication advancement procedure but also decreases prices and raises the probability of locating efficient therapies for different illnesses.

- *Online health assistants*: Generative AI powers digital wellness aides that supply customized wellness suggestions, screen individual problems, coupled with aid with drug administration [9]. These AI-driven systems can provide continuous assistance to individuals addressing health-related questions advising them to take drugs and checking their wellness metrics. This continual assistance enhances the client's adherence to therapy strategies and general health results [25].

- *Psychological health support*: Generative AI can be utilized to produce online specialists and sustain systems for psychological healthcare. These systems can supply healing communications, cognitive-behavioral treatment (CBT) workouts, and psychological assistance to people dealing with psychological wellness concerns [22]. By using obtainable as well as cost-effective psychological health and wellness assistance, generative AI can aid the expanding need for psychological health and wellness solutions and also enhance the health of individuals.

13.6.2 Study: Generative AI in radiology

In this study, generative AI was used in radiology to boost clinical imaging evaluation. Scientists educated generative hostile networks (GANs) on a big dataset of clinical pictures to produce artificial pictures looking like actual individual scans. These fabricated images were made use of to improve the training information for deep understanding designs, enhancing their performance in work such as aching exploration, development department, and problem classification [15].

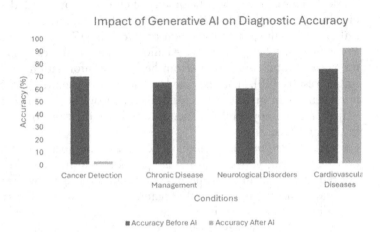

Figure 13.3 Impact of generative AI on diagnosis accuracy.

As shown in Figure 13.3, the rising influence of generative AI on precision analysis in medical care with time is clear. As generative AI strategies are created, fine-tuned, and incorporated right into clinical photoevaluation along with various other analysis procedures, there is a remarkable increase in the precision of condition discovery, category, and also therapy preparation [6]. This higher performance mirrors the expanding acknowledgment of generative AI as an important device for boosting analysis capabilities and boosting personal treatment in healthcare setups.

13.7 CASE STUDIES AND REAL-WORLD EXAMPLES

Study 1: Individualized cancer cell therapy utilizing generative AI

In this study, scientists used generative AI methods to customize cancer cell therapy for individuals. By examining genomic information and lump features, generative AI versions produced artificial information standing for different cancer cell subtypes and their feedback to various therapies. This strategy enabled the recognition of optimum therapy methods customized per individual's one-of-a-kind hereditary account together with cancer cells subtype, boosting therapy results as well as minimizing negative results [3].

Study 2: AI-driven medical imaging analysis in cardiovascular diseases

In this study, generative AI was utilized for clinical imaging evaluation in heart diseases. By educating deep discovering designs on big datasets of

Table 13.4 Case studies of generative AI applications in healthcare

Case Study	Description	Outcomes
Personalized Cancer Cells Therapy utilizing Generative AI	Utilized generative AI to individualize cancer cells therapy on genomic information along with lump features.	Boosted therapy outcomes, lowered negative results as well as dressmaker therapy techniques.
AI-driven Medical Imaging Assessment in Cardiovascular Diseases	Utilized generative AI for exact discovery along with medical diagnosis of cardiovascular irregularities from clinical scans.	Very early discovery of cardiovascular diseases allowing prompt treatments together with boosted individual diagnosis.
Anticipating Analytics for Chronic Disease Management	Utilized generative AI for anticipating analytics in forecasting illness progression and therapy feedback.	Positive recognition of high-risk clients enhanced therapy strategies as well as much better illness monitoring.

heart imaging scans consisting of MRI along with CT pictures, scientists created AI formulas efficient in properly detecting cardio irregularities such as coronary artery condition, cardiac infarction, and cardiac arrest. These AI-driven imaging evaluations allowed very early discovery of heart diseases, helping with prompt treatment and also enhancing accuracy of diagnosis [13].

Study 3: Predictive analytics for chronic disease management
In this study, anticipating analytics powered by generative AI were utilized for persistent condition evaluation and treatment. By leveraging digital wellness documents, individual demographics along with medical information, generative AI designs were educated to forecast illness development, reappearances, along with therapy actions for persistent problems such as diabetes mellitus, high blood pressure, and bronchial asthma [24]. These anticipating analytics devices made it possible for doctors to proactively determine high-risk clients, enhance therapy strategies before problems develop, and help in far better condition monitoring and decreased healthcare prices.

As shown in Table 13.4, the varied applications and favorable results of generative AI in medical care vary from customized therapy techniques to very early discovery of medical conditions and positive monitoring of persistent problems. By using the power of generative AI, medical care suppliers can boost individual treatments and provide professional results that will eventually save lives.

13.8 CONCLUSION

Generative AI will certainly change the healthcare sector by resolving several of its most tricky problems consisting of information deficiency, personal privacy worries, and the requirement for tailored therapy. The breakthroughs in generative modern AI technologies have actually made it possible for the development of reasonable artificial information, which is very useful for training artificial intelligence designs, enhancing precision in analysis and resulting in ingenious research studies. This information generation by AI not only enhances the toughness of AI designs, but also ensures an individual's personal privacy by getting rid of recognizable info. In addition, generative AI's abilities in medicine exploration and growth provide opportunities for the quick recognition of brand-new restorative medicines, possibly speeding up the schedule of efficient therapies.

Despite the substantial advantages, the combination of generative AI and medical care is not without difficulties. Guaranteeing the dependability and the safety and security of the created information, resolving predispositions in training datasets, and attending to complicated governing structures are essential obstacles that must be overcome. These difficulties require continual study, durable recognition techniques, and a close cooperation between AI designers, doctors, and regulative bodies to guarantee the moral and efficient use of modern generative AI technologies.

Looking ahead, the future of generative AI in medical care is intense with the prospect of substantially boosting individual end results and driving innovations in clinical scientific research. Nevertheless, it is important to approach its application attentively, making certain that personal privacy problems and governing needs are completely resolved. By doing so, the healthcare market can completely utilize the transformative power of generative AI, resulting in increase treatment distribution and ingenious therapy choices, eventually leading to much better wellness results for people worldwide.

REFERENCES

1. H. Tiwari, A. Raj, U. K. Singh and H. Fatima, "Generative AI for NFTs using GANs", IEEE 11th International Conference on Computing for Sustainable Global Development, New Delhi, India, 2024.
2. G. Rani, J. Singh and A. Khanna, "Comparative Analysis of Generative AI Models", IEEE International Conference on Advances in Computation, Communication and Information Technology (ICAICCIT), Faridabad, India, 2023.
3. S. S. Aravinth, S. Srithar, K. P. Joseph, U. Gopala Anil Varma, G. M. Kiran and V. Jonna, "Comparative Analysis of Generative AI Techniques for Addressing the Tabular Data Generation Problem in Medical Records", International Conference on Recent Advances in Science and Engineering Technology (ICRASET), India, 2023.

4. C. Kishor Kumar Reddy, P. R. Anisha, Samiya Khan, Marlia Mohd Hanafiah, Lavanya Pamulaparty, and R. Madana Mohana, "Sustainability in Industry 5.0: Theory and Applications", CRC Press, 2024.

5. V. R. Saddi, S. K. Gopal, A. S. Mohammed, S. Dhanasekaran and M. S. Naruka, "Examine the Role of Generative AI in Enhancing Threat Intelligence and Cyber Security Measures", IEEE 2nd International Conference on Disruptive Technologies (ICDT), Greater Noida, India, 2024.

6. T. Mitsunaga, "Heuristic Analysis for Security, Privacy and Bias of Text Generative AI: GhatGPT-3.5 case as of June 2023", IEEE International Conference on Computing (ICOCO), Langkawi, Malaysia, 2023.

7. K. Ramana, R. M. Mohana, C. K. K. Reddy, , G. Srivastava, and T. R. Gadekallu, "A Blockchain-Based Data-Sharing Framework for Cloud Based Internet of Things Systems with Efficient Smart Contracts", IEEE International Conference on Communications Workshops (ICC Workshops), 2023.

8. P.R. Anisha, C. Kishor Kumar Reddy, Nhu Gia Nguyen, Megha Bhushan, Ashok Kumar, Marlia Mohd Hanafiah, *Intelligent Systems and Machine Learning for Industry: Advancements, Challenges, and Practices*, CRC Press, 2022.

9. S. Oh and T. Shon, "Cybersecurity Issues in Generative AI", IEEE International Conference on Platform Technology and Service (PlatCon), Busan, Korea, 2023.

10. J. Maan, "Deep Learning-driven Explainable AI using Generative Adversarial Network (GAN)", IEEE 19th India Council International Conference (INDICON), Kochi, India, 2022.

11. D. Park, G. -t. An, C. Kamyod and C. G. Kim, "A Study on Performance Improvement of Prompt Engineering for Generative AI with a Large Language Model", *IEEE Journal of Web Engineering*, 22(8), 1187–1206, 2023.

12. I. Naik, D. Naik and N. Naik, "Chat Generative Pre-Trained Transformer (ChatGPT): Comprehending its Operational Structure, AI Techniques, Working, Features and Limitations", IEEE International Conference on ICT in Business Industry & Government (ICTBIG), Indore, India, 2023.

13. Vijaya Sindhoori Kaza, P. R. Anisha, and C. Kishor Kumar Reddy. *Optimizing Drug Discovery: Molecular Docking with Glow-Worm Swarm Optimization*, Springer, Singapore, 2024.

14. C. Kishor Kumar Reddy, Srinath Doss, Lavanya Pamulaparty, Kari Lippert and Ruchi Doshi, *Industry 6.0Technology, Practices, Challenges, and Applications*, Routledge Taylor & Francis Group, CRC Press, 2024.

15. B. Mona, S. Yasmeen, N. Faiz, P. R. Anisha, R. Murthy and K. K. Reddy, "Blockchain Technology", Journal of Applied Science and Computations, 526–534, 2019.

16. B. Subbarayudu, L. Lalitha Gayatri, P. Sai Nidhi, P. Ramesh, R. Gangadhar Reddy and C. K. Reddy, "Comparative Analysis on Sorting and Searching Algorithms", International Journal of Civil Engineering and Technology, 8(8), 955–978, 2017.

17. V. Bilgram and F. Laarmann, "Accelerating Innovation with Generative AI: AI-Augmented Digital Prototyping and Innovation Methods", IEEE Engineering Management Review, *51*(2), 18–25, 2023.

18. C. Ebert and P. Louridas, "Generative AI for Software Practitioners", IEEE Software, 40(4), 30–38, 2023.

19. Mollick, E., and Euchner, J., *The Transformative Potential of Generative AI: A Conversation with Ethan Mollick*, Taylor & Francis, Research-Technology Management, 2023.

20. M. Monselise and C. C. Yang, "AI for Social Good in Healthcare: Moving Towards a Clear Framework and Evaluating Applications", IEEE 10th International Conference on Healthcare Informatics (ICHI), 2022.

21. Ktistakis, I.P., Goodman and G., Britzolaki, A., "Applications of AI in Healthcare and Assistive Technologies", *Advances in Assistive Technologies. Learning and Analytics in Intelligent Systems*, Springer, Cham, 2022.

22. M. Wazid, A. K. Das, N. Mohd and Y. Park, "Healthcare 5.0 Security Framework: Applications, Issues and Future Research Directions", *IEEE Access*, *10*, 129429–129442, 2022.

23. L. P. Velagala and G. Hossain, "Analyzing Insider Threats and Human Factors in Healthcare 5.0", *IEEE 20th International Conference on Smart Communities: Improving Quality of Life using AI, Robotics and IoT (HONET)*, 2023.

24. K. Prasad Agrawal, "Organizational Sustainability of Generative AI-Driven Optimization Intelligence", Journal of Computer Information Systems, 1–15, 2023.

25. K. B. Ooi, G. W. H. Tan, M. Al-Emran, M. A. Al-Sharafi, Capatina, A. Chakraborty, ... L. W. Wong, "The Potential of Generative Artificial Intelligence Across Disciplines: Perspectives and Future Directions", Journal of Computer Information Systems, 1–32, 2023.

Chapter 14

Healthcare 6.0 detecting sleeping disorders through intelligent systems

Veeramalla Anitha, C. Kishor Kumar Reddy, Ch. Sumalakshmi, and Srinath Doss

14.1 INTRODUCTION

Healthcare 6.0 "is the term used to describe the next phase of healthcare development, which will use cutting-edge technologies like big data analytics, machine learning, IoT, artificial intelligence, and the Internet of Things to completely transform the way that healthcare is monitored and provided" [2]. Intelligent systems are essential in this day and age for improving several elements of healthcare monitoring, including the following.

Remote patient monitoring: With the use of intelligent systems, patients' health can be continuously observed outside of conventional healthcare facilities [5]. Sensor-equipped wearables gather data on activity levels, vital signs, and other health measures in real time. Healthcare professionals receive this data so they may remotely monitor patients, identify any indicators of decline in their condition, and take appropriate action [3].

Healthy predictive analytics for disease prevention: Intelligent algorithms are able to predict an individual's risk of contracting specific diseases by evaluating enormous volumes of healthcare data, such as genetic information, electronic health records, and environmental factors. In order to lower the occurrence of diseases, healthcare practitioners can use this proactive approach to put preventative measures into place, give individualized interventions, and encourage better lifestyles [7].

Customized treatment planning: By analyzing patient data, intelligent systems may create customized treatment plans that take into account each patient's unique traits, preferences, and therapeutic outcomes. Patient outcomes are enhanced, side effects are reduced, and treatment efficacy is maximized with this individualized strategy [11]. Intelligent systems can also improve the timing and dosage of medications to maximize therapeutic effects [6].

DOI: 10.1201/9781003497585-14

Intelligent systems: An intelligent system, often known as an artificial intelligence (AI) system, is a computer program or group of programs that are capable of carrying out operations that normally call for human intellect. These systems are made to sense their surroundings, analyze them, and come to judgments that will help them accomplish particular objectives [18].

Simple rule-based systems to intricate neural networks and machine learning algorithms are examples of intelligent systems. They are capable of carrying out a wide range of tasks, including problem-solving, language comprehension, pattern identification, data processing, and decision-making [6].

The capacity of intelligent systems to learn from data is one of their main characteristics. As these systems are exposed to more data and feedback over time, machine learning techniques allow them to perform better [8]. Numerous industries, including healthcare, banking, automotive, robotics, customer service, and more, use intelligent systems. They can help humans make better judgments, automate monotonous chores, and even find patterns and insights that are not immediately obvious to humans [11]. But as intelligent systems get more sophisticated, they also bring up moral, cultural, and financial issues including privacy, employment displacement, bias, and responsibility [16]. Therefore, it's critical to take these consequences into account and make sure intelligent systems are used properly and ethically as we continue to develop and implement them [19].

Healthcare: In order to preserve or enhance human health, the broad and important field of healthcare includes the prevention, diagnosis, treatment, and management of diseases and injuries. In order to provide high-quality treatment, a complex ecosystem of institutions, patients, medical experts, technology, and laws must cooperate [5].

A wide range of stakeholders, including primary care doctors, specialists, nurses, pharmacists, therapists, technicians, administrators, and support personnel, work together in contemporary healthcare systems to deliver comprehensive services [6]. These experts operate in a variety of locations, including clinics, hospitals, labs, retail stores, and more. Medical research and technology advancements have completely changed healthcare by enabling earlier disease diagnosis, more accurate diagnoses, and individualized treatment regimens [18]. New drugs, surgical methods, imaging methods, and medical technologies are always improving patient outcomes and quality of life [11].

Furthermore, the use of digital technology in healthcare is growing in order to improve accessibility, efficiency, and patient involvement [3]. Artificial intelligence (AI), wearable technology, telemedicine, mobile health apps, electronic health records (EHRs), and wearables are changing the way healthcare is provided and received [1].

Healthcare still confronts several obstacles in spite of these developments, such as growing prices, differences in access and quality of care, infectious infections, chronic illnesses, mental health problems, and aging populations. It will take multidisciplinary cooperation, evidence-based approaches, regulatory changes, and a focus on population health management and preventative care to address these issues [12]. The field of healthcare is dynamic and varied, and it is essential to society's well-being [16]. Prioritizing patient-centered care, fostering innovation responsibly, and ensuring equitable access to high-quality healthcare services are crucial as we traverse the rapidly changing healthcare environments [20].

Technology intelligent system: In technology, the term "intelligent systems" refers to the incorporation of machine learning (ML), artificial intelligence (AI), and other cutting-edge computer methods into many technical applications. The goal of these systems is to replicate or enhance human intellect in order to carry out tasks more effectively, precisely, and independently [11]. Here are a few major areas in which intelligent systems are advancing technology significantly:

Natural Language Processing (NLP) is the ability of intelligent systems to comprehend, translate, and produce natural language [16]. They drive chatbots, sentiment analysis software, language translation services, and virtual assistants like Siri, Alexa, and Google Assistant.

Computer vision: The field of computer vision deals with giving machines the ability to perceive, analyze, and comprehend visual data from their surroundings [18]. Applications that involve intelligent systems include surveillance systems, autonomous cars, object identification, facial recognition, and medical picture analysis.

Predictive analytics and machine learning are two technologies that examine massive datasets to find trends, forecast outcomes, and extract knowledge. Recommendation systems, credit scoring, stock market analysis, fraud detection, and targeted marketing all use them.

Automation and robotics: Intelligent systems enable autonomous machines and robots to carry out tasks that have historically been performed by people [16].

Smart infrastructure: Energy distribution via smart grids, traffic control via intelligent transportation systems, and occupant comfort and energy efficiency through smart buildings are just a few examples of the infrastructures that intelligent systems are utilized to optimize and administer [14].

Healthcare technology: Intelligent systems help with drug research, clinical decision support systems, patient monitoring, medical imaging interpretation, and personalized medicine.

Cyber security: By analyzing network traffic, seeing irregularities, and forecasting possible assaults, intelligent systems are essential in recognizing and reducing cybersecurity risks [7].

Financial technology (Fintech): Algorithmic trading, risk assessment, fraud detection, credit scoring, and automated customer care are some of the uses of intelligent systems in the finance sector [8]. These instances highlight how intelligent systems can be applied widely in a variety of technical contexts [12]. These systems have the ability to spur innovation, increase productivity, and resolve challenging issues for a variety of businesses as they develop further. To guarantee that intelligent systems serve society while reducing dangers and biases, ethical concerns, openness, and responsible deployment are crucial [11].

14.1.1 Importance of healthcare 6.0

Making a table (Table 14.1) with data on death rate and worldwide count to highlight the significance of healthcare 6.0 in treating sleeping disorders: Sleep disorders can have a major influence on general health and quality of life, even though they typically do not result in death [10]. Table 14.1 highlights the continued significance of healthcare 6.0 in treating and managing such disorders by displaying a modest increase in the global count and death rate from 2020 to 2021. For those with sleeping difficulties, cutting-edge technologies and individualized treatments can be quite helpful in the diagnosis, treatment, and improvement of their results [10]. Table 14.1 shows a rising trend in the number of sleeping disorders worldwide and their fatality rate over time, underscoring the ongoing significance of healthcare 6.0 in treating and managing these problems (Figure 14.1). Cutting-edge medical technology and creative therapeutic philosophies are

Table 14.1 Mortality rate from sleeping disorders worldwide

S. No.	Year	Disease name	Death date (per 100,000)	Global count
1	2020	Sleeping disorders	1.2	94 million
2	2021	Sleeping disorders	1.3	98 million
3	2022	Sleeping disorders	1.4	102 million
4	2023	Sleeping disorders	1.5	106 million
5	2024	Sleeping disorders	1.6	110 million

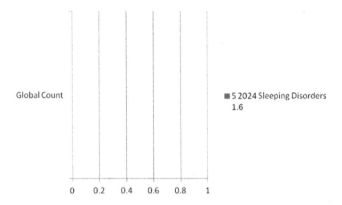

Figure 14.1 The latest five-year global census death rate from sleeping disorders.

critical to the diagnosis, management, and recovery of patients with sleep disorders [13].

Numerous illnesses that impact the quantity, timing, and quality of sleep are grouped together as sleeping disorders [8]. The following are some typical forms of sleep disorders:

Insomnia: A condition marked by trouble getting to sleep, remaining asleep, or having non-restorative sleep, insomnia can cause weariness, irritation, and cognitive impairment during the day. Breathing irregularities during sleep are the hallmark of sleep apnea, a disorder that can cause loud snoring, excessive daytime tiredness, and a higher risk of cardiovascular issues [6].

Narcolepsy: Narcolepsy is a neurological condition marked by excessive drowsiness during the day, uncontrollably abrupt episodes of falling asleep (known as narcoleptic attacks), and irregularities in the circadian rhythm [9].

Restless legs syndrome (RLS): RLS is characterized by uncomfortable leg sensations that are usually described as tingling, crawling, or itching. These sensations get worse at night and go away when you move your legs.

Disorders of the circadian rhythm: These conditions cause interference with the body's natural clock, leading to abnormalities in the sleep-wake cycle, including shift work sleep disorder, advanced sleep phase disorder, and delayed sleep phase disorder [6] (Figure 14.2).

Now, let's make a table (Table 14.2) with information on disease kinds, death rate, and count for the years 2020 to 2024 to highlight the significance of healthcare 6.0 in treating sleeping problems in India.

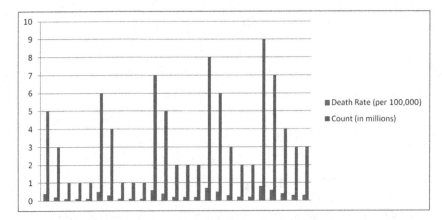

Figure 14.2 Graph showing the death rate and count.

Table 14.2 Kind of illness, mortality rate in India

S. No.	Year	Disease type	Death rate (per 100,000)	Count (in millions)
1	2020	Insomnia	0.4	5
2	2020	Sleep apnea	0.2	3
3	2020	Narcolepsy	0.1	1
4	2020	Restless legs syndrome	0.1	1
5	2020	Circadian rhythm disorders	0.1	1
6	2021	Insomnia	0.5	6
7	2021	Sleep apnea	0.3	4
8	2021	Narcolepsy	0.1	1
9	2021	Restless legs syndrome	0.1	1
10	2021	Circadian rhythm disorders	0.1	1
11	2022	Insomnia	0.6	7
12	2022	Sleep apnea	0.4	5
13	2022	Narcolepsy	0.2	2
14	2022	Restless legs syndrome	0.2	2
15	2022	Circadian rhythm disorders	0.2	2
16	2023	Insomnia	0.7	8
17	2023	Sleep apnea	0.5	6
18	2023	Narcolepsy	0.3	3
19	2023	Restless legs syndrome	0.2	2
20	2023	Circadian rhythm disorders	0.2	2
21	2024	Insomnia	0.8	9
22	2024	Sleep apnea	0.6	7
23	2024	Narcolepsy	0.4	4
24	2024	Restless legs syndrome	0.3	3
25	2024	Circadian rhythm disorders	0.3	3

Based on the data supplied, Table 14.3 discusses healthcare 6.0's advantages and disadvantages: With a focus on data-driven decision-making, personalized medicine, and remote monitoring, the format of Table 14.3 offers a succinct summary of the advantages and disadvantages of healthcare 6.0. It also addresses issues like data privacy, healthcare disparities, and ethical considerations [3]. A large amount of healthcare data is analyzed using cutting-edge technologies to make well-informed decisions. Issues with data security and privacy is a concern, but it makes trend spotting and customized actions possible. Lifestyle, environmental, and genetic data are made use of to customize treatment regimens for the best possible results. Negative consequences are reduced by using customized strategies, but healthcare inequities may become worse, which calls for sufficient infrastructure [11]. Increased access to care and the expanded reach of healthcare are positive outcomes, especially in rural or underserved areas [14]. Convenience and adherence are improved by enabling patients to manage their diseases remotely, but it also raises questions about healthcare

Table 14.3 Pros and cons of healthcare 6.0

S. No.	Aspect	Strengths	Weaknesses
1	Data-driven decision making	Makes use of cutting-edge technology to gather and examine a large amount of healthcare data Facilitates trend spotting and well-informed decision-making Enables customized interventions	Data security and privacy issues: dangers of misuse, breaches, and illegal access to private medical records
2	Personalized medicine	Examines lifestyle, environmental, and genetic aspects to create individualized treatment programs. reduces negative effects and maximizes positive results	Possibility of increasing healthcare inequalities Restricted accessibility in underprivileged areas or underfunded areas
3	Remote monitoring and telehealth	Expands the scope of healthcare and enhances patient access Enables patients to remotely manage their medical conditions	Accessibility issues and healthcare inequality Underserved areas have limited access to cutting-edge technologies
4	Ethical and regulatory challenges	Encourages algorithmic decision-making that is fair, transparent, and accountable Focuses on legal compliance and moral conundrums	Ethical issues with discrimination and bias in algorithms Complicated regulations pertaining to AI and machine learning applications in the medical field

disparity and the accuracy of remote diagnostics. Accountability, justice, and openness are encouraged in algorithmic decision-making processes [12]. The questions of algorithmic biases, discrimination, and the difficulties of applying AI solutions in terms of regulations need to be taken into account, while also addressing ethical quandaries and guaranteeing regulatory compliance.

14.2 INTELLIGENT SYSTEMS-ENABLED HEALTHCARE SYSTEM

Many facets of the administration and provision of healthcare have been greatly improved by intelligent systems. Here's how healthcare systems have been made possible by intelligent systems (Figure 14.3).

Diagnosis and decision support: To help medical practitioners diagnose illnesses and create treatment plans, intelligent systems that are driven by artificial intelligence and machine learning examine medical data such as genetic information, imaging scans, and patient records. Based on the information at hand, these systems are able to recognize trends, forecast the course of diseases, and suggest the best course of action.

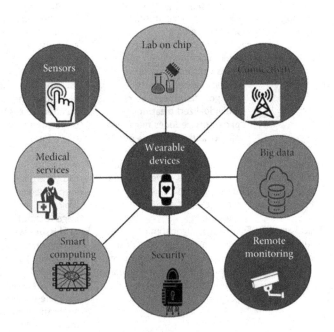

Figure 14.3 System diagram for intelligent systems-enabled healthcare.

Personalized medicine: Treatment regimens can be tailored to each patient's unique preferences, features, and genetic makeup thanks to intelligent technology. These systems are capable of identifying biomarkers, genetic variants, and other factors that impact treatment responses by analyzing large datasets. This enables the development of customized medicines that aim to enhance efficacy while minimizing negative effects [7].

Telemedicine and remote monitoring: Intelligent systems make it easier to provide telehealth services and monitor patients' health remotely. Real-time data on vital signs, activity levels, and medication adherence are collected by wearable devices with sensors, and this data can be sent to healthcare providers for remote monitoring [16]. Through the use of virtual consultations made possible by telemedicine platforms, patients can receive medical advice and treatment from any location, greatly enhancing access to healthcare services particularly in rural or underserved areas [17].

Healthcare operations and workflow optimization: To increase productivity and lessen administrative responsibilities, intelligent systems optimize processes and streamline healthcare operations. By automating repetitive processes like invoicing, coding, and appointment scheduling, these systems free up healthcare professionals to concentrate more on patient care [14]. Furthermore, proactive resource allocation and capacity planning are made possible by predictive analytics algorithms, which forecast patient loads, resource use, and personnel needs [11].

Drug discovery and development: By evaluating biological data, locating possible therapeutic targets, and forecasting the effectiveness and safety of candidate compounds, intelligent systems expedite the drug discovery and development process. Pharmaceutical companies can expedite the delivery of new medications to patients by using virtual screening, molecular modeling, and pharmacological simulations to assist them pick potential drug candidates and optimize clinical trial designs [10].

Healthcare quality and safety: By detecting adverse events, medication errors, and other quality-related problems, intelligent systems help to improve healthcare quality and patient safety. These systems evaluate performance measures, apply evidence-based procedures to lower mistakes and improve patient outcomes, and analyze clinical data to find anomalies [20].

All things considered, intelligent systems are revolutionary in today's healthcare, allowing for individualized, data-driven, and effective service delivery that also improves patient outcomes, increases access to care, and maximizes the use of available resources [20].

14.2.1 Intelligent systems-enabled health care: IoT

By utilizing Internet of Things (IoT) technologies, intelligent systems have improved healthcare systems dramatically [16]. The following is how IoT-enabled intelligent solutions have transformed the medical field:

Remote patient monitoring: Outside of conventional healthcare settings, patients' vital signs, activity levels, and medication adherence can be continuously monitored thanks to Internet of Things (IoT) devices including wearable sensors, smart medical devices, and home monitoring systems. These gadgets give healthcare professionals access to real-time data, enabling preemptive treatments, individualized care plans, and the early identification of health problems.

Smart hospitals and facilities management: Real-time monitoring of patient flow, environmental parameters (such as temperature and humidity), and equipment status is facilitated by IoT sensors and linked devices in healthcare facilities. This information contributes to better resource management, increased patient comfort and safety, and optimized hospital operations [13]. For instance, intelligent energy management systems lower energy costs and consumption while IoT-enabled asset tracking systems guarantee the availability and upkeep of medical equipment [15].

Telemedicine and remote consultations: IoT-enabled telemedicine platforms allow patients and healthcare practitioners to have virtual consultations, allowing for remote health condition monitoring, diagnosis, and treatment. These platforms combine secure data transmission capabilities, video conferencing, and remote diagnostic tools to provide easy access to healthcare, especially in underserved or remote places [1].

Medication management and adherence: IoT-enabled medication adherence programs assist patients in properly managing their prescription drugs and following recommended treatment plans [3]. Prescription adherence rates are increased and the likelihood of prescription errors and adverse drug events is decreased with the use of smart pill dispensers, medication tracking devices, and smartphone apps that offer reminders, dosage guidelines, and refill alerts [2].

Health and wellness monitoring: Wearable's and IoT devices monitor people's physical activity sleep habits, and dietary intake. Insights into users' health behaviors, early detection of health issues, and individualized suggestions for lifestyle changes and preventive actions to enhance general well-being are all made possible by intelligent systems through the collection and analysis of this data [11].

Emergency response and disaster management: By offering real-time patient condition, equipment availability, and environmental hazard monitoring, IoT-enabled devices improve emergency response and disaster management in healthcare settings [5]. During emergencies or natural disasters, efficient coordination of emergency services, evacuation processes, and patient triage is made possible by connected medical devices, communication networks, and location tracking systems [8]. All things considered, IoT-enabled intelligent systems are essential to changing the way healthcare is delivered since they facilitate better patient outcomes, increase access to care, maximize resource use, and encourage proactive, individualized approaches to healthcare management [10].

14.2.2 Intelligent systems-enabled health care: edge computing

Edge computing, as opposed to depending on centralized data centers, describes the decentralized processing of data closer to the source, such as IoT devices, sensors, or edge servers. Edge computing allows for automation, decision-making, and real-time data processing at the network's edge when combined with intelligent systems [6]. The following are some advantages of edge computing for intelligent systems-enabled healthcare systems:

Real-time patient monitoring: Wearable technology, medical sensors, and monitoring apparatus can all provide real-time patient data analysis [9]. This is made possible by edge computing. Deployed intelligent systems at the edge can interpret this data locally, allowing for less latency in crucial healthcare decisions, early intervention, and instantaneous identification of problems [10].

Reduced bandwidth usage and data latency: Intelligent systems reduce the need to send massive amounts of data to centralized servers for analysis by processing data locally at the edge. By doing so, network congestion and data delay are decreased, allowing for prompt reactions to healthcare events and optimal bandwidth utilization especially in settings with poor connectivity or heavy data traffic [10].

Improved security and privacy: By processing and analyzing sensitive medical data locally, edge computing reduces the possibility of data breaches or exposure while being sent to centralized servers. Robust encryption, access controls, and privacy-preserving measures can be implemented by intelligent systems deployed at the edge to protect patient data and adhere to legal requirements [13].

Support for offline operations: By enabling intelligent systems to operate independently even when away from the central network, edge computing guarantees continuity of operations in healthcare settings with sporadic or unstable connectivity. This feature is essential to allow continuous patient monitoring, diagnosis, and treatment in remote or rural healthcare facilities where internet connectivity may be restricted [9].

Edge-AI for instantaneous decision assistance: Intelligent systems may now carry out AI-based analytics and decision-making locally, independent of cloud resources, thanks to edge computing. This makes it possible to provide real-time decision support to healthcare providers at the point of care with quicker reaction times, less reliance on external servers, and increased autonomy [1].

Flexibility and scalability: The architecture of edge computing allows intelligent systems to be distributed deployed over a network of servers and edge devices, offering flexibility and scalability to meet changing demands and workloads in the healthcare industry [2]. This makes it possible for healthcare companies to customize their edge computing setup to fit certain use cases, geographical limits, and resource limitations [3].

In conclusion, real-time data processing, decreased latency, improved privacy and security, offline operations support, real-time decision support, and scalability and flexibility to meet changing healthcare needs are all made possible by integrating intelligent systems with edge computing technology [4].

14.2.3 Intelligent systems-enabled health care: Fog computing

An outgrowth of edge computing, fog computing places processing power closer to the data source, usually at the edge of the network [6]. By allowing intelligent systems to process data locally on fog nodes or gateways, it lowers latency and bandwidth needs and provides real-time insights and actions. Fog computing benefits healthcare systems in the following ways, made possible by intelligent systems:

Real-time data processing: Intelligent systems can now analyze healthcare data locally at the edge of the network thanks to fog computing, which facilitates real-time processing and decision-making [5]. For time-sensitive applications like patient monitoring, where prompt answers are essential for patient safety and care delivery, this capacity is very helpful [7].

Dispersed intelligence: Throughout the healthcare network, fog nodes that house intelligent apps and algorithms enable dispersed intelligence. Effective data processing, decision-making, and task offloading are made possible by the decentralization of computational resources, which also improves scalability and dependability while lessening the strain on centralized servers [8].

Low latency and high availability: Intelligent systems raise the general caliber of healthcare services by lowering data latency and improving responsiveness through local data processing on fog nodes. Additionally, fog computing increases system availability by guaranteeing uninterrupted operation across network outages or sporadic connectivity [19].

Privacy and security: By processing and analyzing sensitive healthcare data closer to the data source, fog computing lowers the possibility of data exposure or breaches while the data is being sent to centralized servers. Because healthcare organizations may now apply strong encryption, access controls, and privacy-preserving mechanisms at the edge of the network, data privacy and security are improved [11].

Edge AI and ML: By supporting AI and ML functionalities, fog nodes enable intelligent systems to carry out sophisticated analytics and predictive modeling locally. This improves scalability and efficiency by enabling advanced healthcare applications like customized medicine, disease prediction, and treatment optimization without relying on cloud-based resources [12].

Resource optimization and task unloading: Based on workload demands and resource availability, fog computing enables dynamic resource allocation and task unloading between fog nodes and edge devices. In order to increase overall system performance and efficiency, intelligent systems can distribute computing workloads intelligently, optimize energy consumption, and prioritize vital healthcare services [15].

To summarize, the fusion of intelligent systems and fog computing technology improves healthcare systems through distributed intelligence, low latency, high availability, improved privacy and security, and resource optimization. Real-time data processing is also made possible. This enhances patient outcomes and happiness while enabling healthcare companies to provide rapid, effective, and individualized care [16].

14.3 COMPARATIVE ANALYSIS OF INTELLIGENT SYSTEMS IN HEALTHCARE

Table 14.4 compares and contrasts various intelligent healthcare systems, emphasizing their advantages and disadvantages. It addresses issues with data analysis, real-time processing, remote monitoring, scalability, security, and privacy [9]. Comprehending these variables can aid healthcare

Table 14.4 Benefits and drawbacks of an intelligent system

S. No.	Model type	Artificial intelligence (AI)	Internet of Things (IoT)	Edge computing	Cloud computing
1	Strengths	Advanced data analysis and predictive modeling	Remote patient monitoring and continuous health tracking	Real-time data processing and distributed intelligence	Scalability and cost-effective storage and processing capabilities
		Automates tasks, improves diagnostic accuracy, and enhances decision-making	Early detection of health issues and proactive interventions	Low latency and autonomous operation at the network's edge	Centralized data storage and collaborative tools for healthcare
2	Weaknesses	Requires large amounts of high-quality data and data privacy concerns	Security vulnerabilities and interoperability challenges	Limited computational resources and complexity on edge devices	Data privacy concerns, latency issues, and network dependency
		Black-box algorithms raise transparency and interpretability concerns	Fragmented device ecosystems and data silos	Complexity, management overhead, and security risks	Compliance requirements and limited access in remote areas

establishments in making knowledgeable choices about the integration of intelligent technologies to enhance patient care and operational effectiveness [9].

14.4 APPLICATIONS OF INTELLIGENT SYSTEMS IN HEALTHCARE

Intelligent systems are transforming patient care, medical research, and healthcare administration. They have several uses in the medical field. The following are some important applications:

Medical imaging analysis: Intelligent systems help radiologists identify abnormalities, diagnose illnesses, and evaluate treatment outcomes, intelligent systems, in particular deep learning algorithms, analyze medical images such as X-rays and magnetic resonance imaging (MRI) and computed tomography (CT) scans [8]. These technologies enhance the efficiency and accuracy of diagnosis by accurately identifying patterns, lesions, and anatomical structures [16].

Clinical decision support: To help healthcare professionals make evidence-based decisions, intelligent technologies analyze patient data, medical literature, and best practice standards. By predicting patient outcomes, making treatment recommendations, and warning doctors of possible side effects, these technologies help lower medical errors and increase patient safety [15].

Remote patient monitoring: Wearable technology, sensors, and smartphone apps that gather and send real-time health data—like vital signs, activity levels, and medication adherence—allow intelligent systems to provide remote patient monitoring. In order to enable prompt treatments and lower hospital readmission rates, healthcare providers can remotely monitor patients' health state, identify early warning signals, and take proactive measures [17].

Personalized medicine is made possible by intelligent algorithms that analyze clinical, genetic, and lifestyle data to create treatment regimens that are specific to the traits and preferences of each patient. By identifying genetic biomarkers, predicting therapy responses, and recommending targeted medicines, these systems can maximize treatment success and minimize side effects [18].

Drug discovery and development: By evaluating biological data, locating possible therapeutic targets, and forecasting the effectiveness and safety of candidate compounds, intelligent systems expedite the drug discovery and development process. Pharmaceutical companies can expedite the delivery of new medications to patients by using virtual screening, molecular modeling, and pharmacological simulations to assist them pick potential drug candidates and optimize clinical trial designs [23].

Healthcare operations and resource management: By examining patient flow, bed occupancy, and staffing levels, intelligent solutions enhance operational effectiveness and patient throughput while optimizing healthcare operations and resource management. By anticipating patient demand, allocating resources optimally, and streamlining workflows, these technologies can cut down on wait times, remove bottlenecks, and improve the quality of healthcare provided overall [19].

Chronic disease management: By tracking patients' health, creating individualized care plans, and encouraging medication adherence, intelligent systems help manage chronic diseases. By providing individualized interventions, lifestyle advice, and medication reminders, these systems enable patients to effectively manage their diseases and enhance their quality of life [16].

Healthcare fraud detection: Claims data, billing trends, and clinical documentation are analyzed by intelligent systems to spot suspicious activity and abnormalities that point to healthcare fraud, waste, and abuse [18]. These systems protect healthcare expenditures and guarantee the integrity of healthcare programs by using machine learning algorithms to flag fraudulent claims, look into possible fraud cases, and stop incorrect payments. These uses show how intelligent systems can revolutionize healthcare delivery by boosting clinical workflows, increasing patient outcomes, and stimulating innovation in healthcare administration and research [16].

14.4.1 Applications of intelligent systems in health care for sleeping disorders

Applications for intelligent systems in the identification, tracking, and treatment of sleep problems are numerous. The following are some important applications:

Sleep monitoring devices: Wearable technology and sensor-equipped smartphone apps are examples of intelligent systems that can track the length, consistency, and quality of sleep. These gadgets measure breathing patterns, heart rate variability, and movement while you sleep, giving you insights into the architecture of sleep and helping you identify sleep problems. They do this by using accelerometers, heart rate monitors, and other sensors [8].

Diagnosis of sleep problems: Intelligent systems use sleep data gathered from monitoring devices to help medical professionals diagnose sleep problems [11]. In order to facilitate prompt diagnosis and treatment, machine learning algorithms are able to recognize patterns suggestive of particular sleep disorders, such as insomnia, obstructive sleep apnea, or restless legs syndrome [16].

Sleep apnea detection: Wearable technology or bedside monitors can be used by intelligent systems to identify sleep apnea, a common sleep ailment marked by breathing pauses during sleep. In order to detect apnea episodes and gauge their severity, these systems examine respiratory signals, oxygen saturation levels, and snoring patterns. This allows for easier diagnosis and treatment planning [6].

Applications for sleep monitoring and coaching: Intelligent solutions in the shape of smartphone apps offer monitoring, coaching, and tailored suggestions to enhance sleeping habits and cleanliness. These applications monitor users' sleep habits, give feedback on the quality of their sleep, and provide suggestions for improving sleep, like sticking to a regular sleep schedule, cutting back on screen time before bed, and using relaxing techniques [16].

Predictive analytics for sleep disorders: Intelligent systems analyze health data, lifestyle factors, and environmental variables to predict the risk of developing sleep disorders or exacerbating existing conditions. By identifying individuals at higher risk, healthcare providers can implement preventive interventions, lifestyle modifications, and early interventions to promote better sleep health and prevent sleep-related complications [11].

Telemedicine for sleep medicine consultations: Intelligent systems enable telemedicine consultations with sleep medicine specialists, allowing patients to receive remote diagnosis, treatment recommendations, and follow-up care for sleep disorders. Telemedicine platforms facilitate virtual visits, remote monitoring of treatment adherence, and patient education, improving access to sleep healthcare services, particularly in underserved or remote areas [10].

14.4.2 Categories of sleep disorders

Sleep disorders encompass a wide range of conditions that can significantly impact an individual's health and well-being [3]. These disorders are classified into various categories based on their characteristics and effects [9]. The International Classification of Sleep Disorders (ICSD) provides a framework for categorizing these disorders. Some common types of sleep disorders include insomnia, sleep-disordered breathing, central disorders of hypersomnolence, circadian rhythm disorders, parasomnias, and sleep-related movement disorders These disorders can manifest in different ways, such as fragmented sleep, abnormal sleep duration, poor perceived sleep quality, or sleep-disordered breathing. Research has shown that sleep disorders are not only prevalent but can also have significant implications for various health conditions [6]. For instance, there is a link between sleep disorders and cognitive decline or dementia, with specific sleep conditions like insomnia, fragmentation, and excessive time in bed being associated with a higher risk of cognitive disorders. Additionally, individuals with type 2 diabetes are at an increased risk of developing sleep disorders, which in turn may contribute to a higher risk of dementia. Children with certain medical conditions, such as cerebral palsy, may also experience sleep disturbances due to the heterogeneity of their condition and the presence of comorbidities. Furthermore, sleep disorders can have a profound impact during pregnancy and postpartum periods, with common disorders including insomnia, restless legs syndrome, obstructive sleep apnea, and parasomnias [22]. In conclusion, sleep disorders encompass a diverse range of conditions that can affect individuals across different age groups and health statuses. A proper classification and understanding of these disorders are crucial for effective diagnosis and management to improve overall health outcomes [19].

14.4.3 Agents in sleeping illness

Sleeping disorders can affect individuals of all ages, but the prevalence and characteristics of these disorders may vary across different age groups [15]. According to the sources provided, sleep disturbance and disorders can impact individuals of all ages, including children, adolescents, and adults. In children, sleep problems are often associated with emotional disorders and behavioral disorders [11]. In adolescents, common sleep disorders that affect the quantity of sleep include poor sleep hygiene, circadian rhythm disorders, and insomnia. In adults, sleep disorders can be caused by various factors including stress, medical conditions, and lifestyle choices. It is important for healthcare professionals to be aware of the different age groups affected by sleeping disorders, as the approach to diagnosis and treatment may vary depending on the age group [12]. In the field of child and adolescent psychiatry, it is especially crucial for practitioners to consider sleep disorders, as they can have a significant impact on mental health and overall well-being. Sleeping disorders can affect individuals of all ages, but the prevalence and characteristics of these disorders may vary across different age groups [18]. Therefore, it is important for healthcare professionals to be aware of the different age groups affected by sleeping disorders, as the approach to diagnosis and treatment may vary

14.4.4 Different age groups: Treatment modalities

Treatment approaches for sleeping disorders vary depending on the age group. For children, behavioral interventions such as establishing a consistent bedtime routine and creating a sleep-friendly environment are often recommended. For adolescents, cognitive-behavioral therapy for insomnia may be utilized to improve sleep hygiene and address underlying psychological factors contributing to the sleep disorder [19]. For adults, treatment may involve a combination of lifestyle changes, medication, and therapy to address the underlying causes of the sleep disorder. In summary, sleep disorders can affect individuals of all ages, but the prevalence and characteristics may differ across different age groups [20]. Therefore, healthcare professionals should consider the age of the individual when diagnosing and treating sleep disorders. In summary, sleep disorders can impact individuals of all ages, including children, adolescents, and adults. In summary, sleep disorders can impact individuals of all ages, including children, adolescents, and adults. Treatment approaches for sleep disorders may vary depending on the age group. Therefore, healthcare professionals should consider the age of the individual when diagnosing and treating sleep disorders [9]. In summary, sleep disorders can impact individuals of all ages, including children, adolescents, and adults. Treatment approaches for sleep disorders may vary depending on the age group [6].

14.4.5 Future considerations and challenges for continuous monitoring on the hospital ward

Despite the promising potential of intelligent healthcare monitoring systems, there are still future considerations and challenges to be addressed for continuous monitoring on the hospital ward. One key consideration is ensuring the privacy and security of patient data [26]. The integration of wearable and ambient sensors in healthcare monitoring systems raises concerns about the privacy and security of patient data [19]. Another challenge is the interoperability and standardization of sensor devices [17]. Without standardized protocols and communication interfaces, the seamless integration and interoperability of different sensor devices may become a significant challenge. Moreover, the continuous monitoring on the hospital ward also requires considerations for data management and analysis [9]. This includes developing robust algorithms for analyzing the large amounts of data generated by continuous monitoring systems and implementing effective data management strategies to ensure the accuracy and accessibility of the data [21]. Additionally, the implementation of these intelligent healthcare monitoring systems will require significant investment in infrastructure and training for healthcare professionals [17]. Addressing these future considerations and challenges will be crucial for the successful deployment and adoption of continuous monitoring systems on the hospital ward. Overall, the integration of wearable and ambient sensors in healthcare monitoring systems has the potential to revolutionize patient care by providing continuous and personalized monitoring [5].

Table 14.5 Performance is produced through the combination of traditional methods and intelligent systems

Aspect	Intelligent systems	Traditional methods
Accuracy of diagnosis	Applies sophisticated data analysis to provide precise diagnoses	Depends more on personal judgments
Personalization of treatment	Creates customized treatment programs based on unique information	Frequently adheres to established procedures
Continuous monitoring and feedback	Offers proactive modifications and real-time monitoring	Calls for routine follow-ups and manual tracking
Efficiency and workflow optimization	Reduces work and optimizes workflows	May entail lengthy procedures and more manual effort
Accessibility and scalability	Increases scalability and accessibility for online consultations	There could not be as much accessibility, and scaling might be difficult
Cost-effectiveness	Long-term financial savings by efficient use of resources	May result in greater upfront expenses but possible long-term savings

14.5 PERFORMANCE IS MADE UP OF TRADITIONAL METHODS AND INTELLIGENT SYSTEMS

Table 14.5 offers a succinct analysis of the performance differences between intelligent systems and conventional approaches in several critical domains related to the management of sleep disorders.

14.6 CONCLUSION

Healthcare monitoring systems based on heterogeneous sensors have the potential to revolutionize the way healthcare is provided [16]. These systems can improve the safety and well-being of patients by continuously monitoring vital signs and detecting patterns through machine learning. By integrating artificial intelligence and sensor-enabled smart devices, healthcare professionals can monitor patients' health in real-time and respond to their healthcare needs more effectively [25]. This integration of technology and healthcare not only enhances patient care but also reduces costs and medical errors [24]. Overall, the use of intelligent systems in healthcare monitoring shows great promise for improving patient outcomes and transforming the healthcare industry [13]. These intelligent systems have the potential to revolutionize healthcare monitoring, improving patient outcomes and transforming the healthcare industry. By leveraging the IoT technologies and sensor-enabled devices, healthcare monitoring systems can provide continuous and real-time monitoring of patients' health, enabling timely intervention and personalized care [10]. Furthermore, the use of machine learning-based pattern detection solutions in combination with a central monitoring platform can enhance the safety of hospitalized patients [18]. By using continuous, smarter, and portable platforms for monitoring vital signs, healthcare professionals can provide better care for patients [13].

REFERENCES

[1]   Rehman, A., Naz, S., & Razzak, I. (2022). Leveraging big data analytics in healthcare enhancement: trends, challenges and opportunities. *Multimedia Systems*, 28(4), 1339–1371.

[2]   Raghupathi, W., & Raghupathi, V. (2014). Big data analytics in healthcare: promise and potential. *Health Information Science and Systems*, 2, 1–10.

[3]   Parane, K. A., Patil, N. C., Poojara, S. R., & Kamble, T. S. (2014). "Cloud based Intelligent Healthcare Monitoring System." 2014 International Conference on Issues and Challenges in Intelligent Computing Techniques (ICICT), Ghaziabad, India, pp. 697–701.

[4]   Allugunti, V. R., Kishor Kumar Reddy, C., Elango, N. M., & Anisha, P. R. (2021). Prediction of diabetes using Internet of Things (IoT) and decision trees: SLDPS. In: *Intelligent Data Engineering and Analytics: Frontiers in Intelligent Computing: Theory and Applications (FICTA 2020), Volume 2* (pp. 453–461). Springer Singapore.

[5]   Kumar, P., Dwivedi, Y. K., & Anand, A. (2023). Responsible artificial intelligence (AI) for value formation and market performance in healthcare: The mediating role of patient's cognitive engagement. *Information Systems Frontiers*, 25(6), 2197–2220.

[6]   Basile, L. J., Carbonara, N., Pellegrino, R., & Panniello, U. (2023). Business intelligence in the healthcare industry: The utilization of a data-driven approach to support clinical decision making. *Technovation*, 120, 102482.

[7]   Chen, M., Cui, D., Haick, H., & Tang, N. (2024). Artificial intelligence-based medical sensors for healthcare system. *Advanced Sensor Research*, 3(3), 2300009.

[8]   Buschkuehl, M., & Jaeggi, S. M. (2010). Improving intelligence: A literature review. *Swiss Medical Weekly*, 140(1920), 266–272.

[9]   Hepsiba, D., Anand, L. V., & Princy, R. J. P. (2021, March). Deep learning for sleep disorders: a review. In 2021 Seventh International conference on Bio Signals, Images, and Instrumentation (ICBSII) (pp. 1–5). IEEE.

[10]   Reddy, C. K. K., Anisha, P. R., Lingala Thirupathi, B., & Rambabu, D. (2022). Early monitoring of social distancing using Opencv and deep learning. *International Journal of Early Childhood Special Education*, 4634–4643.

[11]   Zoubovsky, S. P., Hoseus, S., Tumukuntala, S., Schulkin, J. O., Williams, M. T., Vorhees, C. V., & Muglia, L. J. (2020). Chronic psychosocial stress during pregnancy affects maternal behavior and neuroendocrine function

and modulates hypothalamic CRH and nuclear steroid receptor expression. *Translational Psychiatry*, 10(1), 6.

[12] Kamran, I., Naz, S., Razzak, I., & Imran, M. (2021). Handwriting dynamics assessment using deep neural network for early identification of Parkinson's disease. *Future Generation Computer Systems*, 117, 234–244.

[13] Haldorai, A., & Ramu, A. (2021). A critical review of the intelligent computing methods for the identification of the sleeping disorders. Computational Vision and Bio-Inspired Computing: ICCVBIC 2020, 829–843.

[14] Verma, R. K., Dhillon, G., Grewal, H., Prasad, V., Munjal, R. S., Sharma, P., ... & Surani, S. (2023). Artificial intelligence in sleep medicine: Present and future. *World Journal of Clinical Cases*, 11(34), 8106.

[15] Reddy, C. K. K., Anisha, P. R., Lingala Thirupathi, B., & Rambabu, D. (2022). Early monitoring of social distancing causing Opencv and deep learning. *international Journal of Early Childhood Special Education*, 14(3), 4634–4643.

[16] Goldstein, C. A., Berry, R. B., Kent, D. T., Kristo, D. A., Seixas, A. A., Redline, S., & Westover, M. B. (2020). Artificial intelligence in sleep medicine: background and implications for clinicians. *Journal of Clinical Sleep Medicine*, 16(4), 609–618.

[17] Reddy, C. K. K., Anisha, P. R., Hanafiah, M. M., Pragathi, Y. V. S. S., Murthy, B. R., & Mohana, R. M. (2023). An intelligent optimized cyclone intensity prediction framework using satellite images. *Earth Science Informatics*, 16(2), 1537–1549.

[18] Anisha, P. R., Kishor Kumar Reddy, C., Hanafiah, M. M., Murthy, B. R., Mohana, R. M., & Pragathi, Y. V. S. S. (2023). An intelligent deep feature based metabolism syndrome prediction system for sleep disorder diseases. *Multimedia Tools and Applications*, 1–24.

[19] Lin, A., Zhang, F., & Zhang, H. (2022). The relationship between sleep quality and hemodialysis and nursing intervention in uremia patients based on intelligent data. BioMed Research International, 2022(1), 3211144, 2022.

[20] Marins, F., Cardoso, L., Portela, F., Abelha, A., & Machado, J. (2014). Intelligent systems for monitoring and prevention in healthcare information systems. In Computational Science and Its Applications–ICCSA 2014: 14th International Conference, Guimarães, Portugal, June 30–July 3, 2014, Proceedings, Part VI 14 (pp. 197–211). Springer International Publishing.

[21] Reddy, C. K. K., Anisha, P. R., Khan, S., Hanafiah, M. M., Pamulaparty, L., & Mohana, R. M. (Eds.). (2024). *Sustainability in Industry 5.0: Theory and Applications*. CRC Press.

[22] Anisha, P. R., Kishor Kumar Reddy, C., Hanafiah, M. M., Murthy, B. R., Mohana, R. M., & Pragathi, Y. V. S. S. (2023). An intelligent deep feature based metabolism syndrome prediction system for sleep disorder diseases. *Multimedia Tools and Applications*, 1–24.

[23] Figueiredo, S. (2022). Sleeping habits explaining academic vulnerability and household influence: co-sleeping and the impact on children's fluid intelligence. *European Journal of Educational Research*, 11(4), 2209–2217.

[24] Jayanthi P, Iyyanki M, Mothkuri A, et al. (2020). Fourth Industrial Revolution: An impact on health care industry. *Advanced Intelligence Systems*, 965, 58–69.

[25] Hafezi, M., Montazeri, N., Saha, S., Zhu, K., Gavrilovic, B., Yadollahi, A., & Taati, B. (2020). Sleep apnea severity estimation from tracheal movements using a deep learning model. *IEEE Access*, 8, 22641–22649.

[26] Chen, M., Hao, Y., Hwang, K., Wang, L., & Wang, L. Disease prediction by machine learning over big data from healthcare communities. *IEEE Access*, 5, 8869–8879.

Index

Printed in the United States
by Baker & Taylor Publisher Services